RETHINKING GALATIANS

RETHINKING GALATIANS

PAUL'S VISION OF ONENESS IN THE LIVING CHRIST

Peter Oakes and Andrew K. Boakye

LONDON • NEW YORK • OXFORD • NEW DELHI • SYDNEY

T&T CLARK
Bloomsbury Publishing Plc
50 Bedford Square, London, WC1B 3DP, UK
1385 Broadway, New York, NY 10018, USA
29 Earlsfort Terrace, Dublin 2, Ireland

BLOOMSBURY, T&T CLARK and the T&T Clark logo are trademarks of
Bloomsbury Publishing Plc

First published in Great Britain 2021

Cover design: Charlotte James
Cover image © beastfromeast/ Getty Images

A catalogue record for this book is available from the British Library.

Library of Congress Cataloging-in-Publication Data
Names: Oakes, Peter (Peter S.), author. | Boakye, Andrew, author.
Title: Rethinking Galatians : Paul's vision of oneness in the living Christ /
Peter Oakes and Andrew Boakye.
Description: London ; New York : T&T Clark, 2021. |
Includes bibliographical references and index. |
Summary: "Oakes and Boakye rethink Galatians by examining the text as a vision for the lives
of its hearers. They show how, in tackling the difficulties that he faces in Galatia, Paul offers
a vision of what the Galatians are in their relationship with the living Christ. This offers a new
understanding of the concept of unity in diversity expressed in Gal 3:28. The authors develop
their views over six chapters. First, Oakes maps a route from the letter to a focus on its Galatian
hearers and on Paul's vision for their identity and existence. In the next chapter, Oakes uses
the Christology of Galatians as a way to support the idea of pistis as current relationship with
the living Christ. Boakye then offers three chapters analysing the letter's scriptural quotations
and ideas about salvation and law. Boakye sees a key dynamic at work in Galatians as being
a movement from death to life, as prophesied metaphorically by Ezekiel and as made literal
for Paul in his encounter with the resurrected Christ, trust in whom becomes the route to life.
Life becomes a key category for evaluating law. Boakye also draws Galatians close to Romans
4 in seeing in both texts the promise of the birth of Isaac, with Paul closely tying that to the
resurrection of Jesus. Oakes then argues that the letter has a thematic concern for unity in
diversity. In the first instance this is between Jews and gentiles but, in principle, it is between
any other socially significant pair of groups"–Provided by publisher.
Identifiers: LCCN 2020032740 (print) | LCCN 2020032741 (ebook) | ISBN 9780567074966 (pb) |
ISBN 9780567181114 (hb) | ISBN 9780567697769 (epdf) | ISBN 9780567697752 (epub)
Subjects: LCSH: Bible. Galatians–Criticism, interpretation, etc.
Classification: LCC BS2685.52 .O35 2021 (print) |
LCC BS2685.52 (ebook) | DDC 227/.406–dc23
LC record available at https://lccn.loc.gov/2020032740
LC ebook record available at https://lccn.loc.gov/2020032741

ISBN: HB: 978-0-5671-8111-4
PB: 978-0-5670-7496-6
ePDF: 978-0-5676-9776-9
ePUB: 978-0-5676-9775-2

Typeset by Newgen KnowledgeWorks Pvt. Ltd., Chennai, India

To find out more about our authors and books visit www.bloomsbury.com
and sign up for our newsletters.

CONTENTS

PREFACE

There is a disconnect between most Galatians scholarship and the most prominent use of Galatians in current public discourse. A striking recent example of such use is the editorial for the left-of-centre UK newspaper the *Guardian*, dated 25 December 2019. Under the headline, 'The Guardian View on the Rise of Christian-Nativist Populists: A Troubling Sign of Things to Come', the editorial begins:

> 'There is neither Jew nor Greek, there is neither slave nor free, there is no male and female, for you are all one in Christ Jesus.' These words, written by Saint Paul 2,000 years ago, are central to the Christian faith. They speak of a vocation for the universal and point to an ethic of social justice and solidarity. The Christian tradition's account of the humble circumstances of the birth of Jesus, represented in the nativity scene, is in the same spirit, identifying Christ with the marginal, the maligned and the poor.
>
> It has therefore, for many Christians, been depressing to witness the faith of their churches being used to justify the abandonment of such principles in Europe, Donald Trump's America and beyond. For liberally minded Christians, 2019 was the latest in a succession of anni horribiles, during which a cultural appropriation of their religion did service for aggressive nationalism, xenophobia, homophobia and anti-environmentalism.[1]

The editorial goes on to discuss Poland, Hungary, Italy and Donald Trump, before considering 'straws in the wind', in the form of the use of Christian discourse by Elizabeth Warren and Pete Buttigieg, the 19 December *Christianity Today* editorial calling for Donald Trump's removal, and the Pope's endorsement of Greta Thunberg. The editorial concludes:

---

[1] *The Guardian*, editorial, Wednesday, 25 December 2019, 16.00 GMT. Last modified on Friday, 27 December 2019, 08.07 GMT: https://www.theguardian.com/commentisfree/2019/dec/25/the-guardian-view-on-the-rise-of-christian-nativist-populists-a-troubling-sign-of-things-to-come (accessed 15 January 2020).

Liberal democracies rightly prize the separation of church and state which emerged following the Enlightenment. But as the reactionary right denigrates ideas of human dignity and equality that can be traced back to the first formulations of early Christianity, liberals of goodwill need to unite across the religious/secular divide in 2020.

Scholars and students of Galatians may, probably rightly, suspect that the main exposure the *Guardian* editorial team would have had to scholarship on Gal. 3:28 would be through politically committed, identity-related studies on the text, usually carried out using a type of modern-reader-response approach. Studies from angles that are more historical-critical, and which look at the letter as a whole, have instead tended to foreground topics such as Paul's disputes and his opponents; law, faith and righteousness; use of scripture; Jew-gentile relations; cosmic change; and empire.

Leading recent historical/textual studies of Gal. 3:28, such as those by Bruce Hansen, Karin Neutel and Gesila Uzukwu, do not give extensive attention to the letter as a whole. Conversely, prominent recent attempts to read the whole letter in a way that makes sense of the role of Gal. 3:28 have struggled to find the broadest acceptance, whether the approaches centre on apocalyptic, on empire or on the imperatives of post-Holocaust Jewish-Christian relations. Two recent developments in research on Paul by several scholars, including the authors of the present book, lead us to think that there is now a new, viable historical-critical route to reducing the scope of the disconnect. Our approach centres on seeing Galatians as a vision for the lives of its hearers. In tackling the difficulties that he faces in Galatia, Paul offers a vision of what the Galatians are in their relationship with the living Christ. Although that vision does not actually turn Paul into the ideal advocate for 'a vocation for the universal', it does promote a unity in diversity that Gal. 3:28 expresses and which can very reasonably be seen as engendering in Paul's present-day readers 'an ethic of social justice and solidarity'.

The first of these research developments is a renewed focus on life, resurrection and the living Christ. Boakye explores this in his 2017 monograph, *Death and Life: Resurrection, Restoration and Rectification in Paul's Letter to the Galatians*. Independently, David Downs and Benjamin Lappenga also conclude that Paul has a primary focus on the living Christ, in their 2019 book, *The Faithfulness of the Risen Christ: Pistis and the Exalted Lord in the Pauline Letters*. The other development is what one could call the 'relational turn' in study of *pistis* (faith, trust, loyalty, faithfulness). Zeba Crook and Karl Friedrich Ulrichs each present a type of relational reading of *pistis* in their monographs, respectively, *Reconceptualising Conversion: Patronage, Loyalty, and Conversion in the Religions of the Ancient Mediterranean* and *Christusglaube: Studien zum Syntagma* pistis Christou *und zum paulinischen Verständnis von Glaube und Rechtfertigung*. Oakes presents a relational understanding of *pistis* in his 2015 Galatians commentary. With a different nuance and much more impact, Teresa Morgan also does so in her groundbreaking 2015 study, *Roman Faith and Christian Faith:* Pistis *and* Fides *in the Early Roman Empire and Early Churches*. Oakes responds in an article titled '*Pistis* as Relational Way of Life in Galatians' in the *Journal for the Study of the New Testament*. Nijay Gupta picks up the relational reading of *pistis* in *Paul and the Language of Faith*, and, in a different way, so does Matthew Bates in *Gospel Allegiance: What Faith in Jesus Misses for Salvation in Christ*.

Seeing *pistis* as relational, and seeing that relationship as with the living Christ, refocuses key passages of Galatians away from the past, and beyond the foundational events of the cross and the reordering of the cosmos, towards people, specifically Paul's Galatian hearers, as he sees them essentially being: in Christ (albeit an existence shaped by the cross and new creation). Galatians becomes fundamentally a vision of the life of people in Christ, people who are one in Christ, a vision that combats the divisions that Paul sees as being at the centre of the problems that he finds his Galatian hearers to be facing. Centring our reading of Galatians on this vision puts Gal. 3:28 back at the heart of the letter.

We develop our argument in six chapters. First, Oakes maps a route from the letter to a focus on its Galatian hearers and on Paul's vision for their identity and existence. In the next chapter, Oakes uses the Christology of Galatians as a way to support the idea of *pistis* as current relationship with the living Christ. Boakye then offers three chapters analysing the letter's scriptural quotations and ideas about salvation and law. For Boakye, each of these point in the same direction. He sees a key dynamic at work in Galatians as being a movement from death to life, as prophesied metaphorically by Ezekiel and as made literal for Paul in his encounter with the resurrected Christ, trust in whom becomes the route to life. Life becomes a key category for evaluating law. Boakye also draws Galatians close to Romans 4 in seeing in both texts the promise of the birth of Isaac, with Paul closely tying that to the resurrection of Jesus. Oakes then argues that the letter has a thematic concern for unity in diversity. In the first instance this is between Jews and gentiles but, in principle, it is between any other socially significant pair of groups. Boakye concludes the book, reflectively drawing together many of the key themes.

This book expresses a dialogue between the research trajectories of the two authors, each being affected by the other. We discovered that there might be a prospect for useful progress in study of Galatians by drawing together Oakes's work on relationality and the interests of hearers of the NT with Boakye's work on life as a focus of Paul's thought. We discussed how the present book should be structured, and we read and commented on each other's chapters. However, as will be apparent, our voices and many of our views do differ. Our hope is that the putting together of these distinct but related ideas will help in the building of a set of historical-critical ideas about Galatians that both shed further light on the letter and enable further fruitful dialogue with approaches more oriented around experiences of the range of present-day readers.

We would like to thank our Manchester colleagues, especially members of the Ehrhardt biblical studies research seminar, who have repeatedly listened to and engaged in insightful discussion on the ideas presented in this book. We want to thank the wonderfully supportive and creative Manchester PhD 'lunch' group of c. 2009–13: Isaac Mbabazi, David Harvey, Elif Karaman, Pyung-Soo Seo, Stephen McBay, Sungjong Kim, Soonyi Byun and Richard Britton. We also thank everyone at T&T Clark involved in the production of the book, especially Dominic Mattos and Sarah Blake, not least for their willingness to work positively with the twists and turns of this book's genesis. Finally, we thank our families in a special way, particularly Chi and Janet, who have provided the loving context for everything.

CHAPTER 1
INTRODUCTION: RETHINKING GALATIANS IN TERMS OF THE VISION OFFERED TO THE HEARERS
Peter Oakes

In principle, the chapters of the present book do not need special introduction. Each covers a mainstream issue in the study of Galatians, dealt with in a conventional way. However, the set of studies pushes in a general direction that will feel unfamiliar to many readers accustomed to the most common lines of scholarship on the letter. Galatians has tended to be read from the viewpoint of interest in disputes in the early Jesus movement, or Christian theology, or modern Jewish-Christian relations, or the development of Paul's thought, or particular linguistic features of the text and so on. This book is oriented around the then-current experience of the letter's hearers, as represented by the letter and, particularly, the idealized current experience that the letter presents gentile followers of Jesus as having. Paul uses this idealized life as a key basis for persuasion of his hearers.

Aspects of this approach are already present in scholarship. Then-current experience is a key element, in particular, of the recent resurgence of work on participation in Christ, for instance, in the collection edited by Thate et al. (2014) and in the work of Grant Macaskill (2013, 2019), Jeanette Hagen Pifer (2019) and Michael Gorman (2019). However, as we hope to show, a more extensive focus on current Christian existence, as expressed in the letter, brings a change in the overall feel of the text: a change from a centring on dispute, controversy and death, to a centring on life and unity. Of course, no one can deny that Galatians is argumentative, even polemic, but if we turn things round and look at the experience that it projects for its hearers, which is a key strategic tool in Paul's persuasion, we learn about aspects of the letter that are evidently significant and that also have a constructive relation to modern usage.

This chapter will begin our study by reflecting on a few factors that might help us identify issues that would be prominent for the letter's hearers, as they approach Galatians with an interest in their own actual and potential experience.

In a letter, second-person address is a key form of emphasis. The hearers (Paul's letters were read out to groups) no doubt pay some attention while narrative and argument is being presented but, in many cases, to really catch their attention the author will write, 'You'. In Galatians, there is almost constant use of the second person in the latter half of the letter (4:8–6:18), but Paul uses it very sparingly in the first half, when he is building his main case. What do the Galatians hear when he does address them directly?

Another way in which hearers' attention is drawn is by the use of identifiers that they would see as characterizing them. In Galatians, there are two references to Galatia and Galatian people (1:2; 3:1). Given the main practical topic of the letter, namely, dissuading gentile followers of Jesus from adopting circumcision (2:3-5, 14; 4:21; 5:1-6; 6:12-13), it looks safe to conclude that the hearers in general (although probably with exceptions) would describe themselves as gentile. We would expect their attention to be drawn by terms expressing that identity. In this letter, that particularly means the Greek words *ethnē* (nations, gentiles), *Hellēn* (Greek) and *akrobustia* (uncircumcision, in the sense of lack of circumcision).

Paul rebukes the Galatians. He questions them. He argues with them. However, to persuade people to action generally also needs the presentation of a positive vision to people, a vision of what they essentially are (in the writer's view), a vision of the best they can be. Even as the Galatians process all the rebuke and argument, they will be listening out for what it all means for them, in positive terms, if they buy into Paul's ideas.

Looking at Galatians in view of these three factors reorients interpretation of the letter towards the kind of issues raised in the present book. We will explore each of the factors in turn: second-person address and reference; reference to gentiles; and presentation of a vision for the hearers' existence.

1. You

As well as second-person pronouns (and some relative pronouns) and references to Galatia and Galatians, the hearers are addressed or referred to as *adelphoi* (brothers (and sisters): 1:11; 3:15; 4:12, 28, 31; 5:11, 13; 6:1, 18), as τέκνα μου (my children: 4:19) and, collectively, as *allēlous* (one another: 5:13, 15 x 2, 26 x 2; 6:2). They are also addressed in a range of second-person plural imperatives and are the subject of various second-person plural indicatives (and, in 4:7, a singular). A number of related participles and imperatives are also involved. If we put all of this together, the number of occurrences in each section of the letter (Oakes 2015: v–vi) is as shown in Table 1.1.

In 1:1–4:7, there are only three concentrations of second-person reference: 1:6-9 (x 7), 3:1-5 (x 11) and 3:26-29 (x 8). Apart from these thirteen verses, there are only ten second-person references across the first half of the letter. A related group involves first-person plural references that the hearers would unambiguously hear as including them. There are four of these in 1:3-5. Also fairly unambiguous are 3:14 and 4:6. More ambiguous are 2:4 (x 2), 3:13 (x 2) and 4:5.

The effect of all this is that, in the first half of Galatians, which carries the core of Paul's argument, the hearers' attention is particularly drawn to 1:6-9, 3:1-5 and 3:26-29. What is said to them in these places? What other second-person references are there in the letter, and how do they function?

In 1:6-9, the Galatians are actually only addressed in two verbs, *metatithesthe*, 'you are turning away' (1:6), and *parelabete*, 'you received' the gospel preached by Paul (1:9). Apart from these, the second-person references are to things done to the Galatians. They were 'called' (1:6). They

Table 1.1 **Frequency of second-person and related forms of address in sections of Galatians**

Chapter and verse	No. of occurrences
1:1-10	9
1:11-24	4
2:1-10	1
2:11-21	0
3:1-14	11 (all in 3:1-5)
3:15-29	8 (all but one are in 3:26-29)
4:1-11	10 (all but two are in 4:8-11)
4:12-20	25
4:21–5:13a	26
5:13b–6:10	29
6:11-18	6

are being 'harassed' (1:7). They have had the gospel preached to them by Paul (1:8), and they putatively have a contrary gospel preached to them (1:8, 9). The hearers will have perceived that Paul was surprised and annoyed with them. They will also probably have seen him as impugning their intelligence: he sees them as having replaced a real product with a fake one (1:6-7, cf. 3:1-5; Rom. 1:21-23). Paul then diverts attention away from the hearers, to those who have recently taught them, castigating the teachers in the strongest terms (1:8-9). This somewhat softens the effect of Paul's rebuke of the Galatians, by redirecting primary blame. However, it does so at the cost of regard for the Galatians' agency. Things happen to them: the Galatians are not powerful actors in the situation. This reinforces the impression of having their intelligence denigrated.

In the rest of Galatians 1, the isolated second-person references are more general epistolary ones. 'I declare to you, brothers and sisters' (1:11) is a standard letter-body opening formula. 'For you heard' (1:13) uses a reminder to draw the hearers into listening and provides a shared starting point for exposition. In 1:20, the second person is used in an exclamatory denial that Paul is lying. A more significant second-person pronoun is in 2:5, where Paul's action in resisting circumcision of Titus is, surprisingly, 'so that the truth of the gospel would remain for you'. This links the Galatians in a specific way to the account of the Antioch incident (esp. 2:14). We will return to it when we consider references to gentiles.

The next substantial block of direct address to the Galatians picks up where the first block, 1:6-9, left off. In 3:1 Paul denigrates the hearers' intelligence in the clearest terms, 'O foolish Galatians!' Whereas in ch. 1 the foolishness lay in swapping from something genuine to a fake, now it is an inability to process properly the evidence of their eyes. They had seen (in some manner) Christ crucified but were not acting on the implication of that. According to the preceding verse, if Christ died, and that death was worthwhile, the (Jewish) law cannot be the source of righteousness (2:21). The next verses imply that Galatians had adopted 'works of the law' (3:2, 5). Galatians 3:1 implies that Paul sees such an adoption as a foolish ignoring of the principle of 2:21.

Again, as in 1:6-9, Paul immediately does what might be seen as softening the criticism by shifting the blame, this time to others who had 'cast the evil eye' on them (NRSV: 'bewitched'). Whether this is literal or figurative, it moves some blame to those who caused the problem: if we follow John H. Elliott (2011) in taking it entirely literally, the shift of blame is particularly complete. However, as in 1:6-9, this is again at the expense of the Galatians' agency. Again, they are acted upon, rather than independently acting.

To an extent, Paul continues throughout the letter this strategy of diminishing the Galatians' agency. By the end of the letter, it is very much the other teachers who are blamed for the situation, rather than the Galatians (esp. 4:17; 5:7-12; 6:12-13). This clearly has some rhetorical advantages. Paul can follow a strategy of seeking to distance the Galatians from his opponents' influence and draw them back under his. However, this can only go so far. The Galatians also need to act. Paul needs to encourage them to take some control of their destiny and decide to follow what he believes to be the secure route towards a positive outcome.

In a way that probably helps this, the tone and approach shifts subtly in 3:2. The argument of 3:2-3 is, indeed, yet another appeal to the idea of foolishness.

> Just this one thing I want to learn from you: Was it by works of law that you received the Spirit, or by a message of trust? Are you so foolish that, having begun in the Spirit, you are now ending in the flesh? (3:2-3; Oakes 2015: 103)

One subtlety is that Paul has moved from accusing them of foolishness to appealing to their judgement of what would constitute foolishness. This is a significant step towards rebuilding a sense of agency. A second step is that the field on which he expects them to base their judgement is one which is directly accessible to them, namely, their experience. They can judge whether their community experience of the Spirit was initiated by Paul's preaching of trust in Christ or by their following of his opponents' preaching of the necessity of works of the law. Paul presses this argument more specifically in 3:5, applying it to their community perception of having experienced miracles.

Paul's turn in 3:1-5 to direct address to the Galatians also coincides with the appearance of a new actor, the Spirit. After a long narrative about Paul's gospel, then a recounting of an argument with Peter, Paul's turn to the Galatians is also a turn to focus on their experience of the life of the Spirit. Narrative and argument give way to current life, a life in which God is now present among the Galatians by the Spirit.

After 3:5, Paul builds a series of arguments to which we will return when we focus on the term 'gentiles'. By the time the Galatians next hear a series of direct addresses, in 3:26-29, they have been listening to a lengthy explanation of the valuable but time-limited role of the law. Paul transitions dramatically out of this explanation with a *pantes*, 'all', a sudden and sustained switch to the second person, and a bold new statement of the Galatians' identity.

> For you are all sons of God (πάντες γὰρ υἱοὶ θεοῦ ἐστε) through trust, in Christ Jesus. For as many of you as were baptized into Christ, you have put on Christ. (3:26-27)

This is packed with assertions about the Galatians' identity as followers of Jesus. Paul describes a past event and present identity. Like 3:2-5, the past event is one that the Galatians can recall from their community life. They were baptized. Paul characterizes this as baptism 'into Christ' (εἰς Χριστόν). It is described as if it is a mode of spatial entry. As such it follows on naturally from the preceding 'in Christ Jesus' (ἐν Χριστῷ Ἰησοῦ, probably to be read as a separate clause from διὰ τῆς πίστεως, 'through trust': Oakes 2015: 130). The believer comes to be 'in Christ' through having moved 'into Christ' in the baptismal ritual. It also fits with Paul's interpretation of baptism as being a 'putting on' of Christ. Christ becomes like a garment surrounding the believer. All in all, there is a strong sense of spatiality of Christ, as a sphere one inhabits (cf. Schliesser 2016).

However, Christ remains a living, active person. We see this as early as 1:1, where Paul writes that he was commissioned 'through Jesus Christ and God the father', both of whom are clearly alive and acting. Similarly, in 2:20, Christ 'lives in' Paul. The sense is of a continuing relationship rather than of being inhabited by the memory of a dead person. The continuing activity of Christ in people is also signalled by the Spirit's identification with Christ. In 4:6, because the Galatians are God's sons, God sent 'the Spirit of his son' into the Galatians' hearts. As in 3:26-27, sonship of God is linked to relationship with Christ. When, in 3:2-5, the Spirit is the active force in the Galatian community, this is equivalent to Christ being active in the community: the Spirit is the Spirit of Christ. In 3:26-37, past baptism begins present experience of life, in the living Christ, as children of God. This leads on to the statement about the Galatians' current existence that most directly addresses the issue of gentile identity in relation to Judaism.

> There is no Jew or Greek. There is no slave or free. There is no male and female. For you are all "one" in Christ Jesus. If you are of

Christ, then you are Abraham's seed, heirs according to the promise. (3:28-29)

Again, note that, in addressing the Galatians directly, Paul's focus is on their current existence. Again, they are 'in Christ'. They are also 'of Christ', which appears to be the determinative factor in being 'Abraham's seed'. In 3:16, Paul has said, with great emphasis, that 'the seed' of the promises to Abraham is Christ, is singular. In 3:29, a second-person plural is used to assert that the Galatians, a group, are this seed. The paradox is, in Paul's view, resolved by the Galatians all being 'of Christ', which is synonymous with being 'one', 'in Christ' (3:28).

This is not just a theoretical oneness. For Paul, the oneness means the abolition of social polarities, whether of ethnicity, servitude or gender. The one most pertinent to the issue in Galatia is the ethnic one: in Christ there is already no Jew or Greek, so requiring Greeks to take action to become like Jews is nonsensical. Given the factors of gender and control of the body that are issues for circumcision, the other two polarities do also have some relevance to this (Oakes 2015: 69, 128–9). However, the naming of the other two polarities probably also both generalizes the ending of divisions (D. Campbell 2005: 108) and shows the paradoxical nature of Paul's assertion. There are clearly still enslaved people and free people. There are clearly still men and women. The continuing distinctions are most obvious in society's sharp differentiation in the power and resources made available to each group. Paul's vision is, in a sense, utopian (for discussion of this text in relation to a wide range of issues in ancient utopianism, see Neutel 2015). Yet, it is also deeply practical, if only in a messy, partial sense. The Galatians are to live in the scope of this vision. Most immediately, that frees gentile Galatians from the need to accept circumcision. However, the accepting of that form of freeing also lays on them the responsibility to live in the other dimensions of that ending of polarities. How far they got, in their communities, in removing distinctions in power and resourcing we do not know (except that it did not go as far as, for instance, systematic freeing of slaves). However, wherever gentile Christians take the vision of Galatians as licence not to practice circumcision and other aspects of Jewish law, it should also summon them to life more widely determined by this abolition of polarities.

As we have seen, there is a surprising switch from 'we' to 'you' in 3:25-26, as Paul jumps from an account of the arrival of trust into life under the law to the Galatians' identity as sons of God. A remarkably similar switch happens in 4:5-6. Christ redeems those under law so that 'we' might receive adoption (4:5). The next words are, 'Because you are sons' (4:6). At the same assertion of sonship as in 3:26, Paul switches to address the Galatians in the second person. The structural parallels then continue. The assertion of sonship is followed by declaration of a past event in the life of the hearers: God having sent the Spirit of his son into their hearts. The spatial dynamics, however, are inverted: Christ, in the Spirit, enters the Christian, rather than the Christian entering Christ. Also parallel is the end point of the passage: Christians are heirs, although this time 'through God' rather than in Christ (4:7). One is tempted to seek a further parallel in the occurrences of *doulos*, 'slave' (3:28; 4:7). It looks difficult to make, although perhaps an enslaved person might read an in-principle free existence into each. Anyway, 4:6-7, which returns again to the use of the second person at the end of the letter's main argument, is, like the second-person passages before it, focused on the Galatians' current existence, which is in relationship to the living Christ.

The second half of the letter is full of instructions, hence full of second-person address. The instructions are delivered in various modes. Galatians 4:8-10, in effect, reverts to showing of foolishness – being free, are you reverting to slavery?! – to dissuade from calendrical observance. Paul adds a note of personal frustration (4:11), which sets the stage for an encouraging of loyalty to him, grounded in the Galatians' past welcome for him, and with the goal of 'forming Christ' in them (4:12-20). In 4:21, those inclined to adopt the law are called to a hearing of the 'law', that is, of scripture, that opposes such adoption and encourages expulsion of Paul's opponents (4:22-30). In 4:31–5:1, the Galatians are again presented as free, with Paul's opponents' way viewed as a return to slavery. Gentile circumcision is presented in 5:2-4 as an alienation (*katēgēthēte*) from Christ and as rendering him useless to them. As in 1:6-9, the Galatians' behaviour is again laid at the door of Paul's opponents in 5:7-12, with strong reminiscences of the earlier passage in the references to calling (5:8) and harassment (5:10), and in Paul's extreme vituperation of his opponents (5:12). In 5:13, the Galatians are yet again reminded that they are free. However, paradoxically, this time it is made the basis of slavery to each other in love. Love and being led by the Spirit are set in contrast to mutual destruction and 'the works of the flesh' (5:13-26; 'flesh' having been paralleled with 'works of the law' in 3:2-3). Further encouragements to mutual support follow (6:1-10). Paul uses a second-person pronoun to pointedly draw attention to the large letters he uses to write in their case. 'See with what large, to you, letters I write with my own hand' (6:11) is the Greek word order. The Galatians are given the impression

Table 1.2 **Frequency of occurrence of terms for gentiles in sections of Galatians**

Chapter and verse	No. of occurrences
1:1-10	0
1:11-24	1
2:1-10	5
2:11-21	4
3:1-14	3
3:15-29	1
4:1-11	0
4:12-20	0
4:21–5:13a	1
5:13b–6:10	0
6:11-18	1

in 6:12-13 that Paul's opponents are 'taking them for a ride'. In 6:17, Paul uses a third-person imperative to ward off attacks. The final verse, 6:18, wishes Christ's grace to be with the Galatians' spirit.

It is not surprising that the second half of the letter, a half full of instructions, relates mainly to the Galatians' present existence, addressed by many imperatives or equivalents for them. More notable is the present indicative of many second-person references in the first half of the letter. In both halves of the letter, the Galatians' attention, drawn to direct references to themselves, is drawn to assertions about their current existence.

2. Gentiles

Just as the use of the second person in a letter draws a hearer's attention, so does the use of terms relating to a hearer's identity. In this case, among the Galatian hearers, there appears to be at least a substantial majority identity as non-Jews. The occurrence of terms for gentiles are distributed as shown in Table 1.2.

The pattern is roughly the opposite of the distribution of second-person references. In particular, the last occurrence of *ethnē*, 'gentiles', is in 3:14 and the second and last occurrence of *Hellēn*, 'Greek', is in 3:28. After that the only direct reference to gentiles is in the repeated formula about the lack of significance of either circumcision or *akrobustia*, 'uncircumcision'. It is very striking that all three of the final references to gentiles are in versions of that formula (3:28; 5:6; 6:15). Terms for gentiles are rare in the second half of the letter, but where they do occur, it is in the formula that Paul hammers home more than anything else in Galatians.

If the hearers' attention is drawn to occurrences of terms for gentiles in Galatians, what do they hear there?

The one occurrence in ch. 1 is in v. 16. Paul's Damascus revelation is aimed at him 'gospelling' God's son among the gentiles (ἵνα εὐαγγελίζωμαι αὐτὸν ἐν τοῖς ἔθνεσιν. Contrary to Joshua Garroway's recent bold proposal (2018: 52), the immediate reference to the gentiles must make this equivalent to Paul's preaching of his εὐαγγέλιον to the gentiles, as in the revelation of 1:11-12, the expression of 2:2 and the agreement of 2:7). The Galatians hear that Paul's initial call itself is for their sake, as gentiles. Having heard about Paul's gospel as divine revelation, the Galatians then hear about its human verification. Paul sets out two strands of this in 2:1-11: an agreement with James, Peter and John; and the trying out of a test-case, the arrival in Jerusalem of the Greek Titus. As mentioned above, in 2:5, Paul ties this testing of his gentile gospel directly to the Galatians. He refused to give way to opponents in Jerusalem 'so that the truth of the gospel would remain for you'. This also ties the Galatians into Paul's dispute with Peter at Antioch, who Paul confronted because he could see that Peter was 'not walking in line with the truth of the gospel' (2:14). Paul presents himself as the champion of gentile rights in the communities of followers of Jesus.

The dispute also draws attention to the flip side of Paul's Jerusalem agreement. The leading apostles had agreed that Paul had 'the gospel of the uncircumcised' (2:7, τὸ εὐαγγέλιον τῆς ἀκροβυστίας). The leaders' handshakes verified that he and Barnabas were to go to the gentiles: the Jerusalem leaders were to go instead to the circumcised (2:9, ἡμεῖς εἰς τὰ ἔθνη, αυτοὶ δὲ εἰς τὴν περιτομήν). The Galatian gentiles should hear this as meaning that no one from James, Peter or John should be coming and preaching a gospel to them: the agreement was that this was for Paul to do. The point is brought home in Antioch when the arrival of 'certain people from James' causes Peter and some other Jewish followers of Jesus to stop eating with gentiles. The Galatians would probably identify with the gentiles in this story, suddenly affronted by the change of practice by Peter and other distinguished guests.

Paul not only defends gentile rights but also uses gentile identity as his route to confronting Peter. Paul asserts to Peter, 'You being a Jew, live in a gentile manner and not in a Jewish manner' (2:14). The Galatians hear Paul representing Peter as, in some sense, having taken on a gentile way of life and having left behind a Jewish one. The only clue to that in the preceding text is that Peter, left to his own devices, 'was eating with the gentiles' (2:12): presumably he and Paul, and certainly the people from James, saw this is not behaving in a Jewish manner. Another possible contribution to what Paul means by 'living in a gentile manner' is the transition that he and Peter appear to undergo in 2:15-17, from not being 'by nature' 'sinners from among the gentiles' (2:15) to the possibility of being found to be 'sinners' (2:17). This could tie up with the previous idea if, as Christina Eschner argues, their taking on of trust in Jesus Christ (2:16) led them to re-evaluate the boundary-marking nature of the law, a move that led them to re-evaluate both their own status and, in particular, the status of gentiles in Christ, which led Paul and Peter to view them as proper people to eat with, thus contravening the expectations of most Jews around them, even if Peter and Paul's view of Jewish food norms had not, in essence, changed (2019: 465–6).

Surprisingly, by the end of Galatians 2, Paul has not yet actually said anything about gentiles and their potential relationship with God. Even though he has already made nine of his fifteen references to gentiles, the hearers have so far learned very little about gentile status in Christ. Mostly they have heard Paul asserting the link between his gospel and gentiles. The Galatians have also heard about Titus the Greek not being circumcised (2:3) and about Paul's assessment of Peter as living in a gentile manner (2:14). They have heard Paul criticize Peter as, in effect, attempting to 'compel the gentiles to live in a Jewish manner' (2:14). In 2:15 the hearers may be somewhat irked to hear gentiles characterized as 'sinners', although they may note that Paul sees himself and Peter as somehow taking on that status through trust in Christ (2:17).

Only at 3:8 does gentile status in Christ start to be discussed explicitly. However, we ought to see this as beginning slightly earlier, at 3:6. The *kathōs*, 'just as', that links 3:6 to 3:5, draws 3:6 into the web of second-person address in 3:1-5. The Galatians expect what is said in 3:6 to relate to them. This carries the hearers forward into the argument of 3:6 onwards. The occurrence of the identity label *ethnē*, 'gentile', in 3:8 (x 2) and 3:14 combines with the passage's link to the second-person address of 3:1-5 to make the Galatians really sit up and take notice of this argument, as applying strongly to them.

The same effect happens at the conclusion of the argument. In 3:26-29, the gentile identity marker *Hellēn*, 'Greek', sits right in the middle of the next concentration of second-person address. Again, the identity marker and the second-person address work together to draw the hearers' attention. The Galatians are thus drawn deeply into both the set-up and the pay-off of the argument of 3:6-29 (which then runs on to 4:7).

The argument runs from Abraham to inheritance. More specifically it runs from Abraham who 'trusted God and it was reckoned to him as righteousness' (3:6) to 'you' (4:7) – you, singular – you Galatian gentile – who are 'a son' and hence 'an heir through God'. The unique switch to the second-person singular really draws the hearers' attention at this point. The inheritance is bound up with Abraham. The conclusion in 3:29 is that the Galatian gentiles, being 'of Christ', are therefore 'Abraham's seed, heirs according to promise'. The Galatians' status is of double sonship: sons of Abraham (3:7, 29) and sons of God (3:26; 4:6-7). (At this point, I want to say 'sons and daughters'. That is certainly the reality in terms of the gender of people in Christ. The two complications in doing so in Galatians are that ancient sonship ties specifically into inheritance rights, a key issue here, and that Paul uses 'son' as a term to parallel Jesus and his followers in their relationship to God.) The passages inextricably enmesh this with being 'in Christ' (3:14, 26, 28) and having the Spirit of Christ, God's son, in them (3:14 again, 4:6), which, as 3:2-5 shows, means the Spirit as experienced in the Galatian community (cf. also 5:13-25). All the language of righteousness (3:6, 8, 11, 21, 24), blessing (3:8-9, 14), the removal of curse (3:10, 13) and life (3:11-12, 21) ends up in a current status and experience that Paul presents the Galatians as having as followers of Jesus.

Paul wants them to appreciate and maintain that status and experience. He particularly stresses the implication of their status as ending the distinction between Jew and gentile. The letter's two further occurrences of terms for gentiles both reinforce the point that 'there is no Jew nor Greek' (3:28). Each takes the form οὔτε περιτομή τι . . . οὔτε ἀκροβυστία ἀλλὰ . . . (neither circumcision something . . . nor uncircumcision but . . .; 5:6; 6:15). The boundary between Jew and gentile (concretized in terms of the issue of circumcision, the matter most directly at stake in the letter) is rendered insignificant. Something else is made significant instead. In 5:6, 'in Christ Jesus' what 'matters' (*ischuei*) instead is 'trust working through love'. This ties in well with the social unity implied in 3:28 and then worked out in the ethic driven by love and the Spirit in 5:13–6:10. In 6:15, what 'is something' instead is 'new creation'. This is a dramatic innovation that has launched major theological theories such as J. Louis Martyn's 'apocalyptic' reading of Paul (1985, 1995, 1997, 2000). However, in the context of seeing 6:15 in relation to 3:28, I am struck again by the dramatic *pantes*, 'all', of 3:26: 'You are all sons of God, through trust, in Christ Jesus.' Somewhere between the idea of new creation of a person in Christ and the idea of new creation of the cosmos, what could well strike the Galatian hearers is the drama seen in the sudden appearance of communities of sons and daughters of God, through the arrival of Christ.

3. Vision

Despite all the rebukes, questions and imperatives, the Galatians would have heard in the letter a strong present indicative. The passages highlighted by the use of second-person reference and the identity term 'gentile' reinforce this. Paul cajoles, but he does so with provision of an underlying vision of present life in Christ, a life which the Galatians in principle have and are urged to maintain. Paul's vision, which he views as having come from God, offers a vision for the Galatians' life. Scholarship has gone down many paths that have tended to obscure the present indicative aspect of the letter, submerging it under a mass of polemic. The present indicative is universally observed in Romans. It is there in Galatians too. We hope that the following chapters will help to bring it out more clearly.

CHAPTER 2
THE *PISTIS* OF THE
RELATIONAL CHRIST
Peter Oakes

Jesus Christ is the person most frequently named in Galatians. 'Christ' occurs thirty-eight times, sixteen of which are with 'Jesus' and three with 'Lord'; there is one further occurrence of 'Jesus' (6:17) and two of 'Lord', as well as four of 'son'. The number of references to Christ is surprisingly high, given that the letter centres on Paul struggling with Galatians in relation to his opponents, involving issues of 'law' and 'faith' which might be imagined to be abstract matters, not tied to Christ in particular.

Beginning with Christ turns out to be a particularly useful way into the letter because the most debated issue relating to Christ in Galatians is tied into two of the most far-reaching theological proposals that have been made about the letter – and indeed about Paul's ideas – in the past half century. The issue is the apparently innocuous question of how to translate the phrase *pistis Christou*, which occurs at a crux of the letter at 2:16. In that verse, it also appears as *pistis Iēsou Christou*, as it does again at 3:22. The related ἐν πίστει . . . τῇ τοῦ υἱοῦ τοῦ θεοῦ (by trust in the Son of God?) occurs at 2:20. Some would also include 3:26, διὰ τῆς πίστεως ἐν Χριστῷ Ἰησοῦ (through trust in Christ Jesus?), but we will read the syntax differently. *Pistis* has a range of meaning, such as trust, belief, loyalty, faithfulness, credit or proof (Morgan 2015: 6–7). Attaching it to the genitive *Christou* produces something like 'trust of Christ' or 'faithfulness of Christ'. The first of these translations is ambiguous: is Christ trusting? (making *Christou* what some would call a 'subjective genitive') or is someone trusting Christ? (with *Christou* as what some would call an 'objective genitive'; for criticism of these terms, see Porter and Pitts 2009: 47–8). The second translation is unambiguous: it is clear that it is Christ who is faithful. Most English translations of 2:16 opt for 'faith in Christ' (e.g. NIV, NRSV main text). What raises the stakes dramatically is that this is part of what is, for most Protestantism, the definitive soteriological expression 'justified by faith in Christ' (2:16, NIV). The idea of 'justification by faith', key for Luther and other reformers, is an abbreviated form of 'justification by faith in Christ'. This means that when the NRSV footnotes the alternative, 'the faith of Christ', much may ride on it, since this alternative is presumably offered specifically to enable 2:16 to be read as speaking of being justified by Christ's own faith.

After setting out a few of the many alternative approaches that have been taken to the *pistis Christou* question, this chapter turns to the Christology of Galatians. We will go through the references to Christ twice: first in their order in the text and argument of Galatians; then in what one could call the chronological order of the underlying narrative of Christ's existence that these references present (we also gather references that do not relate to identifiable points in that narrative). We conclude that this Christology consistently presents a Christ in relationship with his people. We then discuss what the *pistis* of such a Christ should be understood as being. That will not give us a definitive answer to what the term means in each of its occurrences in Galatians: among other factors, that depends on the syntax of those texts, as Porter and Pitts (2009: 47–8) argue, rather than just on how *Christou* modifies *pistis*. However, the way in which Galatians presents Christ does have significant effects on some of the key issues in the debate.

1. *Pistis Christou*: Faithfulness, apocalyptic, gospel, spheres, gift and relationship

The seminal 1983 study by Richard Hays, *The Faith of Jesus Christ* (the edition cited here is Hays (2002)), argued that the poetics and underlying narrative of Galatians, together with a range of exegetical considerations such as the repetitive redundancy that a 'faith in Christ' translation produces in 2:16, should lead us to read *pistis Christou* as the faithfulness of Christ to God, expressed especially through his self-giving on the cross (2002: xxx). This reshapes Pauline soteriology, shifting the main basis of justification away from human belief in Christ onto Christ's own actions. For Hays this makes a more effective contrast to justification by works of the law: now justification stems not from any human action or disposition but from an act of God in Christ (xlvii). Hays himself does not see this as undermining the idea of trust in Christ in Galatians: he, like N. T. Wright, who takes a similar position, holds together Christian faith and Christ's faithfulness even though a shift in the significance of each has occurred (Hays 2002: 211; Wright 2013: 839).

The second and more radical challenge to the Lutheran position builds on Hays's reading of *pistis Christou* in a further direction (aspects of which Hays disagrees with; see later). J. Louis Martyn (1997) moves Paul's soteriology far away from the stress on personal salvation inherent in the Lutheran idea of justification by faith in Christ. For Martyn, the key point about Paul's vision is that it is apocalyptic. Martyn takes this as not only meaning that it is revealed by God (the Greek *apokalyptō* means 'reveal'), which is uncontroversial among scholars, but also that Paul's soteriology is centrally one of cosmic destruction and renewal: the cross ends the old cosmos and brings a new one into being. Martyn's key text is 6:14, which he reads as announcing 'the horrifying crucifixion of the cosmos' (572), producing 'the end of all religious differentiations, such as the differentiation of holy, circumcised people from profane and uncircumcised people' (561). He makes the basic soteriological act an objective, cosmic one.

Hays, and particularly Wright, have resisted key aspects of Martyn's apocalyptic construct. In particular, they insist on a strong degree of continuity in God's covenant before and after the cross, as opposed to the sharp discontinuity in Martyn's system (e.g. Wright 2013: 1481). Opposition to all the versions of reading *pistis Christou* as 'faithfulness of Christ' has come from various scholars, such as James Dunn and Barry Matlock. They offer a range of arguments largely based on exegesis of the texts in question (e.g. Matlock 2009). A key line of argument that Dunn (2008) has used is to link *ek pisteōs Christou* (by faith in/of Christ, 2:16; cf. 3:22) to the other uses of *ek pisteōs* (in Gal. 3:7, 8, 9, 11, 12, 24; 5:5), arguing that those refer to human faith, generally in Christ, and that the links between those texts and 2:16 and 3:22 imply that *pistis Christou* should be read in that way too. A particularly contentious text has been 3:11, which cites Hab. 2:4. For both Hays and scholars who disagree with him, such as Francis Watson, this text is seen as particularly supporting their case (Hays 2002: 140; Watson 2009; see discussion later).

As typically happens for biblical studies questions that have two competing answers, scholars have been creative in proposing ways of arguing for 'both of the above' (Hooker 1990; Morgan 2015: 272) or for 'neither of the above', presenting a series of alternative solutions. For Sam Williams, *pistis Christou* is a Christ-type faith in God (1997: 69–70). For Preston Sprinkle, it is the gospel and its content (2009: 180; see esp. 1:23 cf. 1:16). Benjamin Schliesser takes an approach related to Martyn's apocalypticism but which reads both *pistis* and *Christos* as 'spheres of influence' (2016: 283), an approach which, in particular, takes very seriously the parallel between *pistis Christou* and being 'in Christ' (see later).

An influential recent move has been John Barclay's new angle into a 'faith in Christ' reading via the concept of gift. Seeing this as a central feature of Paul's theology, Barclay reads *pistis Christou* as 'faith in (what God has done in) Christ' (2015: 371; his parenthesis). Another major recent development is Teresa Morgan's wide-ranging study of *pistis* and *fides*, the Latin term that she sees as overlapping particularly closely with it (2015: 7). Morgan sees *pistis* as always, to an extent, incorporating several relational senses (273). This leads her to affirm both 'faith in Christ' and 'faithfulness of Christ' senses as present in the occurrences of *pistis Christou* in Galatians. This emphasis on relationality is also seen in the work of Karl Ulrichs, for whom *pistis Christou* formulates 'in justification contexts, the fellowship with Christ that is conceived of in a participatory way' (2007: 251; Oakes's translation of 'in Rechtfertigungskontexten die partizipatorisch gedachte Gemeinschaft mit Christus'). As with almost all German-speaking scholarship, Ulrichs combines this with a sharp rejection of 'faithfulness of Christ' readings (250). In a recent article, I use Septuagintal evidence to support a relational reading and argue both that Paul generally has a trusting and/or loyal way of life in view in his use of *pistis* (with Crook 2004: 244; Williams 1997: 65) and that the relationship in view in Galatians was between the living Christ and people (Oakes 2018). In presenting the Christology of Galatians, this chapter will be using that to extend the argument that *pistis Christou* represents the relationship between people and the living Christ (probably theirs with him; possibly his with them, or both).

2. The presentation of Christ in the sequence of Galatians

Christ appears in every chapter of Galatians. There are particular concentrations of occurrences in the opening verses and in 2:15–3:1, 3:13-16, 3:21–4:6, 5:1-6 and 6:12-18. Conversely, there are few references in the narrative of 1:18–2:14, 3:2-10, 4:8-31 and 5:7–6:10, although the references that do occur in those sections often play key roles. More broadly, the references to Christ repeatedly carry the argument of Galatians forward in crucial ways.

Paul begins the letter by relating his apostleship to Christ and God: Paul is 'an emissary not from people, nor through a person, but through Jesus Christ and God the Father' (1:1). Differentiation between God and Christ then comes in the note that God raised Christ from the dead (1:1). However, God and Christ share in providing grace and peace (1:3). Christ is then unusually characterized as the one 'who gave himself for our sins, to rescue us from the present evil age' (1:4). In these few verses, Paul has already tied himself to Christ, Christ to God and Christ to the salvation of Paul and his hearers. In 1:6 and 1:10, Paul further links himself and his message to Christ. The Galatians were called 'in the grace of Christ' (1:6, see later) and Paul is 'Christ's slave' (1:10). Paul reinforces this link in the account of his calling. His message came through 'a revelation of Jesus Christ' (1:12), involving God choosing to 'reveal his Son to me' (for this reading of *en emoi*, see Oakes 2015: 57–8) so that Paul might 'proclaim him' among the gentiles (1:16).

The subsequent narrative of 1:18–2:14 only indirectly involves Christ: James is 'the brother of the Lord' (1:19); the 'assemblies of Judaea' are 'in Christ' (1:22); and the freedom that Paul and his Galatian hearers have is also 'in Christ Jesus' (2:4). However, the narrative ends with the Antioch incident leading into a speech by Paul that is packed full of language about Christ. Righteousness only comes through *pistis* of Jesus Christ, knowledge about which leads Christian Jews, such as Paul and Peter, to trust in Christ so as to gain righteousness that way (2:16). Paul denies that being 'found to be sinners' while 'seeking to be considered righteous in Christ' makes Christ 'a servant of sin' (2:17). Paul asserts that he has

> been crucified with Christ. I am no longer alive. Christ is alive in me. For the life I now live in the flesh, I live by trust in the Son of God [de Boer reads, 'faith, that of the Son of God'; 2011: 140, 162], who loved me and gave himself for me. I do not set aside the grace of God, for if there is righteousness through law, then Christ died for nothing. (2:19-21)

Paul now turns directly to the Galatians. What makes their behaviour so surprising is that 'Jesus Christ was presented before your very eyes as having been crucified' (3:1). After an argument from the Galatians' experience of the Spirit (3:2-5), followed by a comparison and link made with Abraham (3:6-9), a discussion about the Law and a curse leads, according to Richard Hays and others, to Christ coming back into the argument in 3:11 in a citation of Hab. 2:4:

> Because no one is considered righteous before God by means of law, it is clear that (δῆλον ὅτι) 'the one who is righteous on the basis of *pistis*

will live' [or 'the righteous one will live on the basis of *pistis*': ὁ δίκαιος ἐκ πίστεως ζήσεται].

For Hays, who prefers the second of these readings of Habakkuk, the verse is only wholly intelligible if Paul's use of the text holds together three senses of it:

(a) The Messiah will live by (his own) faith(fulness).
(b) The righteous person will live as a result of the Messiah's faith(fulness).
(c) The righteous person will live by (his own) faith (in the Messiah). (Hays 2002: 140)

Francis Watson responds by arguing that Paul repeatedly associates the expression *ek pisteōs* with righteousness but never directly with life (2009: 160). He concludes that the first of the readings of Habakkuk is correct and that, consequently, 'the righteous one' is not to be read as the Messiah, that is, Christ (161–3). We can add that Gal. 3:11 begins with a recapitulation of the conclusion of 2:16, 'no one is considered righteous before God by means of law' (for δῆλον ὅτι as a fixed formula, 'it is clear that'; see Wakefield 2003: 162–7, 207–14; de Boer 2011: 202–3; Oakes 2015: 110–11). This suggests that the topic of 3:11 is of unsuccessful and successful bases for righteousness of people before God. (In my commentary, Greek word order led me to favour the second reading of Hab. 2:4 (2015: 110–12). Arguments such as Watson's and the comparison with 2:16 have changed my mind.) We should add that, even with the second reading of Hab. 2:4, the link between Gal. 3:11 and 2:16 still stands and a reference to Christ is far from necessary.

However 3:11 is read, Christ certainly returns to the argument in 3:13.

Christ redeemed us from the curse of the law, becoming a curse on our behalf, because it is written, 'Cursed is everyone who hangs on a tree', so that the blessing of Abraham would come to the gentiles in Christ Jesus, so that we would receive the promise of the Spirit through trust. (3:13-14)

Boakye will discuss (in Chapter 3) the use of Deut. 21:23. The key points about 3:13-14 for us here are that Paul interprets Christ's death as removing the legal curse and that this somehow enables gentiles to receive Abraham's blessing and the Spirit.

The argument of 3:15-29 centres on a radical Christological rereading of the Abrahamic promise narrative. Paul sees Christ as 'the seed' who was to share in Abraham's blessing (3:15-16). The arrival of Christ, as Abraham's seed, signalled the arrival of *pistis*, which also meant the end of the Law's role as a *paidagōgos* (a slave protecting a child and helping facilitate their basic education) (3:19-25). The promise of God was 'given on the basis of trust in Jesus Christ to those who trust' (3:22; 'via the faith of Christ to those who believe' (Martyn 1997: 353)). Christians 'were baptised into Christ', 'have put on Christ', are now 'all "one" in Christ' (3:28) and are 'of Christ' (3:29). This oneness in Christ, expressed socially through the 'no Jew nor Greek . . . no slave nor free . . . no male and female' formula of 3:28, makes people Abraham's 'one' seed, hence Abraham's heirs.

Galatians 4:4-6 narrates a double sending.

> But when the fulness of time came, God sent out his Son, born of a woman, born under law, so that he might redeem those under law, so that we might receive adoption. Because you are sons, God sent out the Spirit of his Son into our hearts, crying out, 'Abba, Father'!

Although brief, this is the most extensive narration in Galatians of the Christ-event. It picks up the note about time from 3:19-25 and the idea of redemption from 3:13, with the broader redemptive background of 2:16-21 and 1:4. The repetition of 'God sent out' forms a tight link between the sendings of God's son and of 'the Spirit of his son', an identification which further tightens the link and brings the Spirit closely into the understanding of the process by which Paul sees Christians as continuing to relate to Christ. By linking the Spirit with Christ, Paul also effectively brings Christ somewhat into the sections of the text where Spirit language predominates over references to Christ, namely, 3:2-5 and 5:13-23. The parallel between the two sendings is also part of the way in which this part of Galatians 4 is driving towards calling Paul's hearers not to make moves that he sees as a retreat back into practices (4:8-11) from which Jesus has brought about redemption.

The next appearances of Christ in the text are in the unexpected realm of identity of Paul and his hearers. In 4:14, Paul notes that the Galatians received Paul 'as if I were an angel of God, as if I were Christ Jesus'. This must be more than a generalized compliment to the Galatians' hospitableness. The links with Paul's weakness and his proclamation of the gospel (4:13-14) look too pointed for that (and cf. 6:17: Paul's closing appeal to his bearing the 'marks of Jesus'). A few verses later, Paul is in repeated birth-pangs for the formation of Christ in the Galatians (4:19). Again, this must be more than a general hope for Paul's hearers becoming better people. Given the letter's other language about mutual indwelling, there must be some more substantive sense in which Christ is to be formed in them.

Paul heads off in other directions in 4:21-31, including surprisingly making use of the idea of Abrahamic descent in ways other than the patterns worked out at such length in Galatians 3. However, the issue of freedom in the Sarah, Hagar, Isaac, Ishmael account brings Paul back in 5:1 to the issue of gaining freedom, hence back to Christ as the redeemer. As in 4:7-11, the aim is to prevent Paul's hearers reverting to practices that he sees as slavery, here specified as gentile adoption of circumcision (5:3). Paul brings Christ into his plea as a particular motive for not doing this: 'If you get circumcised, Christ will be of no use to you' (5:2); 'You were alienated from Christ, those of you who are being considered righteous by means of law. You fell away from grace' (5:4). Paul then returns to the logic of 3:28 to give the theological grounds for this motive: 'for in Christ Jesus neither circumcision matters, nor uncircumcision' (5:6). Paul goes on to specify what does matter 'in Christ', namely, 'trust, working through love'. This sets up much of the dynamic of the handling of moral issues in the rest of the chapter.

There are two brief references to Christ in the next few verses. Having objected to the actions of his opponents, Paul expresses confidence, being 'persuaded about you, in the Lord, that you will not think otherwise' (5:10). The reference to 'the Lord' here is presumably something such as an expression of confidence that the sovereignty of Christ means that Christ will maintain the Galatians in right thinking. In 5:11, Paul refers to 'the scandal of the cross':

If I am still preaching circumcision, why am I still persecuted? In that case the offence of the cross would be done away with.

For Paul, there is something about Christ's central act, his death on the cross, that is incompatible with the preaching of the need for gentile circumcision.

Since the Spirit is specified in 4:6 as τὸ πνεῦμα τοῦ υἱοῦ αὐτοῦ, 'the Spirit of his Son', which is sent by God but not specified, in Galatians, as 'the Spirit of God', we might wonder whether, in 5:13-23, the Spirit to some extent stands in for Christ, making Christ present in these verses despite the lack of explicit reference to him. It is certainly the case that there is a very direct link made back to Christ in 5:24: the people 'led by the Spirit' (5:18) are clearly the same as those 'of Christ' (5:24), a point followed by a switch to describing these people as those who 'live by the Spirit' (5:25). A couple of verses later Paul switches back to characterizing behaviour in relation to Christ, with the enigmatic 'Bear one another's burdens, and so you will fulfil the law of Christ' (6:2, see later in this chapter).

The letter closing includes two references to the cross as, specifically, 'the cross of Christ' (6:12) and 'the cross of our lord Jesus Christ' (6:14). In 6:12-14, Paul appears to be back in the territory of 5:11: the opponents' preaching of circumcision is to avoid suffering or loss that Paul associates with preaching of the cross. In 6:14, the cross is, more broadly, the locus of 'the world' being 'crucified' to Paul, and Paul to 'the world' (note that this is an event happening to Paul; he may well see his experience as paradigmatic for Christians, but Martyn looks unreasonable in seeing it as implying an event happening to the cosmos; see earlier). At the end of his peroration, Paul appeals to his bearing τὰ στίγματα τοῦ Ἰησοῦ, 'the marks of Jesus', on his body (6:17). 'Our lord Jesus Christ' is the source of grace in the final benediction (6:18).

3. The underlying Christological narrative and references to Christ that are non-narrative

We will now turn the process round and look at the Christological assertions of Galatians in chronological order in terms of what the letter indicates about the existence of Christ. Some readers may detect my long-standing enthusiasm for Norman Peterson's *Rediscovering Paul: Philemon and the Sociology of Paul's Narrative World* (1985), in which he, very illuminatingly, runs through the 'poetic sequence' and the 'referential sequence' of the letter. Another pair of points of inspiration is the interest in underlying narrative in the work of Hays and Wright. However, in a manner that will, I hope, be embraced by scholars who are sceptical of reframing letters as if they are narratives, our interests here are more basically analytical than narratological: unlike Peterson, our interest is not in examining how Paul reorders the chronological sequence as he makes his argument. We are essentially just trying to construct an organized picture of the set of ways in which Christ is presented by Paul.

There is no overt set of chronological indicators for statements about Christ in the letter. However, it looks reasonable to identify five time periods, albeit with various overlaps among them. The five are:

a. Prior to Christ's birth

b. Birth, death and resurrection of Christ

c. Christ in relationship with Christians: the period starting from when this began

d. Christ in Paul's calling and existence: the period beginning with Paul's encounter with Christ

e. Christ in the Galatians' calling and existence: the period beginning with the Galatians' encounter with Christ

To bring in all the references to Christ in the letter, we then need a sixth category:

f. References to Christ without direct links to chronological stages of Christ's existence

An example is 'the gospel of Christ' (1:7). Such a reference to Christ is unlikely to have an identifiable location in an underlying narrative of the life (or afterlife) of Christ.

3a. Prior to Christ's birth

There is virtually nothing in Galatians that could be thought of as description of pre-existence of Christ. This is partly an effect of there being a lack of direct Christological discussion in the letter. Despite the large number of references to Christ, Christ is rarely the main subject of discussion. However, there is one crucial way in which Christ comes into argument relating to the period prior to his birth. Christ is stated to be, along with Abraham, the object of the promises spoken to Abraham:

> The promises were spoken to Abraham and to his seed – it does not say 'and to the seeds', as if to many, but as to one: 'and to your seed', who is Christ. (3:16)

A few verses later, Christ is 'the seed . . . to whom the promise was made' (3:19). However, Christ does not play any active role until 'God sent' him 'out' (*exapesteilen*) as a person being born (4:4).

All this leaves open the question of whether any of it is evidence of pre-existence. The note associating Christ with the promise to Abraham could function simply prophetically – God could make promises to Christ who God knew would be born – or through an anthropology of general human partial pre-existence as seeds within an ancestor (cf. Heb. 7:4-10). In support of the latter case, we could say that it makes Paul's mode of argument look less strange: if there was a common view that Abraham was effectively full of thousands of seeds of his descendants, Paul's point would be that, in using the singular noun 'seed', God was indicating that he would pick just one out of that crowd. Paul's phraseology then looks less arbitrary than it does without assuming that anthropological theory.

It is also uncertain whether 'sending' language implies pre-existence with God, from which position Christ is viewed as arriving. The verb here, *exapostellō*, is used in Acts 12:11 of God sending an angel, which probably carries the thought of the angel existing and travelling from God to earth. Such a thought about Christ in Gal. 4:4 could imply pre-existence, although it clearly could not directly parallel what happens to the angel because Christ is then born. In Acts 22:21, Paul speaks of God sending him (from Jerusalem) to the gentiles, clearly not carrying a sense of arrival from a supernatural realm. The Septuagint Greek translation of the Psalms has examples of use of *exapostellō* of God sending a range of people and objects (e.g. Ps. 17:15 (MT 18:14); 42:4 (43:3); 104:26 (105:26)), without implication of their pre-existence. The discussion on either side of the question is somewhat akin to scholars' discussion of Johannine 'sending' language, although with much less textual data to draw on.

3b. Birth, death and resurrection of Christ

Although silent about any possible pre-existence, Galatians is explicit about Jesus's birth.

> But when the fulness of time came, God sent out his Son, born of a woman, born under law. (4:4)

Even though births and mothers become important in Paul's argument in 4:19-31, he does not appear to pick up on the gendered reference to Christ's birth in 4:4. The reference to being 'born of a woman' looks more likely to be intended as a statement of Jesus's human identity, an identity which is then further specified as being 'under law'. Paul picks that up straightaway to link Jesus's birth to redemptive activity: 'so that he might redeem those under law' (4:5). This is characteristic of Galatians. The Christology is used to serve soteriology, often then moving on quickly to a point of dissuading the Galatians from following Paul's opponents, as happens here in 4:8-11. In

4:5, the referent of 'those under law' is complicated by the pronouns in the next two clauses: 'so that we might receive adoption' and 'because you are sons' (4:6). The move from 'they' to 'we' to 'you' broadens the group who are redeemed beyond being only Jews. Somehow the predominantly gentile Galatians are drawn into this, as indeed into the earlier law-related rhetoric of 3:11-14. In any case, the move here that is most typical of Galatians is that Christ's sonship becomes the basis of the sonship of Christians (male and female; see 3:28). Just as birth under law serves a redemptive purpose in relation to law, Christ's very sonship is made the basis of redemption expressed in sonship terms.

The arrival of Christ at a particular point of time is also a motif of 3:19-25. As in 4:4-6, the arrival is seen instrumentally. It is for a redemptive purpose. In 3:19-25, this is effectively expressed through the equation that Paul makes between the arrival of Christ and the arrival of *pistis*. The law was 'added' until 'the seed', that is, Christ, arrived (3:19). People were 'guarded under the law . . . until the coming *pistis* would be revealed' (3:23). The 'law was our *paidagōgos* until Christ' (3:24; see earlier for *paidagōgos*). 'With *pistis* having come, we are no longer under a *paidagōgos*' (3:25). Christ and *pistis* are brought together in redemptive statements such as 'you are all sons of God through trust, in Christ Jesus' (3:26; taking διὰ τῆς πίστεως and ἐν Χριστῷ Ἰησοῦ as complementary expressions of how people are 'sons of God', although taking the whole phrase together as 'through trust in Christ Jesus' would, of course, be far from alien to the thought of Galatians). Again, the Christology of Christ's arrival is expressed to produce soteriology.

An enigmatic expression which, on some theories, relates to either Christ's ministry or death, or both, is 6:2: 'Bear one another's burdens, and so you will fulfil the law of Christ.' Dunn argues that this refers 'to the Jesus tradition as indicating how Jesus interpreted the law in his teaching and actions' (1993: 322, cf. 323). A comparison of burden-bearing with the descriptions of Christ's action on the cross at 1:4, 2:20 and 3:14 supports the idea that 'the law of Christ' here relates especially to what was seen in his death (Oakes 2015: 179–80). However, Paul's surprising use of the term 'law' here means that we need to be a bit cautious about how certain we can be of a link simply to Christ's life, death or words (see, e.g., de Boer 2011: 378–81).

As with references to Christ's birth, references in Galatians to Christ's death are also for the sake of soteriology. There are several such texts in Galatians. The first is 1:4, where Christ's death is implied by the expression 'gave himself for our sins'. That the 'for our sins' is intended redemptively is then made explicit by the explanation 'to rescue us from the present evil age'.

This is also the one text about Christ's death that might, to some extent, function as evidence for Richard Hays's reading of the event of the cross as an act of obedience (2000: 240): this rescue was 'according to the will of our God and Father' (1:4). This sounds rather like Phil. 2:7, in which Christ is ὑπήκοος μέχρι θανάτου, 'obedient through to death', with the obedience undoubtedly being directed towards God rather than death. However, Gal. 1:4 is more likely to be an expression of God's will to redeem, rather than of Christ's obedience to God's will. Among other factors, this is supported by the relationship to the reference in 1:3 to 'God our father', which encompasses Paul and the Galatians. If Paul intended to stress Christ's obedience to God, 1:4 would more likely have referred to 'the will of God *his* father'. In any case, 1:4 would be a very thin base in Galatians for an argument that the letter's central idea of *pistis* in relation to Christ is that of Christ's obedience to God in Christ's death on the cross.

There is quite a gap between 1:4 and the next reference to Christ's death, in 2:20-21. The cross is often read into the 'justification by faith' text in 2:16, but it is not explicitly there. The links between 2:16 and 2:20-21 do show that Paul's thought makes links between Christ's death and the route to righteousness. Paul's way of thinking on this is also indicated by the key passage relating righteousness to faith in Romans (3:21-31). There, the link between righteousness, faith and Christ's death (viewed in sacrificial terms) is directly expressed. However, Galatians predates Romans. Although the relationship between Gal. 2:16 and 2:21 does give weight to the idea that Christ's death is part of the thought of 2:16, it is not certain that the earlier text of Galatians does actually include the fuller ideas worked out in Romans – although it might well do so. As noted earlier, some scholars introduce the idea of the cross into Gal. 2:16 as being inherent in *pistis Christou*: John Barclay seeing *pistis Christou* as centred on trust in the event of the gift expressed on the cross; and Richard Hays seeing *pistis Christou* as expressing Christ's faithful death.

Christ's death is emphasized in 2:20-21, again with soteriological effect. Paul, relating to himself aspects of the ideas of 1:4, writes of 'the Son of God, who loved me and gave himself for me'. As we saw with the motif of Christ's birth, here too the move from Christology to redemption is followed by an application to attack the message of Paul's opponents, which is implicit as he continues, 'I do not set aside the grace of God, for if there is righteousness through law, then Christ died for nothing' (2:21). The people who arrived at Antioch from James, and the teachers in Galatia who are encouraging gentile circumcision, are viewed as annulling Christ's death through their actions that Paul sees as a setting aside of grace. Paul then goes straight on to apply this to his Galatian hearers: 'Oh foolish Galatians! Who has cast the evil eye on you – you to whom Jesus Christ was presented before your very eyes as having been crucified?!' (3:1).

The third text that to some extent narrates the event of Christ's death is 3:13. 'Christ redeemed us from the curse of the law, becoming a curse on our behalf, because it is written, "Cursed is everyone who hangs on a tree." ' Event and redemption are immediately tied together here. The relationship to the Galatians' lives is further explained in 3:14, 'so that the blessing of Abraham would come to the gentiles in Christ Jesus, so that we would receive the promise of the Spirit through trust'. Again, Christ's death is narrated for the sake of soteriology, which is applied to the Galatians.

A text which describes effects of Christ's action, but without specifying what that action is, is 5:1, 'For freedom Christ has set us free.' However, the similarity to the concept of 'rescue' in 1:4 suggests that 5:1 may also be alluding to Christ's death. Galatians 5:1 is clearly soteriological. Also, in keeping with the pattern we have been observing, it leads on to a call for the Galatians to resist the teaching of Paul's opponents, 'Stand firm then and do not be subject again to a yoke of slavery. Look, I Paul say to you that, if you get circumcised, Christ will be of no use to you' (5:1-2).

Christ's death is referred to in other texts in Galatians. However, they speak of relationship to Christ's death, rather than narrating that death itself, so they will be dealt with in section 3f.

The resurrection of Christ is directly referred to only once in Galatians, but it is right at the beginning. It is striking that Paul, at that point, chooses to characterize God as the one 'who raised' Jesus Christ 'from among the dead'. Boakye explores this in Chapter 4.

3c. Christ in relationship with Christians: The period starting from when this began

The next stage of the underlying Christological narrative is that Christ becomes a figure who is in continuing relationship to a concrete group of people. The starting point of this stage is not specifically defined in the letter. It could be seen as beginning with the first encounter of people with Christ in his ministry. It could be seen as beginning with the resurrection, as an event which puts Christ into a mode of existence in which concepts such as being 'in Christ' might be seen as making better sense. However, all we know from Galatians is that, by the time there are Christians, their life is 'in

Christ' and relates to Christ in various further ways. There is no end point, in Galatians, to this stage in the Christological narrative: unlike letters such as 1 Thessalonians and Philippians, Galatians does not refer to eschatological events which could be seen as moving matters on to a further stage.

The largest set of links between Christ and Christian existence comes in texts that characterize that existence as being 'in Christ' (*en Christō*) or similar formulations. Galatians 1:22 refers to 'the assemblies of Judea that are in Christ'. In 2:4, people 'spy on our freedom, which we have in Christ Jesus'. Galatians 2:17 speaks of 'seeking to be considered righteous in Christ' (for this reading, see Oakes 2015: 82–4). The result of Christ's death in 3:13 is that 'the blessing of Abraham would come to the gentiles in Christ Jesus' (3:14). Galatians 3:26-29 expresses this participation in Christ using both 'in Christ' and a range of other formulations.

> For you are all sons of God through trust, *in Christ Jesus*. For as many as were *baptized into Christ*, you have *put on Christ*. There is no Jew nor Greek. There is no slave nor free. There is no male and female. For you are all *"one" in Christ Jesus*. If you are *of Christ*, then you are Abraham's seed, heirs according to the promise. (Emphases added)

Echoing 3:28 is 5:6, 'in Christ Jesus neither circumcision matters, nor uncircumcision'. Galatians 5:24 repeats the terminology of 3:29 in describing Christians as 'those who are of Christ Jesus'.

Being 'in Christ' probably refers to an all-encompassing relationship with the living Christ, in which the Christian is dependent on Christ. Few scholars would deny this as such. However, as we saw when looking at theories on *pistis Christou*, many would put significant emphasis elsewhere in their explanation of the role of Christ in Galatians, so it is worth us reflecting on the grounds that there are in Galatians for seeing the 'in Christ' relationship as one involving the living Christ.

A starting point for our argument is in 1:1: Christ having been 'raised . . . from among the dead'. From the start of Galatians, the reader has been made aware that Christ is a currently living being (Downs and Lappenga 2019: 86). Of course, that in itself does not imply that the living Christ relates to people. In the Graeco-Roman world, many figures were viewed as having, in some sense, an ongoing, heroized afterlife (although here I agree with N. T. Wright that the transition to such afterlife would not be described using terms that would be translated as 'raised from the dead' (2003: 32–7)) but would not relate substantially to living people. However, Christ is shown to be active on the Galatians' behalf in the letter's opening grace wish: 'Grace to you and peace from God our Father and the Lord Jesus Christ' (1:3). The living Christ sends grace and peace to the Galatians. The resurrected Christ also acts on behalf of Christians in texts such as Rom. 8:34. Paul's belief that Christ is now alive sharply increases the likelihood that when he uses phrases that indicate relationship to Christ, Paul has the current, living Christ in mind.

A second stage of argument draws on 2:20. 'Christ lives in me', Paul writes. This is conceptually surprising if one takes 'in Christ' in some kind of spatial sense, which cautions us against going too far in that direction. If Christ is a 'sphere' (Schliesser 2016: 283), 2:20 makes it hard to avoid also seeing Paul, or a Christian more generally, as also being a 'sphere'. However, the dependency noted earlier means that the sense in which Paul can say 'Christ lives in me' (2:20) is not quite symmetrical with the sense in which Paul is 'in Christ'. Christ is not fundamentally dependent on Paul (although God does entrust a gospel message to Paul (2:7) so, in that sense, puts his work in Paul's hands). One indication of the asymmetry of the relationship is that Paul far more frequently speaks of people being 'in Christ' than of Christ being in people. Paul does speak quite often of the Spirit being in people (3:2-5, 14; 4:6, 29; 5:17-25). However, even if the Spirit is very closely identified with Christ (4:6; 'the Spirit of his Son'), indwelling by a Spirit does not mean that the Spirit's existence is determined by location in the people in the same way that the Christian's existence is determined by location in Christ. All this means that the sense in which Christ might be seen as a 'sphere' is not quite the same sense in which Paul or other people might be indwelt 'spheres' (although there may well be an analogy between them). However, the point for us here is that all the indicators of Christ or the Spirit living in Christians represent ideas of Christ and the Spirit as living, active beings. This further supports the idea that 'in Christ' represents a relationship with Christ as a living, active being.

A third stage of argument draws on Christ being trusted. Christ is the object of Christian trust in Galatians, irrespective of the view that is taken about *pistis Christou*. Writing of Christian Jews in 2:16, Paul asserts, ἡμεῖς εἰς Χριστὸν Ἰησοῦν ἐπιστεύσαμεν, 'we trusted in Christ Jesus'. Another example which links trust to Christ (but which is caught up in the *pistis Christou* debate) is 2:20, ἐν πίστει ζῶ τῇ τοῦ υἱοῦ τοῦ θεοῦ, which I would read as 'I live by trust in the Son of God'. In fact, whatever view is taken of *pistis Christou*, the expression connects *pistis* to Christ in a manner that, one way or another, is central to Christian existence. In 3:22, however one reads that verse, Christ becomes the basis for what was promised being given to Christians, ἵνα ἡ ἐπαγγελία ἐκ πίστεως Ἰησοῦ Χριστοῦ δοθῇ τοῖς πιστεύουσιν, 'so that the promise would be given on the basis of trust in Jesus Christ to those who trust' (de Boer reads, 'so that the promise from the faith of Jesus Christ be given to those who believe'; 2011: 218). Morgan demonstrates that *pisteuō* generally includes the idea of trusting, rather than merely belief (2015: 273). In Galatians, that certainly appears to be the case. In both 2:16 and 3:22 (and especially in 2:20, if it is read as earlier), *pisteuō* does not just denote cognitive assent but also some sort of commitment of trust in Christ. Again, this supports the idea that Christ is probably being viewed as a living being who can be trusted for future actions, rather than just belief and trust in the effects of the past actions of a being who no longer acts. Again, this bolsters the probability that the 'in Christ' relationship is seen as involving a living Christ.

A final form of argument for our case is from the contexts of the various 'in Christ' references themselves. These all work well if the phrase expresses relationship with the living Christ, whereas they variously work less well if they involve Christ only as a past actor. To take the first instance in the letter: characterizing communities as 'the assemblies of Judea that are in Christ' (1:22) makes most sense if Christ is a living being to whom the groups relate.

One particular aspect of the pattern of 'in Christ' language in Galatians is that it and *pistis* language several times appear to be equivalent to each other. This is especially clear in 2:16-17.

> . . . knowing that a person is not considered righteous on the basis of works of law, except through trust in Jesus Christ, even we trusted in Christ Jesus, so that we would be considered righteous on the basis of trust in Christ . . . If, while seeking to be considered righteous in Christ . . .

The key consequence of our argument is that both the participation and *pistis* language of Galatians are read as primarily referring to relationship to the living Christ in what is, by the time of Galatians, his post-resurrection existence.

3d. *Christ in Paul's calling and existence*

We move on to the period beginning from Paul's encounter with Christ. This period starts a few years later than the period of 3c, then exists as part of it.

The letter begins with an act in which Christ is involved.

> Paul, an emissary not from people, nor through a person, but through Jesus Christ and God the Father who raised him from among the dead. (1:1)

Christ is somehow part of the process that appoints Paul to ministry.

Paul writes that his gospel came 'through a revelation of Jesus Christ' (1:11). This assertion is presumably referring to the event of Paul's initial calling, which he also puts in terms of revelation. He speaks of when

> God – who . . . called me, through his grace – was pleased to reveal his Son to me, so that I might proclaim him among the gentiles. (1:15-16)

In 1 Corinthians, Paul puts this in terms of the risen Christ appearing to him (in an irregular manner: 1 Cor. 15:8). This is probably to be understood in Gal. 1:15 too and is, of course, reinforced, at second hand, by the various accounts in Acts (9:5; 22:8; 26:15). In Paul's view, the encounter of 1 Cor. 15:8 and, almost certainly, of Gal. 1:15 was an event in which the living Christ appeared to Paul.

Christ is the object of Paul's service. He is 'a slave of Christ' (1:10). The thought here is probably of a living person, whom Paul is serving. In 5:10, Paul also uses a form of the 'in Christ' idea, probably applied to himself. 'I am persuaded about you, in the Lord, that you will not think otherwise at all': an incidental indication of Paul's participation in Christ, with the use of the title 'Lord', as possibly emphasizing something of Christ's authority, although Paul's use of the title is sufficiently common that we should be cautious about reading much into its use here.

3e. Christ in the Galatians' calling and existence

There is surprisingly little directly under this heading. The origins of the Galatian Christian communities are narrated more in terms of their encounter with Paul than their encounter with Christ (4:13-14). However, their calling is probably described as having been 'in the grace of Christ' (ἐν χάριτι Χριστοῦ: the term 'Christ' is present in almost all manuscripts but apparently missing in P46 and in some church fathers such as Tertullian). That could be seen as an action of the living Christ in supplying grace, but that may be an over-reading, given the frequency of the link between 'grace' and 'Christ'. However, we have already noted 1:3, in which 'grace' comes to the Galatians from 'the Lord Jesus Christ', which is a clearer signal of Christ's ongoing action. Galatians 1:3 also increases the likelihood that 6:18, 'the grace of our Lord Jesus Christ be with your spirit', implies an action by Christ.

Galatians 5:2-4 speaks of potential departure from Christ.

> Look, I Paul say to you that, if you get circumcised, Christ will be of no use to you. I testify again to every man who gets circumcised that he is under obligation to do the whole law. You were alienated from Christ, those of you who are being considered righteous by means of law. You fell away from grace.

Although it would also be possible to see this departure as being a giving up of benefits brought through the Christ's cross, the expression would work particularly well if referring to breaking a relationship with the living Christ.

One further text relating Christ and the Galatians is 4:19. Paul writes that he is 'again in pains of childbirth until Christ is formed in you'. Although this could relate to building in the Galatians the character that had been seen in Christ, it would fit more fully into the overall discourse of Galatians if, instead, it related somehow to the degree of fullness of Christ's living in them, as he lived in Paul according to 2:20.

Overall, for both Paul and the Galatians, texts from the period of the awareness of Christ suggest that the living Christ is active in their lives.

3f. References to Christ without direct chronological links to Christ's existence

There are also points in Galatians about Christ that do not tell us about the underlying Christological narrative of the letter but which are part of the range of ways in which Christ is brought into aspects of the letter's thought.

Christ is presented as the basic descriptor of the gospel. Galatians 1:7 accuses Paul's opponents of 'wanting to pervert the gospel of Christ'. The description of the gospel as *tou Christou* could be taken in various ways, seeing Christ as the gospel's basis, origin or content. Under any of these options, the message that Paul sees as generating Christian life is a message tightly identified with Christ. This fits with Paul's description of his commission, which is 'that I might proclaim him among the gentiles' (1:16).

A very specific way in which Christ determines Christian existence in Galatians is that the cross of Christ becomes the site or mode of the Christian's transformation. Galatians 5:24 reads, 'Those who are of Christ Jesus have crucified (*estaurōsan*) the flesh, with its passions and desires.' On its own, 'crucified' in this text might be taken as a somewhat general metaphor, communicating that Christians had dealt with their fleshly passions violently, completely and, maybe, publicly. However, this text needs to be seen alongside two others in Galatians relating to Paul. In 2:19, he writes, 'I have been crucified with Christ' (*Christōi sunestaurōmai*). In 6:14, he writes of 'the cross of our Lord Jesus Christ, through which the world was crucified (*estaurōtai*) to me, and I to the world'. In 2:19-20, Paul is probably presenting himself as paradigmatic in his transformation to a life lived for God, through Christ living in Paul: paradigmatic in the first instance for Christian Jews but, given the parallels drawn in Galatians 3, also for Christian gentiles. Note, for instance, the transition from 2:20 to a general statement in 2:21, then in 3:1 to a rebuke towards the Galatians. The points about the world in 6:14 are also no doubt intended to induce others to see things the same way as Paul. If the texts relating to Paul are indeed paradigmatic, then identification with Christ on the cross is being presented as a key element of Christian existence. It also makes it more likely that the crucifying of the flesh in 5:24 is part of this mode of thought too, so that the crucifying of the flesh is not so much a self-mortifying act as an act of transformation through identification with the crucified Christ.

The converse of this is that Paul sees the message of circumcision for gentiles as effectively being a dodging of the effects of the cross. He asks, 'If I am still preaching circumcision, why am I still persecuted? In that case the offence of the cross would be done away with' (5:11). Later, he claims that his opponents 'are compelling you to be circumcised, only so that they would not be persecuted for the cross of Christ' (6:12). In contrast, the cross is Paul's only boast: 'May I never boast, except in the cross of our Lord Jesus Christ' (6:14). He also ends the letter with the personal claim that 'I bear the marks of Jesus on my body' (6:17).

It is unlikely that any of the texts in this subsection add to the evidence of Christ being living and active at the time of the letter. However, they do help strengthen the picture of a Christ who is being depicted for soteriological reasons. We have seen in prior sections how the soteriological story in Galatians is generally a relational one.

4. A relational Christ and the *pistis* of that Christ

The presentation of Christ in the sequence of argument in Galatians and the underlying Christological narrative of Galatians point in closely related directions. This is not very surprising, but it is significant where scholars might try to play off the argument against the underlying narrative. Understanding these directions is also important for issues in Galatians that involve Christ.

The sequence of references to Christ in Galatians begins with Christ validating Paul and his message (1:1, 10, 12). From almost the start (1:4) and explicitly from 1:12, 16, Christ actually is Paul's message, with Christ seen as a self-giving redeemer figure (1:4). Christian identity as being 'in Christ' comes in in 1:22 and 2:4, which links this with freedom. Trust in/of Christ and being in Christ are made the source of righteousness in 2:16-17. Paul personalizes this in 2:18-20, linking it to Christ living in him and the cross of Christ being something in which Paul participates. In 3:13-14, Christ's cross redeems 'us' from the curse of the law, which enables the Spirit to come to gentiles. In 3:15-25, Christ is Abraham's seed whose arrival brings *pistis* and righteousness. Christians are in him and thus one (3:26-29). In 4:5, Christ's incarnation redeems 'those under law' and brings his Spirit and adoption (4:5-7). Paul then uses this to attack what he sees as regression to slavery, involving calendrical elements (4:8-11). The attack is reinforced in 5:1-4, tying regression from Christ to gentile circumcision. Existence in Christ privileges neither circumcision nor lack of it, but trust and love (5:6). Galatians 5:11 links preaching of circumcision to avoidance of 'the scandal of the cross'. Galatians 5:24 asserts that those 'of Christ Jesus' have 'crucified the flesh'. Galatians 6:12 reinforces the idea that Paul's opponents' message of circumcision is preached to avoid persecution on account of the cross which, in 6:14, redefines the relationship to the world. Paul ends back with a self-identification with the sufferings of Christ (6:17).

The underlying Christological narrative of Galatians begins with Christ's mysterious involvement, of some kind, in the promises to Abraham (3:16). It leads onto birth for the sake of redemption (4:4-7), an arrival which is also interpreted as the arrival of *pistis* (3:23-26). Christ's death is a self-giving, again for the sake of redemption (1:4; 2:20-21; 3:13). Christ is then raised by God (1:1). From about this time onwards an existence 'in Christ' comes about (1:22; 2:4, etc.), which is characterized by trust in Christ (2:16) and some kind of sharing in the cross (2:19; 5:24; 6:14). Christ (2:20) and the Spirit of Christ (4:6) live in the Christian.

Both the set of references to Christ in the sequence of Galatians and the underlying Christological narrative present a consistent picture: this is a relational Christ. More specifically it is a Christ in relationship with his people. Christ's story is shaped around them. He loved them. He acted to free them, through his death. He relates to them now in mutual (although not symmetrical) indwelling, in a bond of *pistis*: trust, loyalty.

Contrary to Hays, Christ is not presented in Galatians as primarily in a *pistis* relationship with God. The identity of interest and action between Christ and God in Galatians does indeed imply a close linkage, but the relational expressions of the letter are between Christ and his people, rather than Christ and God (a point argued by Ota (2016: 3), although his emphasis on the cross is persuasively corrected to the resurrected Jesus by Downs and Lappenga (2019: 86)). Contrary to Martyn, Christ is not presented in Galatians as one who acts primarily in relation to the Cosmos. The Christ of Galatians acts primarily in relation to his people.

Some might respond to these arguments by pointing to the genre and circumstances of Galatians. They could say that it is a letter, written to affect its Galatian hearers, so our exercise of examining the references to Christ was bound to show a Christ who engaged with issues about the hearers, so our study does not invalidate the idea that the real underlying Christological structure is one of Christ's relationship to God and/or Christ's action in regard to the Cosmos. However, we do need to follow the actual evidence in the letter and, when it comes to it, even the use of the term *pistis* itself is part of the letter's message to its Galatian hearers. The whole question of *pistis Christou* is bound within the realm of the evidence in the letter (although secondary appeal can be made to other sources): the *pistis* of Christ in Galatians is itself an element of the rhetoric of Galatians. The Christ of Galatians is a Christ in relationship with his people. The *pistis* of that Christ is a relationship between Christ and his people.

Our investigation of the Christology of Galatians can take us as far as that conclusion. It cannot, in itself, get us beyond that to a decision about whether this *pistis* of Christ is primarily a matter of the trust of Christians in Christ, and their loyalty to him, or primarily a matter of Christ's loyalty to Christians, or an equal balance of the two. To see if progress can be made on that question requires consideration of other factors in the argument of the letter (with some thought about other letters where relevant). I have argued elsewhere (2018: 270–2) that what we can say, which may help push the balance of probabilities in one direction, is that Galatians does unambiguously make reference to Christians' trust in Christ (2:16;

3:22) but does not unambiguously reference Christ's loyalty to Christians, although it does reference his love for them (2:20), which would imply *pistis* towards them.

A further conclusion that our Christological study has led to is that Christians relate to the current, living Christ and that this is the sense of the 'in Christ' language and *pistis* language in the letter. This conclusion contrasts, in formal terms at least, with the views of both Hays and John Barclay, both of whom see the *pistis* idea as tied specifically to the cross. For Hays, it is Christ's faithfulness to God in the event of the cross. For Barclay, it is the Christian's trust in the gift of God expressed in Christ's self-giving on the cross. Both of these scholars do, in fact, speak strongly of Paul seeing Christians as having a relationship with the risen Christ (Hays 2002: xxxi–xxxii; Barclay 2015: 500–501). However, the reading presented here does differ from theirs in the key time reference of *pistis*. Here *pistis* equates to participation in Christ, primarily as a current being. Thus, in our reading 2:16 sees righteousness as primarily coming through current relationship with Christ, rather than primarily either through trust in the cross or through Christ's faithfulness on the cross. That is not to deny that Paul expects relationship with Christ to include trust in the cross as a key element (e.g. 2:21 implies that such trust should dissuade from adoption of legal practices that divide Jews from gentiles). However, my argument is that *pistis Christou* is primarily current relationship with the living Christ, rather than primarily belief in the effects of a past event. Trust in Christ's cross is part of relating to the living Christ, but the centre is the relationship itself.

CHAPTER 3
SCRIPTURE AND PROMISE
Andrew K. Boakye

The social harmony and oneness Paul sought for the Galatian house churches were predicated on their shared experience of baptism into Christ, the activity of the Spirit, the transvaluation of community ethics and, above all, love. One aspect of this broader enterprise evidenced in Galatians was demonstrating how the Jesus community was the ultimate fulfilment of God's purposes. While Galatians (like all Paul's writings) addressed a specific socio-theological problem, we ought not to think of the argument as a 'knee-jerk' response to the crisis instigated by the rival infiltrators in Galatia. The letter's rhetoric clearly aims to persuade gentiles that embracing Jewish ritual and cultic practice is not required for justification, but this rhetoric functions within the contextual tapestry of Israel's redemption history. As such, it reflects some degree of Paul's ruminations about the salient questions of identity within that historical context. This brings us to the subject matter and argument of this chapter.

Paul often quotes, alludes to or draws parallels with Hebrew scripture (usually the Greek version of it), and there are diverse, albeit related, reasons for this. One key connective thread in considering how scripture aids and abets Paul's – often very convoluted – polemical pathways is the idea of 'continuity', and this looms particularly large in the argumentative foreground of Galatians. By continuity, we refer to the apostle's attempt to demonstrate that the death and resurrection of Jesus (and its associated theological, soteriological, ecclesiological and ethical ramifications) are continuous with the divine will outlined in the Jewish biblical tradition. The rhetorical pay-off for Paul from showing continuity between his arguments and the scriptural text barely needs spelling out; if he can successfully demonstrate that his position rightly finishes what the Law and Prophets say God began, then his opponents are not arguing against Paul, but God.

Scholars see consistency in Paul's recourse to Jewish scripture in an array of structural motifs. Moyise in his helpful little book groups the Pauline scripture quotations under the following headings:

- God's plan to include Gentiles
- The faith of Abraham
- Israel's blindness
- The mystery of election
- The character of God
- Jesus Christ
- Adam
- Atonement
- The Christian life
- New and old (2001: 75)

Aris groups the quotations in Galatians into four groups as follows:

A. A sequence of six quotations in the argument of the first 14 verses of chapter 3.
B. Gal. 3:16.
C. Two quotations in chapter 4 (vv. 27 and 30) in the discussion of the bond- and the free woman.
D. The quotation of Lev. 19:18 in chapter 5:14, where St Paul insists that the whole law is fulfilled in one word 'Thou shalt love thy neighbour as thyself.' (1969: 9)

Garlington (1997) proposes that Paul's attempt to 'curse his opponents' in Gal. 3:10-13, where we find the densest collection of Jewish scripture citations, is actually rooted in Gal. 2.17-18, where Paul casts those threatening the unity in the Galatian churches as 'ministers of sin' and 'transgressors'. As such, the OT texts are to validate his relegation of the agitators to the status of the enemies of God, especially in view of the citations speaking to the issues of apostasy and perseverance (85–121). Stanley suggests that Paul's point of departure is primarily rhetorical; Paul based his arguments on scripture because

> he knew that he would eventually have to offer a counterargument to the ideas put forward by his 'opponents'. Apparently, Paul had concluded that a stark assertion of his own authority (i.e., a direct command) would be ineffective, since many of the Galatians were solidly aligned with the circumcision party. But he could trust that the Galatians would recognize the authority of the Jewish Scriptures,

especially since the practices that they were being encouraged to adopt were rooted in the sacred texts of Judaism. (2004: 120)

In this chapter, I will also assume a reasonably systematic sequence in Paul's argumentative trajectory. While Stanley rightly suggests that Galatians is a counter-thesis to a proposal that likely drew its rhetorical impetus from Jewish scripture, the nature of the polemic (especially in Galatians 3–4) strongly implies a significant back story influencing the argument's direction. The shape of the argument was certainly determined by the disruption in Galatia, but the details uncover Paul's commitment to a deeper core tenet – the death and resurrection of Jesus was the critical flash-point to which the scriptures had always pointed, and the role of the scriptures could only be truly grasped retroactively in light of it.

As hinted earlier, Paul makes the most profuse appeal to Jewish scripture in Gal. 3:10-13, which itself forms the core of an argument effectively beginning in 3:6 and running through to 3:29, and about which Silva rightly points out a hornet's nest of exegetical complexities (2001: 251; for an assessment of the broader difficulties with use of scripture in Galatians, see Stanley 2004: 115–18).

This chapter will argue that Paul's recourse to the Hebrew Bible in Galatians principally intends to demonstrate that justification is an expression of new life that is (1) triggered by Abrahamic faith, a faith which is (2) exemplified in the birth of Isaac as the archetypal 'son of Abraham'. The miraculous birth of Isaac is (3) the 'promise of the Spirit' in Gal. 3:14b (a key point to which we will need to return in the next two chapters), the same Spirit received because of the hearing of faith (3:2) and actively experienced within the community (3:5). The rationale for this position is the introductory co-text of the scripture citations. As Cosgrove acutely observes, Paul has provided readers with some index of the importance of the issues he wishes to address (1988: 5–6):

> *This only* I wish to learn from you; did you receive the Spirit from the works of the Law or from the hearing of faith? (Gal. 3:2; emphasis added)

The one aim of Paul's cross-examination of the Galatian gentiles was to elicit from them how they believed the Spirit was received by them and was active in their midst. Did the Spirit originate and work among them in the community because the Galatians responded with faith in Christ to the

Gospel they heard or because they observed the works of Torah? Though the question has already been effectively answered in the thesis statement of Gal. 2:16, it is rehearsed here rhetorically to introduce a more concentrated answer which Paul will corroborate with a focused scriptural tapestry – the Galatians received the Spirit in the same way that Abraham was counted as 'in the right' before God (3:6). The biblical quotations demonstrate how as a result the two events – receiving the Spirit and being counted right before God – are critically related.

1. Galatians 3:6: Abraham and the Spirit

Paul opts for what seems like a curiously oblique way of responding to the enquiry contained in Gal. 3:2-5. To establish a case for his use of the Hebrew Bible in Galatians, our initial step is to unpack his recourse to Abraham. What is the significance of postulating that the Galatians' possession by the Spirit is in some fashion analogous to Abraham coming into right relation to God?

At one level, Abraham is a key figure in Israel's religious history. He was widely regarded as the progenitor of Israel, as *Pss. Sol.* 9:8-9 records:

> You are God and we are the people whom you have loved, for you chose the descendants of Abraham above all the nations.

Abraham's descendants were heirs of God's promise (Sir. 44:21) and the people with whom God would keep the covenant (*4 Ezra* 3:13-15); Abraham is an exemplar of righteousness (*Jub.* 23: 10), able to keep the Law even before it was written (*Jub.* 24:11), when an unwritten Law was in force (*2 Bar.* 57:2). Of course, Abraham accepted circumcision as a seal of the covenant (Gen. 17:1-14), and his story could well have played into the hands of Paul's opponents. Consequently, some scholars reasonably speculate that the introduction of Abraham into Paul's argument in Galatians was a counter-strategy to see off the challenges of the agitators (Lührmann 1992: 57; Martyn 1997: 163).

A more specific explanation for why Paul drew on the Abraham narratives is to posit the exemplary character of the patriarch's faith (e.g. Betz 1979: 141). R. Longenecker presses the point somewhat further saying that Abraham's faith was

qualitatively like that called for in the Christian gospel and so stands
as the prototype of human response to God and his activity on behalf
of humanity. (1990: 113)

Scholars have offered diverse accounts for why Abraham is central
to Paul's thesis in Galatians. Philip Esler (2006), noting the import of
Abraham to the ethnic identity and collective memory of first-century
Judeans, argues that Paul's opponents were offering his converts the
exalted status of Abrahamic descent as a reward for becoming Judeans
through circumcision. Paul's rebuttal in Galatians 3 was to install a
'counter-memory' in his audience's hearts, arguing that Abraham's true
heir was Christ and those in Christ (23–34). Demonstrating significant
parallels between the calling and missions of Paul and Abraham, Pamela
Eisenbaum suggests that Paul is Abraham *redivivus*. She claims that Paul,
like Abraham, was birthing heirs for God and validating the gentiles' claim
to a share in Abraham's inheritance through his gospel (2009; 2000: 130–
45). G. Walter Hansen (1989) classes Galatians as a form of deliberative,
forensic rhetoric based on the 'rebuke and request' formulations in the
epistle. He proposes that the Abraham section of Galatians 3 is Paul's way
of proving that the Bible has addressed the quandaries in Gal. 3:2 and
Gal. 4:9. O'Brien rightly states that Paul took up the example of Abraham
because he is the lynchpin of the Jewish position. If the Apostle's gospel
did not work vis-à-vis Abraham, then it must be false, for Abraham was
the fulcrum for Second Temple Jewish issues of identity and future hopes
(O'Brien 2004: 376). I wish to suggest another pathway, stemming from
the function of the conjunctive *kathōs* which effectively turns Gal. 3:6
into an answer to the debate of 3:2-5. The context of the citation from
Gen. 15:6 is critical, as per Richard Hays's (1989) great contribution to the
study of the use of the OT in the NT – the observation that the context
of the cited passage is imported as well as the text itself. Though many
scholars are deeply critical of Hays's methodology (1–33; for a critique of
Hays, both in support of and against his position, see Litwak 2005: 61–5),
it is appropriate here. Quoted to answer a seemingly unrelated question,
to ignore the original context of Gen. 15:6 would make Paul's appeal to
Abraham seem rather arbitrary. Abraham's 'trust' was not some vague
notion that God was not lying to him. He trusted in God's promise that
Sarah would bear him a son despite both of them being well advanced in
years. It was this belief that God 'counted as righteousness'.

Contextually, Paul has already established that justification occurs by faith in the Messiah, and that for himself as a Jewish believer, this incorporates dying to Law and being reanimated by the life of Christ (2:16-20). If the Law could effect justification, Jesus's death would be superfluous (2:21). As per the thesis statement of 2:16, no one is justified on the basis of works of Law, so Jesus's death was far from superfluous. The Galatians' acquaintance with Jesus's death then becomes the subject of 3:1 and the preamble for the 'one thing Paul wants to learn from the gentile believers' in 3:2. The rhetorical interrogation of 3:2-5 intimates that the necessity of Jesus's death was related to how people receive the Spirit, who was clearly active within their community (3:5). The implication, underscored further in 3:14, seems clear – being justified before God on the basis of faith and receiving the Spirit were related events (Williams 1987: 97). To this end, the *kathōs* (just as) which connects 3:6 to vv. 2–5 causes the Genesis quotation to act as a confirmatory statement to the three faith versus law/flesh questions in vv. 2–5. It acts as more than just a citation formula (contra Betz 1979: 140). The rhetorical net effect is summed up thus: 'Israel's most celebrated patriarch "was reckoned righteous" through faith, independently of Law, proving that you do not need the Law to be counted righteous.' As suggested, the connection with the Spirit is emphasized in 3:14, when the 'promise of Spirit received through faith' is effectively equated with the 'blessing of Abraham' (contra Lee (2013: 182–211), who argues rather that 'justification' is the blessing of Abraham and the Sprit is both the evidence of and means by which the blessing is perpetuated).

Just how radical Paul's use of Gen. 15:6 is becomes clear when he develops the point in Gal. 3:17-18. God forged the covenant with Abraham 430 years before the Law existed, so the covenant was clearly a Law-independent contract. In stark contrast, Jewish writers typically appealed to Gen. 15:6 to exemplify the need to 'uphold' the Law. For example, the author of *1 Maccabees* writes:

> [50] Now, my children, show zeal for the law, and give your lives for the covenant of our ancestors. [51] "Remember the deeds of the ancestors, which they did in their generations; and you will receive great honour and an everlasting name. [52] Was not Abraham found faithful when tested, and *it was reckoned to him as righteousness*? (*1 Macc.* 2:50-52; emphasis added)

Paul's use of the Bible, here and more generally, is an agenda-specific enterprise. The actual passages he cites, the hermeneutic methodology he employs to read them and whether he imports the context of the cited text or not are all governed by the need of the hour. In Galatians, that meant ensuring that the basis for induction into the Abrahamic covenant was thoroughly irrespective of a person's ethnic categorization. What mattered was faith, as the next segment brings into sharp focus.

2. Galatians 3:6-9: Who are the true sons of Abraham?

The argument presented in this chapter is corroborated by the next stage of Paul's response. Having brought into focus the promise of the birth of Abraham's son by Sarah, Paul outlines two things: (1) that the true sons of Abraham are those born as a result of faith in a promise (see later on Gal. 4:23, 28) and not merely the result of natural biological procreation (the controversial statement of Rom. 9:6-9 should be housed in the same context); (2) the 'son born of faith' becomes a model for justification – new life emerging from faith in divine promise. This account of things argues in a different direction from Richard Hays et al., for whom Abraham's faith does not foreshadow the faith of the believer, but the faithfulness of Christ himself (Hays 2002: 168–76). The first premise is established in Gal. 3:7; 'know, therefore, that those of faith, these are the sons of Abraham'. The particle 'therefore' (Gk. *ara*) should be understood as inferential here, so that the conclusion is drawn from 3:6 (Schreiner 2010: 192–3). To be part of Abraham's family requires one to have *pistis*, not to be a Torah keeper.

The second premise is established by the biblical quotation in Gal. 3:8, which appears to be a blend of Gen. 18:18 and 12:3 (Dunn 1993: 165). The promise is repeated in various forms throughout Genesis, but the second-person reference to Abraham stems from Gen. 12:3, while *hai phulai* (the tribes) of Gen. 12:3 is replaced with *ta ethnē* (the nations) from the alternative version in Gen. 18:18. That the '*scripture* foresaw God's justification of the nations by faith and preached the gospel before to Abraham' (emphasis added) is initially a cumbersome way of saying simply that divine foresight is written into the biblical text so that, even when read in Paul's own day, its prophetic significance stands (e.g. Bruce 1982: 156–7). Perhaps more importantly, it paves the way for the inference of 3:9, that those sharing in the blessing of Abraham are 'those of faith' (*hoi ek pisteōs*), which is critical for the next step of the argument.

So then, the question governing this segment is answered – the true sons of Abraham are those who trust in the divine promise. As already suggested, the context of Gen. 15:6 is crucial here – as shall become clear, 'those of faith' are those who, like Abraham, have faith in the promise to make life – this is the faith that must be mimicked by the Jesus communities. The dense and exegetically thorny compendium of scripture citations in Gal. 3:10-13 aim to expound the critical connection between faith and life – the paradigm already determined by Abraham's faith.

3. Galatians 3:10-13: The blessing of life and the curse of death

At one level, Paul appears to have selected the biblical quotations in Gal. 3:10-13 for reasons of lexical continuity. Sanders is critical of Paul's methodological steps, adjudging the apostle to have simply located in the Septuagint verses that contain terms pertinent to his argument which he could manipulate (1983: 421). While Sanders is correct that the lexical connections are important to the overall argument Paul presents, to suggest that they are the totality of the argument's rhetorical potency is to over-extrapolate the evidence.

Others see Paul harnessing the Jewish exegetical technique *gezerah shawah* by which analogies are drawn between different verses on the basis of common words (Bruce 1982: 166; though Trick rightly questions whether gentile audiences would have been acquainted enough with Jewish exegetical methodologies to make the requisite connections – see Trick 2016: 140; cf. Stanley 2004: 123). For what Paul is attempting, he interweaves four biblical citations in as many verses, which collectively embody the following motifs: (1) the language of 'curse' which stands in contrast with the blessing language of Gal. 3:8-9 (cf. 3:14); (2) the verb *zēsetai* (will live); (3) the opposition of Law and faith; (4) a resolution in 3:14 reconnecting the paradigms which introduced the chapter – the origin of the Spirit and the Abrahamic covenant. Paul's word choices here point in a specific direction – the key to interpreting this section of Paul's argument is establishing the historical-theological context from which he writes. As an increasing number of scholars are recognizing, the appropriate context for comprehending Gal. 3:10-13 is exile as punishment for idolatry and apostasy on one hand, and reward for obedience and faithfulness to God on the other. These ideas are outlined in the closing chapters of Deuteronomy, with which Paul is manifestly well acquainted (see the fascinating discussion in Kahl 2010: 253–7; see further Wright 1992: 265–7; 1995: 30–67).

Not all those writing on Paul are convinced by contextual schemes like this, which require extrinsic validation. Normand Bonneau, for example, insists that the logic of the curse language can be established from earlier in the epistle, especially the incident in Antioch in 2:11-14 (1997: 71–8). Whilst clearly related, the precise trajectory of Gal. 3:10-13 seems difficult to fully appreciate purely on the basis of the Antioch incident. With the contextual parameters of exile in place, our analysis will demonstrate that 'life' is a headline for the blessing God extends to those with faith.

Galatians 3:10 (quoting Deut. 27:26)

Paul has established in 3:9 that *hoi ek pisteōs*, literally 'those of faith', are the ones who share in this blessing from Abraham (Johnson Hodge surmises that when *hoi ek pisteōs* points to gentiles entering the covenant family, it refers to those 'born' out of the faithfulness of Abraham to the divine promises in Genesis (2007: 85)). Verse 10 addresses those at the opposing end with the equivalent phrase *ex ergōn nomou*, who are literally those 'of works of Law' and whom Paul relates have incurred a curse, pronounced by the author of Deuteronomy (27:26). This curse, however, the last uttered by Moses on Mount Ebal in Deuteronomy 27, is said to come upon those who do not remain in the words of the Law, which appears to argue in the opposite direction to Paul. Paul clearly considered this curse to be upon Israel – his assertion that *Christ* provides redemption from it, means it must have been upon them until the time of Christ (Gal. 3:13a). Some interpreters read 'under a curse' as parallel to the later expressions 'under law' (3:23; 4:4) and 'under tutors and governors' (4:2). Braswell, for example, sees these expressions as 'spheres of power and dominion to which the people therein enclosed are made subject and under whose sway, reign, and jurisdiction they live' (1991: 76; cf. Wilson 2005: 362–92). As such, those *ex ergōn nomou* are not 'accursed', but under a 'threat' of curse as those living within the sphere in which the curse principle is operative. The curse 'reigns as the power which enforces the law's boundary-function of keeping the Jews within the fence as a peculiar people set apart from the nations' (Braswell 1991: 76). Galatians 4:21 would seem to militate against equating 'under the curse of the Law' with 'under Law'; Paul could scarcely be asking if anyone wanted to be under the 'curse' of the Law.

There is greater difficulty in trying to assess 'why' Paul adjudged Israel to have incurred the curse. The majority position among scholars is still that Paul understood the Law to curse everyone who did not keep it 'perfectly' (see Schreiner 1984: 151–60; Schreiner offers a useful survey of the various scholarly stances on why the curse was sustained). Hunn offers a clarification on the impossibility of perfect Torah observance. Her article suggests that Paul does not 'assume' in v. 10 that no one can keep the Law perfectly, but rather he demonstrates in vv. 10b–12 that the Law curses everyone under it. The impossibility of perfectly keeping the Law will follow from this – it is not assumed but is an implicit conclusion (Hunn 2015: 253–66). One valid contention against this position is the presence of rituals directed at atoning for error within Torah's cultic system itself. Schreiner contests this on the grounds that, Christ having come, OT sacrifices no longer atone (2010: 205). This, however, does not address how Paul could say that the entire Law is fulfilled in loving one's neighbour (Gal. 5:14, citing Lev. 19:18), which does not require perfect legal observance. Also, though Paul considered his own execution of Torah to be faultless (Phil. 3:6), he still maintained that there is no one righteous (Rom. 3:10, citing Ps. 13:1, LXX) and that he routinely struggled to meet Torah's demands (Rom. 7:12-25; scholars generally suspect that Rom. 7:12-25 is not a Pauline self-disclosure. Even if the subject of the passage refers to the proverbial 'everyman', it seems unthinkable that Paul could exclude himself). M. Cranford has argued that the so-called implied premise (i.e. that no one can perfectly hold to the demands of the Torah) misconstrues the debate of Galatians 3 altogether (1994: 242–58).

Another position on this controversial passage is espoused by proponents of what has been dubbed 'the radical perspective' on Paul, chief among whom are John Gager, Lloyd Gaston and Stanley Stowers, and all of whom were influenced by Krister Stendahl (Gager was Stendahl's student at Harvard). Their stance has its origins in a creative rereading of the Pauline texts that aims to resolve many of the quandaries associated with the caustic sounding things Paul says about the Jewish Law, of which Gal. 3:10-13 is clearly an example. Their work, especially Gaston's, sets out to challenge and counteract much anti-Semitic discourse, presumed to have been fuelled by a manipulation of more conventional readings of Paul (see Chapter 5 on 'Law and Spirit'). Two premises are common to the approaches of these commentators: first, the belief that the Torah was and remains the pathway through which Israel entered into and was sustained in covenant relationship with God; it was 'gentile' inclusion into covenant relation to the one God which was predicated on the Christ event, and both covenants were to perpetually coexist in order to establish the people of God. Second, and by extension of the first premise, Galatians is only correctly understood as a message to a 'gentile' audience. As such, Paul's apparently harsh statements regarding Torah criticize Jews and Jewish believers rebelling against this 'two-covenant' scheme – not Jews and believing Jews in general, and certainly not the Torah itself. Gaston writes:

> One would not expect the Apostle to the Gentiles to be engaged in a dialogue with Judaism, but rather with Gentile Christians, explaining how such central concepts as Torah relate to them. (1987: 4)

Gager (2000) asserts that readers' failure to keep the target audience in mind and the erroneous assumption that Paul is challenging the Law as it pertains to Jews are the proximate causes of the faulty exegesis which 'radical perspective' theorists attempt to counter. Interestingly, he cites Sanders's handling of Gal. 3:10 as an example of this perceived oversight:

> At one point Sanders (rightly) observes that in Gal. 3.10 Paul is arguing 'to discourage Gentiles from accepting circumcision', but in the next sentence the subject of the sentence changes from the particular, Gentiles, to the universal, one. 'In [Gal.] 3.10 Paul argues, citing Deut. 27.26, that one who accepts the law must keep all the laws and that failure to keep them all brings a curse.' This tendency to slip from the particular (Gentiles and the law) to the universal (the law itself and all of humanity, including Jews) when reading Paul illustrates the enormous power of established paradigms. (52)

In Gager's reading, it is the gentiles who do not 'abide by all the things written in the book of the Law', and thus, they who are cursed by the Law. It is the gentiles who are released from the curse of the Law by Christ, and who jeopardize their salvation if they embrace the Law (88). Indeed, wherever Paul appears 'anti-Israel', he is speaking of the Torah as it relates to gentile Christ believers. Naturally, this introduces the difficulty that Paul on occasion would have to be writing things he knows not to be true because he is addressing gentiles, a proposition which seems difficult to uphold; despite some of the questions the 'radical perspective' undoubtedly answers, it would appear to raise several more.

A more likely solution to the interpretation of Gal. 3:10ff is the suggestion of James M. Scott that Daniel's prayer of confession (Dan. 9:1-19) is indicative of the prevailing view of Second Temple Jews – that Israel's stubborn disobedience led to her remaining in some manner of ideological or 'spiritual exile', even though her physical exile (most recently from Babylon) was over (1993b: 645–65). N. T. Wright has steadily argued, amid a torrent of scepticism, that the notion of continuing exile was central in Jesus's own day. The scepticism hails in large part from the paucity of NT evidence for such a position. Assessments of Wright's thesis are available (most recently in Scott (2017), which includes several essays in support of Wright's position). Wright argues further that, for Paul, it was the death and resurrection of Jesus that truly brought the exile to an end, in finalistic fashion extinguishing the dissociative and marginalizing effects of consecutive pagan hegemonies (1991: 139–48; 1994: 225; see the excellent critical discussion, in support of Wright et al., in Watson 2004: 427–33). As such, the curse referred to in Deut. 27:26 was upon the 'entire nation of Israel' for her continual flouting of the Law more broadly (see further Scott 1993b: 657–9); it did not refer to any one individual's inability to perform all 613 dictates of Torah. While this position is not without its difficulties, it helps make good sense of both Paul's context and Israel's broader redemptive-historical narrative in scripture (for a critique of Wright, Scott et al., see Silva 2001: 257).

What is of further interest in this citation is that the LXX of Deut. 27:26 does not contain the refrain *gegrammenois en tō bibliō* (written in the book). Paul appears to have added the thoroughly Deuteronomic phrase (cf. Deut. 29:21; 31:26; Josh. 1:8; 2 Kgs 14:6; Neh. 8:1; etc.) to reinforce the view of history commensurate with his intertextual method. Most fully articulated by Martin Noth (1943), this view of history is often called 'Deuteronomistic'. It proposes that the historical flow of large sections of Deuteronomy was more continuous with the history contained in Joshua, Judges, Ruth, Samuel, Kings and Chronicles than it was with the rest of Torah. As such, rather than viewing Deuteronomy as the end of the Pentateuch, it was regarded as the beginning of the Deuteronomist history. At the heart of the Deuteronomistic view of history lies the notion that if Israel complied with the Law, she would invoke blessing; but if Israel rebelled against the Law, the consequence was divine curse. This motif is the kaleidoscope through which this period of Israel's history ought to be interpreted. This view of history influences this entire section of Paul's argument (and some would argue the letter as a whole) as will now become apparent.

Galatians 3:11 (quoting Hab. 2:4)

In Deuteronomy 30, a key chapter in Moses's summation of the blessings and curses which lay on Israel's horizons, the author notably equates blessing with 'life' and curse with 'death':

When all these things have happened to you, *the blessings and the curses* that I have set before you, if you call them to mind among all the nations where the Lord your God has driven you. (Deut. 30:1)

See, I have set before you today *life and prosperity, death and adversity.* (Deut. 30:15)

I call heaven and earth to witness against you today that I have set before *you life and death, blessings and curses.* Choose life so that you and your descendants may live. (Deut. 30:19; all emphases added)

It is this construction of semantic equivalence which Paul seizes upon in what follows. Though there is no direct reference to exile in these verses, the instantiation of life/blessing and crucifixion/curse from the OT intertexts evidence the direction of Paul's thought, continuing and substantiating the life-death contrasts in Gal. 2:19-20 (the details of this will be analysed in the next chapter of this volume).

In Gal. 3:11, Paul incorporates Hab. 2:4 into his argument in a fashion that underscores both how his view of justification operates and how this view is biblically blueprinted – but first a syntactical irregularity must be addressed, one which my co-author Peter Oakes and I do not see eye to eye on!

Galatians 3:11 has two clauses both introduced by the Greek *hoti*, and how the term is translated in each case governs how the statement works. *Hoti* may imply 'that' (as a conjunction) or 'because' (pre-empting an inferential clause). The entire sentence is unintelligible if the *hoti* is translated the same way in each case, leaving interpreters to deduce which translation is pertinent to which occurrence. Most interpreters read the first *hoti* as 'that' and the second as 'because'. F. Thielman (1994) exemplifies the opposite stance, rendering Gal. 3:11, 'But because [*hoti*] no one is justified before God by the law, it is obvious that [*hoti*] "the just shall live by faith"'. Though a novel approach, and grammatically plausible, there are two reasons it ought to be rejected. First, it has Paul begin with a conclusion and argue towards a biblical intertext rather than from it, effectively nullifying his point. Second, the integrity of 3:12 requires a previous conclusive statement regarding faith – in readings like Thielman's, the conclusive statement centres upon Law (127). The verse should read 'and that no one is justified by Law before God is clear because, the righteous will live by faith'. Once more the biblical text, here, courtesy of Habakkuk, corroborates the assertion in the first part of the clause. In so doing, the active verbs correspond – Paul articulates a connection between 'justified' and 'will live', thus, effectively arguing as follows: it is clear that justification does not arise from Law because Habakkuk has stated that those who are justified (i.e. righteous) 'will live' on the basis of faith.

This conclusion is further informed by the Deuteronomistic context already established; the 'life' prophesied by Habakkuk coincides with the 'life' the author of Deuteronomy associates with 'blessing' in Paul's tapestry of citations. In the context of both Deuteronomy and Habakkuk, the people are called to trust in divine action. In Habakkuk's context, the prophet had become so accustomed to righteous people dying at the hands of the corrupt and wicked (Hab. 1:4) that it felt as if God even favoured the wicked (Hab. 1:13)! Thus, God encourages him that the righteous people will not die at the hands of their oppressors – that is, they 'will live' if they trust God (Hab. 2:4). Similarly, the author of Deuteronomy writes with an air of inevitability regarding Israel's self-destructive choices which ultimately lead to exile. Yet they must trust Yahweh. If they reaffirm their allegiance to the divine commands, Yahweh himself will act to restore them (Deut. 30:1-10). The resonance with Paul is clear; trust – perhaps a more helpful rendering of the Greek *pistis* than the more familiar 'faith' – in Jesus is what brings someone into righteous standing with God (for a cogent reading of *pistis* as 'trust', see Oakes 2015: 87–90). Once more, this is not (contra Sanders) Paul simply scrambling for semantically convenient proof-texts; it rather exemplifies Paul drawing the prophetic 'contexts' as well as the prophetic 'words' into his argumentative strategy. A picture should be emerging by now; a true son of Abraham is one that is 'related' to him by faith. This is the same 'family trait' by which Abraham himself is rightly related to God, through which believers receive the Spirit and by which the righteous 'will live'. The case, having been stated positively, is now stated from the other direction.

Galatians 3:12 (Lev. 18:5)

The next biblical quotation in sequence strengthens the idea that Paul, somewhat controversially, aims to convey. Having asserted the centrality of faith in procuring the 'life' of justification, Paul further rules out Torah as a route to it by stating in the opening clause of Gal. 3:12 that Torah is not 'of faith' (*ek pisteōs*; cf. 3:7, 9). The corroborative second clause is taken from Lev. 18:5, a passage which has a hermeneutically complex reception history in Jewish texts. Part of the difficulty in appreciating Paul's use of it here lies in considering whether he reads Lev. 18:5 in one of the diverse ways different communities before him read it, or whether he introduces a unique Pauline spin on it. The most prominent scholarly question in this regard was whether contextually 'will live' was understood eschatologically or simply as the 'this-worldly' result of compliance. Gathercole argues for the former position (2004: 126–45); the difficulties in each of the two positions are explained in Sprinkle (2008: 31–4).

Both Gathercole and Sprinkle do very commendable work in showing the diverse range of treatments of Lev. 18:5 by different Jewish groups; Sprinkle (2008) demonstrates in considerable detail how the *Damascus Document* from the Qumran texts (CD III:15–16) and *Pss. Sol.* 14:1-5 reflect 'eternal life' readings of Lev. 18:5. One of his key assertions is that Paul posits a sharp difference between divine agency and human initiative, as opposed to most Second Temple Jewish authors who see a greater harmony between them. He writes:

> Paul disagrees with all of our Second Temple Jewish interpreters who, whilst agreeing that eschatological life is both now and not yet, believe that the Law is a necessary precondition of eschatological life. (196)

That is, in Sprinkle's reasoning, Second Temple writers generally saw the 'life' of obedience to Torah as a critical component of procuring 'eternal life'. Yet, Sprinkle continues:

> Throughout this study, therefore, we have argued against those scholars who say that Lev. 18:5 was understood by Paul and his contemporaries to refer to 'life in the covenant' or a life regulated by the Law and not to some sort of future life attained as a result of obedience. (196; cf. 94–8)

Sprinkle ultimately stops short of any straightforward, single view of how ancient Jews interpreted Lev. 18:5, and such a stance seems safest. For example, Ezekiel seems to use Lev. 18:5 to refer to the very human agency associated with 'doing the commands', but his treatment of 'life' in Ezekiel 37 has an unambiguous, eschatological dimension.

Other commentators argue that Ezekiel's use of Lev. 18:5 (Ezek. 20:11-13) and Nehemiah's use of the same (Neh. 9:29) were to remind the people that the exile was a consequence of their inevitable rebellion. These same commentators often treat Paul's deployment of Lev. 18:5 as establishing the unavoidable failure of people to perfectly keep the Law and, thus, fall short of divine standards of righteousness – a moral chasm only Christ can bridge (corroborating the view that Paul cited Deut. 27:26 in Gal. 3:10 for the same reason; e.g. Schreiner 2010: 210–15).

Any clear resolution of the questions surrounding Paul's use of Lev. 18:5 remains elusive. In Brian Rosner's rehearsal of the salient issues, he quite rightly shows how a clear solution lies somewhere between evaluating how Second Temple Jewish writers broadly understood Lev. 18:5 and judging how much affinity Paul shared with them (2013: 60–73). However, a further key factor is how Gal. 3:21 relates to the section of the argument beginning with the Bible quotations in Gal. 3:10. The implication of Gal. 3:21 is that no law was ever given which had the capacity to 'produce life' (*zōopoiēsai*). Coupled with the 'will live' of Hab. 2:4 cited in Gal. 3:11, it seems likelier that the life of Lev. 18:5 is the sustenance resulting from observing the Mosaic covenant stipulations (see Dunn 1988b: 612). The contrasting 'life' of Hab. 2:4, therefore, is that which is central to being justified and pre-empts 'eternal life'. Paul's autobiographical testimony substantiates such a view; he died to the Law so he could experience the renewed life of justification (Gal. 2:19). Yet he remained conscious that this life existed in the compromised realm of 'flesh' (Gal. 2:20), where he would remain susceptible to the ravages of sin until the eschaton (Gal. 6:8).

Galatians 3:13 (quoting Deut. 21:23)

The remaining citation in this sequence returns to the curse pronounced by the Law upon Israel as punishment for her defiance of God's demands. If, as Paul writes elsewhere, his duty was to 'preach Christ crucified' (1 Cor. 1:23), he would of necessity have had to re-evaluate Deut. 21:23. How could the Messiah, the most significant figure within the economy of salvation, have died in such ignominious dishonour, under a divine curse? Although the reference in Deuteronomy 21 is to the affixing of a corpse to a tree, there is pre-Pauline evidence that the passage was already being applied to death by impalement. In fragments 3–4 of 4QpNah, the crucifixion of 'the Seekers after Smooth Things' (*dôrshê hā-ḥălāqôt*) at the hands of the Lion of Wrath (which some equate with Josephus's narrative of the crucifixion of eight hundred Pharisees at the behest of Alexander Jannaeus (Josephus, *B.J.* 1.97)) invokes the curse of Deut. 21:23. There is further, though disputed, evidence in 11QTᵃ and certainly *Targum of Ruth* 1:17, which identifies being 'hanged on a tree' as a capital penalty.

The Roman statesman and orator Cicero wrote that the very word 'cross' itself ought to be distanced from the thoughts, eyes and ears of the citizenry (*Rab. Post.* 5.16). Josephus described crucifixion as 'the most pitiable of deaths' (*B.J.* 7.203). Even Seneca, the Stoic philosopher and former adviser to Nero, advised that suicide was preferable to crucifixion, stating:

> Can anyone be found who would prefer wasting away in pain dying limb by limb, or letting out his life drop by drop, rather than expiring once for all? Can any man be found willing to be fastened to the accursed tree, long sickly, already deformed, swelling with ugly weals on shoulders and chest, and drawing the breath of life amid long-drawn-out agony? He would have many excuses for dying even before mounting the cross. (Seneca, *Lucil.* 101:14)

Paul's employment of Deut. 21:23 in Gal. 3:13b, which pronounces a divine curse on anyone hung on a tree, verifies his declaration in the primary clause in Gal. 3:13a. R. Longenecker offers evidence that the assertion may have originated in a pre-Pauline Jewish Christian creedal formula, which is certainly possible (1990: 121–2). Paul's claim is that 'Christ redeemed us from the curse of the Law having become a curse on our behalf' – he 'became' the curse through crucifixion. The 'us' in this statement should be understood as Israel; gentiles were never under Law, but their ultimate redemption was reliant upon Israel's redemption (Romans 9–11 makes gentile redemption dependent on Israel's rejection of the gospel). Two key principles appear to interrelate in how this citation functions. First, the common *katara*- root between the dual use of the noun (curse) in 3:13a and the adjective in the LXX citation in 3:13b (accursed) may be an example of *gezera shawa*. The second, which relates to how Paul attempted to reconcile the notion of a cursed Messiah, is the early Christian tendency to re-evaluate Hebrew scripture in light of Jesus's death and resurrection. In this way, Paul is able to view the Christ event as vicarious; Jesus drew the Law's curse – already established as a punishment on Israel for disobedience in Gal. 3:10 (Deut. 27:26) – upon himself, so as to remove it from Israel (Caneday 1989: 205). As such, he writes that Jesus became a curse *hyper hēmōn* (on our behalf). A similar idea is present in 2 Cor. 5:21 where Jesus is said to have been 'made sin' on our behalf (*hyper hēmōn*). Some scholars connect the *hyper hēmōn* tradition to Isa. 53:9b-11 (see Gilthvedt 2016: 110–12).

Exactly what Paul intends to convey in this portrait is variously debated. Betz treats Gal. 3:13 as a pre-Pauline formula interpreting Jesus's death as a self-sacrificial atonement that spells the end of Torah:

> Due to Christ's incarnation (Gal. 4:4-5) he suffered his death as a human being. Since he was free of sin (cf. 2 Cor 5:21), his death was, in Jewish terms, uniquely meritorious. The result is that 'we' are free from the 'curse of the Law' and indeed from the Law itself. Therefore, Paul can say that Christ is the end of the Law. (Rom. 10:4; Gal. 2:19-20; 3:25; 5:6; 6:15) (1979: 151)

Schreiner reads very explicit substitutionary atonement language, observing:

> In any case, Jesus did not suffer and die for his own transgressions. He died for the sake of his people. We have here the language of substitution. [It is not] persuasive merely to speak of interchange or representation here, if that language is used to rule out substitution. Paul teaches that Christ took upon himself the curse that sinners deserved, that he stood in their place and absorbed their punishment. (2010: 217)

Ardel Caneday, who sees allusions to Deut. 21:23 in Acts and 1 Peter, is adamant about showing that Paul is not proof texting but drawing precisely on the context of Deuteronomy 21. Paul has observed in Israel's experiences deep typological resonances foreshadowing the Messianic age. So, from a salvation-historical perspective,

> Paul argues that Christ hung 'upon the tree' in Israel's place, bearing the curse of the violated covenant and turning away God's wrath from his people by redeeming them out from under the Law's curse. This redemption of believing Jews from the law's curse is epochal in character, for Christ replaces the Law for Jews and in so doing extends to Gentiles the blessing promised to Abraham. (Caneday 1989: 208–9)

On the basis of the structural symmetry between Gal. 3:13-14 and 4:4-6, and the latter passage's use of the term *exapostellō*, which Paul never uses elsewhere, Schwartz detects the instantiation not of the condemned criminal tradition of Deuteronomy 21, but the scapegoat ritual of Leviticus 16. Paul usually employs either *pempsō* or *apostellō* to denote 'send', but this *hapax legomenon*, for Schwartz (drawing on the work of Hatch and Redpath), reflects the typical Septuagintal use of *exapostellō* to render the Hebrew *šlḥ*

(שׁלח), as in the 'sending away' of the scapegoat (Lev. 16:21; the argument is somewhat weakened in that the same Hebrew verb is rendered *apostellō* in the LXX of Lev. 16:10 in reference to the goat. See Schwartz 1983: 260–3).

David Brondos takes a very unconventional line in seeing no semblance of vicarious or substitutionary atonement ideology in Gal. 3:13, claiming rather that these are simply 'doctrines of atonement found in later Christian tradition' read posthumously back into Paul (2001: 32). Rather, Brondos believes that the curse of the Law will be lifted at the *Parousia*. I will suggest that the Pauline claim furthers the argument the Apostle began in Gal. 3:1 by establishing the following: in embracing the curse of death, and overwhelming death with resurrection life, Jesus extinguishes the curse of the Law.

As per the Deuteronomic context of these verses outlined earlier, and as I will argue in the chapter on 'Death, Life and Righteousness', the author of Deuteronomy 30 associates blessing with restoration and 'life', and curse with exile and 'death' (see Deut. 30:1, 15, 19 earlier). Paul never directly mentions exile in Galatians (or anywhere in his letters), but if the curse is understood as 'death', then it becomes clear how Jesus became the Deuteronomic curse – by submitting to death by crucifixion (the notion of a temporary submission to death is seen in Heb. 2:9). That crucifixion implies death ought not need spelling out, but Gal. 2:19 and 5:24-25 demonstrate that an explicit connection exists between the two in Paul's thought.

Paul's argument then is that Jesus took on the curse in death and paved the way for the blessing of life. This blessing of life is referred to as the blessing of Abraham in Gal. 3:14, which can now be procured by gentile believers (3:14a) and Jewish believers alike (3:14b). This verse, at the centre of the third chapter, tying the themes of Abraham, Christ, Spirit and faith and marking off a diffuse section of connected 'biblical' arguments, is a pivotal moment in the letter (Dahl 1977: 133; Williams 1988: 712; Silva 2004: 238). The language of blessing (3:8, 9, 14a) makes way for the corresponding language of promise (3:14b, 16, 17, 18, 19, 21, 22, 29; 4:23, 28), which is determinative for the next three OT insertions.

4. Galatians 3:16; 4:27, 30: Heirs of the promise

Galatians 3:16 (quoting Gen. 22:18)

Perhaps more than any Pauline recourse to the OT in Galatians, the rationale behind drawing on the Genesis narratives in Gal. 3:16 is difficult to reconcile. The most glaring complexity is, in fact, pragmatic; it initially appears that Paul wants a critical Christological inference to rest upon a prophet's use of a word in the singular instead of the plural. To further complicate matters, it is a 'generic' singular – the key noun *spermati* (seed, dative singular), while grammatically singular, clearly implies a multiplicity, as do other grammatically singular words such as 'group' or 'community'. (Though, interestingly, the strategy is not totally alien to rabbinic exegesis; *m.Shabbat* 9.2 not only attempts to formulate an argument by distinguishing between the singular and plural forms of a word, but just as in Gal. 3:16, the word is 'seed'.) So apparently fraught is Paul's logic, Cosgrove argues, that were his intent to validate the Galatian gentiles' entitlement to be the eschatological seed of Abraham, the apostle should have stressed the 'plurality' of Abraham's seed, and not its singularity, as it is in fact conceived in the Old Testament promise text(s) to which he refers (1988: 547). Indeed, according to Genesis 17, the seed of Abraham is 'the nations' (Gen. 17:8) – a nuance Paul is manifestly aware of as Rom. 4:16-17 clarifies (for the range of possible readings of Gal. 3:16, see Pyne 1995: 211–22). What does seem inescapable is that the 'seed versus seeds' contrast aims to refute any exclusive Jewish conceptualization of the seed of Abraham as Israel (Calvert Koyzis 2004: 100).

Though the argumentative reasoning may not be simple to unstitch, Paul's objective in relating that the promise was made to Abraham and to his seed, who is Christ, is vital to the overall polemic. As Gal. 3:13 implies, Jesus having become the curse of death in crucifixion, opened the doorway for the blessing of life. Abraham experienced the blessing of life in the birth of Isaac – a miraculous endowment of life – hence Paul refers to this blessing of life as the blessing of Abraham in Gal. 3:14. Jesus was raised from the dead by God the Father (Gal. 1:1) – a miraculous endowment of life – of which the birth of Isaac was a type. Significantly, the blessing of Abraham is equated with the promise of the Spirit, which brings us right back to the introduction of Abraham into the argument in the first place. The promise to Abraham which Paul recalls from Gen. 15:6, initially fulfilled in Isaac's birth, will be fulfilled anew in the resurrection of Jesus, and the risen life of Jesus will be the energy for the new covenant life. Thus, the inheritance is based on the promise (Gal. 3:18); believers will inherit the life of Jesus because of what God promised to Abraham, and not from 'doing the Law'. With the objective spelled out, we can attempt to make sense of the reasoning behind Gal. 3:16.

Attempting to disambiguate how Paul's argument in Gal. 3:16 is intended to be understood begins with clarifying where specifically in Genesis Paul is quoting from. For there are passages in Genesis where Abraham's 'seed' (or 'descendant' as the Greek could be rendered) refers to a community and times where it refers to an individual son of Abraham. As Collins has shown, the dative of the noun *sperma* occurs sixteen times in the LXX of Genesis – of these occurrences, the ones germane to Abraham are 12:7; 13:15; 15:18; 17:8, 19; 22:18; and 24:7 (2003: 81–2). T. Desmond Alexander (1997) has demonstrated persuasively that Gen. 22:18 is the most appropriate source for Paul's intertext. He goes on to suggest, partly by recourse to the use of the Genesis passage in Ps. 72:17, further grammatical reasons why two of three references to *sperma* in Gen. 22:17-18, including the one Paul cites, refer to an 'individual' and not to Israel (363–7). As such, Paul's method for establishing that the seed is an individual and not the nation may be less farfetched than it initially appears. Boyarin argues that *sperma* has an Aramaic root which best translates as 'family' (1994: 145), a position which may find support in Wright, for whom the family of God is summed up in the Messianic seed (1992: 162–8). The notion of the Genesis promises being fulfilled in a single individual also receives support from the book of *Jubilees*:

> And we returned in the seventh month, and found Sarah with child before us and we blessed him, and we announced to him all the things which had been decreed concerning him, that he should not die till he should beget six sons more, and should see (them) before he died; but (that) in Isaac should his name and seed be called: And (that) all the seed of his sons should be Gentiles, and be reckoned with the Gentiles; *but from the sons of Isaac one should become a holy seed*, and should not be reckoned among the Gentiles. (*Jubilees* 16:16-17, R. H. Charles translation; emphasis added)

This most likely represents what Darrell Bock describes as 'typological' use of the OT (1987: 49). If, as seems likely, Paul treats the Genesis text as referring to an individual, he applies it to the figure most forcefully exemplified by the text. It takes no great stretch of the imagination to see why ancient Christ-believing writers might read Isaac as a prophetic foreshadowing of Christ in Genesis 22 (e.g. Clement, *Paedagogus* I. 5. 23:1-2). In Gen. 22:1-16, Isaac is the 'sacrificial lamb', bound to the wood, situated on a mount and described as his father's 'only son' (for a full treatment of the relation between the *Aqedah* – the story of the 'binding' of Isaac in Genesis 22 – and the expiatory reading of atonement in Paul, see Levenson 1993). As the next OT quotation shows, Isaac is archetypal not only for Christ, but also for those 'in Christ', as the grand conclusion of Gal. 3:26-29 ultimately indicates.

Galatians 4:27 (quoting Isa. 54:1)

The literal seed of Abraham become the subject of a Pauline allegory in Gal. 4:21-31 (for the view that the entire Abraham narrative in Galatians ought to be read allegorically, see Fowl 1994: 77–95). Philo offered an allegorical reading of the Sarah and Hagar story in a few of his works (e.g. *QG* 3.19, 21), where Hagar stood for introductory or secular learning and Sarah for Wisdom (for an extended treatment, see Longenecker 1990: 201–6). John Chrysostom and Jerome expounded Paul's allegory in their commentaries on Galatians, suggesting that Sarah was the blossoming church and Hagar the barren synagogue:

> The synagogue has the Law as its husband, and according to Hannah's prophecy it used to have many children. The church, however, is barren without her husband Christ, and for a long time she lingered in the desert deprived of communication with her spouse. After the synagogue received into her hands the certificate of divorce and turned over all of her husband's assets for the enrichment of an idol, the husband, because his first belt was ruined, wove another one for his loins, an apron made from the Gentiles. As soon as she was joined to her husband, she conceived and gave birth . . . I see no need in us talking about how many Christians there are and how few Jews, since the banner of the cross is resplendent throughout the world and scarcely any noteworthy Jew is found in the cities today. (Jerome [386]; Cain 2010: 189–90)

Momentarily, we will consider ways in which potentially marginalizing readings like Jerome have been challenged; for now, let us consider how Paul's allegory furthers his rhetorical aims.

The story so far reads like this: the Galatian gentiles were possessed by the Spirit in a fashion corresponding to the dynamics of Abraham attaining the right covenant status before Yahweh – both events were predicated on faith and not the works of Torah (Gal. 3:2-5, 6). As such, membership in the covenant family, which means being identified as true sons of Abraham, is ratified by faith (Gal. 3:7-9). This Paul can assert because it is enshrined in the Law and prophets that: (1) the Law has pronounced the curse of death upon Israel for her unrepentant rebellion (Gal. 3:10); (2) the curse is assumed by Christ in his crucifixion (Gal. 3:13) with the effect that the Abrahamic blessing of life might materialize (Gal. 3:14a); (3) by faith, all may share in this life and be counted righteous (Gal. 3:11); (4) the Law is not the origin of this life (Gal. 3:12). Abraham's trust in the promise of a miraculous instantiation of life is repaid in the birth of his son Isaac. (5) This foreshadows another miraculous instantiation of life – the resurrection of the Messiah (Gal. 3:16), trust in whom is the basis of justification (Gal. 2:16, citing Ps. 143:2; Boakye 2017: 131–40). It is proposed here that the next biblical citation establishes how Isaac's birth typifies both the resurrection of Messiah and justification by faith.

Interestingly, scholarly evaluations of the pericope in the major commentaries typically afford comparatively little airtime to analysis of the Isa. 54:1 quotation. A notable exception is Bligh (1969: 401–4). (For a short overview of some of the exegetical positions adopted by commentators, see George 1994: 344–5.) Once the reader identifies the barren woman as Sarah and recalls the ancient context of the restoration of Judean exiles to the holy lands, it is possible to simply say that Paul employs the text as a conversion metaphor. That is, the future 'children of the desolate one' correspond to Jews and gentiles entering the Galatian Jesus community on the basis of faith in Christ. While there must be some truth to this, not least of all because of how Gal. 4:28-29 paves the way for the citation from Gen. 21:10 in Gal. 4:30, there are certain incongruities with Paul's use of Isa. 54:1 which are difficult to ignore.

The most glaring difficulty is that if Paul intends a straightforward resonance between the barren woman and Sarah, the citation becomes awkward, as it suggests that the barren woman's children will ultimately outnumber the 'married' woman. However, in the Genesis narrative, Sarah, the barren one, is the married woman – it is Hagar who is not married. Second, the introductory formula in Gal. 4:27, *gegraptai gar* (for it has been written), sets up the citation to address key questions implied by the co-text, including the difference between birth according to flesh and birth through promise, the identification of Hagar and Sarah with two covenants and what both these things have to do with the present Jerusalem compared to the 'Jerusalem above'. The incorporation of the Isaiah text does not in any immediately obvious sense explain any of these quandaries (though some commentators offer limited resolution to the problem by arguing that Paul is actually associating Isa. 54:1 with the first mention of the barren Sarah tradition in Gen. 11:30, and that such a link was not original to Paul (Juncker

2007: 137)). This, third, is all further complicated in that later Christian writers also integrated Isa. 54:1 into their arguments but in very different ways to Paul. Both Justin Martyr and the author of *2 Clement*, for example, cite the Isaiah passage from the LXX in identical fashion to Paul, but with wholly contrasting hermeneutic emphases. In *2 Clement*, the author claims that Isaiah was speaking of a church that was barren before children were born to it. Justin treats the passage in soteriological fashion – the children born are those of the gentiles who would turn from idolatry and worship Yahweh (*2 Clem.* 2:1-3; Justin Martyr, *Apologia i* 53.5).

Joel Willits (2005) argues impressively that the Hagar-Sarah allegory is to practically demonstrate the eschatological truth of Isa. 54:1, which he sees as an analogue for Paul's situation, that is, the sharp distinction between two genealogical lines – Ishmael and Isaac. Once this is established, Paul can map the former on to the slave children beholden to Torah and the latter to the free children of the New Covenant (188–210).

One of the most sustained and insightful treatments of how Isa. 54:1 works in the context of Gal. 4:21-31 comes from Karen Jobes (1993: 299–320). Central to Jobes's thesis is the adoption of Richard Hays's intertextual method of metalepsis, whereby a word in a text 'echoes' the same word in an earlier text, such that the figurative effect of the echo can lie in the unstated points of resonance between the two texts (Hays 1989: 20). In Jobes's reading, the echo is from the word 'barren'. She argues that Isaiah has taken the usual overtone of barrenness in the Hebrew Bible – namely, death – and reconfigured it, such that birth from a barren womb comes to symbolize the divine manifestation of power in various contexts. This has already become apparent from Isaiah 26, where the prophet combines the barren matriarch tradition with the depiction of Jerusalem as an expectant woman:

> Like a woman with child, who writhes and cries out in her pangs when she is near her time, so were we because of you, O LORD; 18 we were with child, we writhed, but we gave birth only to wind. We have won no victories on earth, and no one is born to inhabit the world. 19 Your dead shall live, their corpses shall rise. O dwellers in the dust, awake and sing for joy! For your dew is a radiant dew and the earth will give birth to those long dead. (Isa. 26:17-19)

On the basis of Isa. 53:10-12, which immediately precedes the text Paul cites, Jobes's interpretation of Paul's thought launches from her treatment of Jesus's resurrection as the event which fulfils Isa. 54:1. I would go further (contra Jobes – and especially in view of the death-focused tenor of Isa. 53:4-12, as Boakye (2017: 152) says) and say that the birth of Isaac 'according to Spirit' ought to be seen in a similar light as a resurrection miracle (Gal. 4:29). Galatians 4:29 is certainly consistent with the 'new life' traditions embedded in Galatians (2:19-20; 3:10-14; 5:24-25), which are themselves all directly or indirectly associated with the presence and work of the Spirit. In other words, Paul's aim is to establish the birth of Isaac as a resurrection miracle, which acts as a 'historical parable' of justification by faith (this is fundamental enough that we will need to return to it in the next two chapters). Isaac was in this sense brought to life by God because of Abraham's faith in the promise – a subject more explicitly central in the thesis of Rom. 4:17-21. In the same way, believers are brought to life, that is, 'justified', by faith in Christ (Gal. 4:28-31), which is made explicit in the concluding section of Romans 4 (vv. 22–25). The precedent for Paul seeing things this way, is, of course, his apprehension of the resurrection of Jesus – the quintessential 'new life' narrative at the heart of much of Paul's theologizing.

The Greek text of Gal. 4:23 and 4:29 exhibit an almost parallel relationship, shedding further light on Gal. 3:14 – the birth of Isaac is the promise of the Spirit, corresponding to the blessing of Abraham:

ἀλλ᾽ ὁ μὲν ἐκ τῆς παιδίσκης κατὰ σάρκα γεγέννηται, ὁ δὲ ἐκ τῆς ἐλευθέρας δι᾽ ἐπαγγελίας. (Gal. 4:23)

[But on the one hand, the one from the slave woman has been born according to flesh, on the other, the one from the free woman through a promise.] (Boakye's translation)

ἀλλ᾽ ὥσπερ τότε ὁ κατὰ σάρκα γεννηθεὶς ἐδίωκεν τὸν κατὰ πνεῦμα, οὕτως καὶ νῦν. (Gal. 4:29)

[But just as then the one being born according to the flesh persecuted the one according to the Spirit, so also it is now.] (Boakye's translation)

The seemingly out-of-place inference of Gal. 3:14, where the Spirit is the substance of what God promised to Abraham, is actually a significant marker for Paul – the Spirit is the conduit of justification life (1 Tim. 3:16); it is by the Spirit that the risen Christ becomes the reanimating energy of the new age (for the Spirit's role in justification, see Macchia 2001: 202–17). The association between life and Spirit is common in Paul (Rom. 8:2, 4, 6, 10, 13; 1 Cor. 15:45; 2 Cor. 3:6; Gal. 5:16, 25; 6:8), and the virtual equation of Christ and Spirit in a number of texts strengthens the point (Rom. 8:9-10; 1 Cor. 6:11; 12:3; 15:45; 2 Cor. 3:3, 17-18).

A second OT quotation adds a controversial practical component to the argument. If the Law (the Sinai covenant) is related to the flesh and slavery, what is the community to make of missionaries, like those opposing Paul in Galatia, insisting that the Law is an essential component of justification?

Galatians 4:30 (quoting Gen. 21:10)

Paul's recourse to the Bible in Gal. 4:30, which he introduces with the question 'what does the scripture say?' (cf. Rom. 4:3), while originating unambiguously from the LXX of Gen. 21:10 (despite some amendments), is an imperative inferred from a claim absent from Genesis 21. The command to cast out the slave woman and her son in Gal. 4:30 derives from Paul's claim in the preceding verse that in the current context, like the ancient context, those born of flesh persecute those born according to Spirit (Gal. 4:29). The logic as it pertains to the Galatian Jesus communities seems unequivocal – the gentiles, being 'persecuted' by those Jewish believers trying to bully them into Judaizing, ought to expel their tormentors from the community.

Susan Eastman (2006) has raised an important challenge to such a reading (a reading consistent with the earlier quotation from Jerome's commentary on Gal. 4:27). She posits that the context of Gal. 4:21-30 is a warning aimed at Galatian gentiles wanting to be under the Law (4:21) and not an exclusive command directed to Paul's loyal followers vis-à-vis those who are going under the Law (313). For Eastman, misunderstanding this has led to an erroneous and exclusivist othering either of Jews in contrast to a superior Christianity or Jewish Christ believers who think gentiles ought to be circumcised in contrast to Jewish Christ believers who do not (the latter being originally proposed by Martyn and taken up by a number of commentators; Martyn 1997: 447–56). Thus, she argues first that Sarah and Hagar are purely metaphors of 'the divine promise that begets children into freedom' and 'the imposition of the Sinai covenant on Gentile Christians', respectively. She then argues, convincingly, that Paul never employs the second-person singular imperative in command against a group and that the target of the command *ekbale* (cast out) is still Abraham, as it was in Genesis – the Galatian gentiles are to 'overhear' in this command a warning not to 'persist in their reliance on the destructive nexus of the law and the flesh' (Eastman 2006: 314). Consequently, the charge to dismiss in Gal. 4:30 is not directed towards the community against the agitators, but towards

Abraham against those gentiles who persist in wanting to be under the Law – and it simultaneously appeals for their reconciliation (314). Bradley Trick, while agreeing that Sarah and Hagar are to be understood metaphorically, argues that they 'represent the testaments that give birth to non-Christian Jews (Sinaitic covenant) and Christian Jews (i.e. the Abrahamic covenant) and say nothing (contra Eastman) of the imposition of the old covenant on gentiles' (2016: 325–6).

While Eastman's linguistic analysis is persuasive, the charge that Paul '[exercising] his authority to evict those who pose a threat to his leadership and his preaching [makes him] no better than the other [rival] missionaries' (2006: 313) is less so; if Paul will demand the expulsion of compulsively sexually immoral believers (1 Cor. 5:13; even if, as Eastman notes, the ultimate goal is their restoration – a prospect which might never materialize and so remain simply an expulsion), expelling promulgators of a dangerously misleading form of the gospel does not seem beyond the realms of probability or unduly 'cliquish and coercive' (313).

Paul's reasoning, however, insinuates a parallel with the ancient context – that is, Hagar and Ishmael ought to be expelled from Abraham's household because Ishmael persecuted Isaac, even though no such scenario exists in Genesis 21. It may be that Paul is referring to Gen. 21:9 ('Sarah saw the son of Hagar the Egyptian . . . playing with her son Isaac') and draws upon on the rabbinic tendency to read 'play' as a euphemism for 'provoke' (Bowker 1969: 224; Betz 1979: 250; Lührmann 1992: 92). Older writers suggest that Paul's claim about Ishmael's treatment of Isaac is related to Ishmael's designation as the 'son of Hagar the Egyptian' in Gen. 21:9. The rationale is that the predicted four hundred years of affliction of Abraham's seed by the Egyptians (Gen. 15:13) commenced with the taunts of Ishmael, the son of an Egyptian woman (Leale 1892: 452).

Whatever Paul's precise historical ploy, the second half of Gen. 21:10 plays straight into his rhetoric, for he has already taken steps to divorce legitimate inheritance rights from those bound to the obligations of the Torah. Earlier in chapter four, the argument rehearsed the themes which resurface in 4:21-31 so as to point towards inheritance; those who are sons (4:6a; cf. 4:22) are recipients of the Spirit (4:6b; cf. 4:29) in a moment of liberation (4:7a; cf. 4:31) by which they become heirs (4:7b; cf. 4:30b). Moreover, the theme of the sons of Abraham was initially determined in Gal. 3:6-9, where they were identified as *hoi ek pisteōs*. The separation of Law and faith is most explicit in 3:12, where the precise opposite claim is made about the derivation of Law to the claim regarding the sons of Abraham – the Law is not of faith (*ho de nomos ouk estin ek pisteōs*). As such, the inheritance cannot be grounded upon the Law (3:18a) without negating the paradigm of response to a promise (3:18b), and God made a promise to Abraham (3:18c), the substance and fulfilment of which is Spirit, received 'through faith' (*dia tēs pisteōs*; 3:14b).

The intertextual dynamics are interesting for a few reasons. Initially, Paul interprets the problem in Galatia by building this narrative of 'the persecuted Gentiles' upon an adaptation of the *haggadah* (Jewish interpretive method aimed at producing edifying, sermonic-style teaching) of Gen. 21:9 – that the interaction between Abraham's first two sons should be viewed as hostile. In a second connected move, he is able to then characterize the gentiles as equivalent to Isaac – no mean feat considering that Hagar and Ishmael are the gentiles in the Genesis account! In a final blow, the Apostle can assert that the gentiles should respond as per the imperative in the ancient text – expel the persecutors, for like the sons of concubines, they will not be heirs of their father's estate. This, of course, reinforces Gal. 3:29 in no uncertain terms – if those demanding gentile submission to the Law are not legitimate heirs, they are not, by Paul's reckoning, truly Abraham's seed (see the account of the 'child of promise' in Watson 2004: 201–9).

5. The Law of love: Gal. 5:14 and the healing of a community

Galatians 5:14 (quoting Lev. 19:18)

The final appeal Paul makes to scripture is certainly appropriate given the conditions in Galatia. Paul's hermeneutical gymnastics are not merely to put his opponents in their place; they are an attempt to heal a family that is socially and theologically fractured. As such, the very suggestion that any adversarial wrangling about the purpose of the Law could be reconciled by the community's mutual *agape* is proactively positive.

The scripture reference remains awkward, nonetheless. To depict how certain community praxis 'fulfils the whole Law' seems confusingly misplaced in a letter purposing in part to reorient the very functionality of the Law and repudiate any notion of its soteriological necessity. Paul is certainly in good company with Jewish writers emphasizing the importance of Lev. 19:18, some seeing it as a summary of the Decalogue or at least containing all the essential moral elements of it (Allison 2010: 353–6). Allison notes the important contributions of J. H. Hertz in *The Pentateuch and Haftorahs* (1950: 495) in this regard and also refers to the work of Pieter van der Horst (1978: 66), who comments that *Pseudo-Phocylides* (a first-century Hellenistic Jewish moral poem) treated Leviticus 19 as either a summary of the Torah or a counterpart to the Decalogue. The synoptic Jesus would concur with the significance of Lev. 19:18 in summarizing Torah, as in Mt. 22:39; Mk 12:31; Lk. 10:27. We read in the *Testament of Issachar*:

> Keep the Law of God, my children; achieve integrity; live without malice, not tinkering with God's commands or your neighbour's affairs. ² Love the Lord and your neighbour; be compassionate toward poverty and sickness. ³ Bend your back in farming, perform the tasks of the soil in every kind of agriculture, offering gifts gratefully to the Lord. (*T. Iss.* 5:1-2)

Philo summarizes the Law in terms of pious duty towards God and just and humane duty towards people:

> And there are, as we may say, two most especially important heads of all the innumerable particular lessons and doctrines; the regulating of one's conduct towards God by the rules of piety and holiness, and of one's conduct towards men by the rules of humanity and justice; each of which is subdivided into a great number of subordinate ideas, all praiseworthy. (*Spec Leg.* 2:63)

However, not only is Paul's agenda manifestly very different to these other authors, but the seeming inappropriateness of the Lev. 19:18 citation is compounded by the introduction in Gal. 6:2 of a 'Law of *Christ*' to be similarly fulfilled (we will return to the Law of Christ when we consider 'Law and Spirit' in Chapter 5). To this point we have ascertained that the Spirit has birthed the true sons of Abraham on the grounds of their faith, independent of Torah. Indeed, Paul will go on to emphasize the dire fate of any gentile opting to submit to circumcision and Law (Gal. 5:2-4), but his stance undoubtedly begged an important question. What would supervise the ethical praxis of those 'sinners from among the gentiles' (Gal. 2:15), who have embraced the Jewish Messiah, but, according to Paul, are not required to embrace the Jewish Torah? (Such an enquiry may have been part of the rhetoric of Paul's opponents). Paul effectively answers in a word – 'Spirit'. Quite how Paul reasons through this will be the subject of Chapter 5 of this volume; for now, the final stage of the argument for which Paul appeals to scripture suggests that loving one's neighbour summates Torah. Elsewhere, and not insignificantly, Christ summates Torah, for example, Rom. 10:4. (For the view that Christ is the embodied Law by which God will judge the world, see Jolivet 2009: 13–30). Birth according to Spirit will give rise to certain characteristics which will galvanize the community, the first of which is love (Gal. 5:22); now we must ask how Spirit, love and the 'Law of Christ' cohere in Paul's thought.

Paul is no stranger to issuing imperatives to love on his own authority (Rom. 12:9-10; 1 Cor. 13:13; 14:1; 16:14; Phil. 1:9; 1 Thess. 3:12; etc.). Moreover, Paul elsewhere cites Lev. 19:18 in support of love as fulfilment of the Law in contexts where he does not say anything terribly abrasive about the Law as a whole (e.g. Rom. 13:9-10).

The curious phrase in Gal. 6:2 provides a clue, for there Paul states:

Ἀδελφοί, ἐὰν καὶ προλημφθῇ ἄνθρωπος ἔν τινι παραπτώματι, ὑμεῖς οἱ πνευματικοὶ καταρτίζετε τὸν τοιοῦτον ἐν πνεύματι πραΰτητος, σκοπῶν σεαυτὸν μὴ καὶ σὺ πειρασθῇς. 2 Ἀλλήλων τὰ βάρη βαστάζετε καὶ οὕτως **ἀναπληρώσετε τὸν νόμον τοῦ Χριστοῦ**.

[Brothers, if also any man might be caught out in some transgression, you the spiritual ones, restore such a one in a spirit of meekness, watching yourself so that you will not also be drawn into temptation. Carry one another's burdens and so *fill up completely the Law of Christ.*] (Boakye's translation; emphasis added)

The parallel with 5:14 is clear:

13 Ὑμεῖς γὰρ ἐπ' ἐλευθερίᾳ ἐκλήθητε, ἀδελφοί· μόνον μὴ τὴν ἐλευθερίαν εἰς ἀφορμὴν τῇ σαρκί, ἀλλὰ διὰ τῆς ἀγάπης δουλεύετε ἀλλήλοις. 14 ὁ γὰρ πᾶς **νόμος** ἐν ἑνὶ λόγῳ **πεπλήρωται**, ἐν τῷ· ἀγαπήσεις τὸν πλησίον σου ὡς σεαυτόν.

[For you were called to freedom, brothers; only not a freedom that is an opportunity for the flesh, but in the context of love, be enslaved to one another. For the entire Law *has been fulfilled* in one message, in the saying: You will love your neighbour as yourself.] (Boakye's translation; emphasis added)

In both passages, a charge is issued to the brethren, calling for interpersonal connection (restoring a transgressor or being enslaved to another believer), and so doing is identified as bringing the Law to fulfilment. (See further Thompson 2011: 126; Green 2014: 35–36).

Initially, Paul warns the Galatian gentiles not to abuse their freedom in Christ to opt for circumcision and be re-enslaved to the Law (5:13b). The proceeding affirmation then seems like a paradox – in the context of love (*dia tēs agapēs*), be enslaved to one another (*douleuete allēlois*). The explanatory 'for' leading into v. 14 introduces the rationale – the entire Law has been fulfilled in the superlative love command of Lev. 19:18. Despite the perfect passive form of 'fulfil', the recourse to scripture creates a future aspect – to love your neighbour as yourself is to be mutually enslaved in the context of love.

Then, in Galatians 6, we read an exhortation to 'the spiritual ones' within the community to gently and carefully restore those caught out in a trespass (6:1). In so 'bearing one another's burdens' (6:2a), the believers will 'completely fulfil' (*anaplērōsete*) the 'Law of Christ' (6:2b). Though, as Wilson neatly summarizes, interpretations of *ton nomon tou Christou* (the Law of Christ) are divergent (2006: 123–44; cf. Strelan 1975: 266–76; Winger 2000: 537–46; Charry 2003: 34–44), we may speculate how Gal. 5:14 and 6:2 relate. By carrying the burden of restoring their wayward brethren, the Galatians demonstrate that they are enslaved to one another in love. It is likely that in Paul's thought process the Christ event was the ultimate act of burden bearing, the supreme expression of being enslaved to someone in love. Paul has, after all, described Jesus in Gal. 2:20 as:

τοῦ ἀγαπήσαντός με καὶ παραδόντος ἑαυτὸν ὑπὲρ ἐμοῦ.

[The one who having *loved* me gave himself up on my behalf.] (Emphasis added)

In other words, if Christ's sacrificial love is a template for the love that unites the community in mutual enslavement (Gal. 5:14), this will be manifest in mutual burden-bearing (Gal. 6:2), such that the Law itself is fulfilled amid the community. Such a view of things is corroborated by Paul's use of Lev. 19:18 in Rom. 13:9-10 to outline love as fulfilment of Torah, especially in light of the earlier statement that Christ is the *telos* (culmination or destination) of the Law (Rom. 10:4a). In what sense then are 'the spiritual ones' (Gal. 6:1) equipped to exhibit this love?

Paul explicates the gentiles' experience of new life emerging from death by crucifixion in a manner that reflects his own (Gal. 5:24-25; cf. Gal. 2:19). Having suffered 'crucifixion', the gentiles are now alive a new way because of the Spirit and, as such, ought to walk in the way of Spirit (5:25). This imperative is embedded in a context of similar exhortations and expectations: 'walk in the Spirit' (Gal. 5:16), be led by the Spirit (Gal. 5:18), 'order your steps by the Spirit' (Gal. 5:25), 'sow to the Spirit' (Gal. 6:8); in 5:22-23 Paul lists a number of virtues (behind which many see fulfilment of Isaianic prophecy, particularly Isaiah 32; e.g. Barclay 1988: 121; Hansen 1994: 178–81; Beale 2005: 1–38) which are the outworking of Spirit possession, the so-called fruit of the Spirit (Betz is correct to challenge the simple equation of the fruit of the Spirit with the 'Law of Christ'; 1979: 286). To address those charged with carrying the burdens of their brethren as *hoi pneumatikoi* (Gal. 6:1), then, seems to make a related claim – *hoi pneumatikoi* are those walking in, led by, ordering their steps by and exhibiting the fruit of the Spirit. It is by the action and power of the Spirit that the faithful ones may emulate the example of Christ's love (cf. Rom. 5:5); as such, the Spirit's power is a key force in the drive for unity in the Galatian fellowship (Rand 1995: 72–92; Oakes 2015: 167). As stated, we will return to the (meaning of) the phrase 'Law of Christ' in the chapter on 'Law and Spirit' – two ideas which the term holds together.

6. Concluding thoughts

Having considered some of the creative and innovative appeals Paul makes to his scriptural heritage, we are left to briefly evaluate how convincing the resultant arguments are. A few considerations ought to suffice.

First, if we are to assume that the implied audience of Galatians are (by and large) gentiles (arguments about their precise identification notwithstanding), then one is left to speculate just how acquainted they would be with the intricacies and nuances of Paul's biblical reflections, theorizing and hermeneutic assumptions. How well did they know the story of Abraham, his struggles to have a son who could be his heir, the divine promises to him or Isaac's relationship with Ishmael? How much sense would the Hagar-Sarah allegory have made? How convincing might Paul's determination that Abraham's seed referred to an individual, the Messiah, and not the nation of Israel have sounded to gentiles? No doubt Paul's original message to the Galatians (Gal. 4:13) would have necessitated some unpacking of Israel's history, for the gospel of Jesus would be incomprehensible divorced from this context. Just how much Paul expounded Israel's convoluted relationship with Yahweh must, nonetheless, remain somewhat cloudy.

Second, the accusations that Paul routinely sacrificed consistency and integrity to successfully manufacture a historical-theological basis for validating gentile induction into the people of God did not originate with the New Perspective campaigners. Long before E. P. Sanders or Heikki Räisänen, Porphyry (third century) and even the great fourth-century bishop John Chrysostom raised critical questions about Paul's hermeneutic strategizing (Jerome's commentary on Galatians incorporates his critique of Porphyry). Even if interpreters are prepared to give Paul the benefit of the doubt when his employment of biblical citations appear unduly maverick, it is difficult not to imagine that he gives hostages to fortune when the plainer reading of the citations seemingly strengthens his opponents' (theoretical) case. For example, the command to expel the slave woman and her son (Gal. 4:30, citing Gen. 21:10) is awkward, for Hagar is the Gentile; similarly, applying the injunctions of Deut. 27:26 to law 'keepers', rather than law 'breakers', might be seen to demand an implausible suspension of logic.

Third, while most Jews of Paul's day would not have denied that gentiles had a place in Yahweh's future, enshrined as it was in Israel's scriptural tradition (Gen. 18:18; Isa. 2:1-4; 66:18-20; Mic. 4:1-2; Zech. 8:23; etc.), the various disputes over gentile integration into God's people suggest a lack of clarity over how their place in that future would manifest (Acts 15:1, 5; Gal. 2:1-5, 11-14; *Pseudo Clementine Homilies* II. 16–17). Indeed, there is evidence that certain Jews, like the author of *Jubilees*, ruled out the possibility of gentile assimilation into God's people altogether, for example, *Jub.* 15:26-27. Paul's highly successful missionary activity meant it did not take long for gentiles to outnumber Jews in the Jesus movement; but ought we assume that the success of Paul's preaching necessarily validates the superiority of his arguments, especially as they pertain to his use of the Bible? Political philosophers of diverse backgrounds have tended to see a clinically sophisticated, albeit cunning and even sinister, culture of thought behind Paul's enterprise, the likes of which they see fit to use in all manner of their own political projects. To this end, the French philosopher and cultural critic Alain Badiou is interested in the potential in Paul for creating a political philosophy aimed at criticizing globalization and capitalism in his *Saint Paul: The Foundation of Universalism* (2003; see further Jacob Taubes, *The Political Theology of Paul*, 2004). We cannot simply rule that Paul's early and even later critics were wrong on the grounds of the successful expansion of the church into the gentile world.

Fourth, as Hans Hübner quite rightly asserts, Paul is in company with other NT authors in taking the view that the Christological reading of Israel's scripture is not simply one of several valid interpretations – it is the only one (Hübner, cited in Gignilliat 2007: 24). A similar paradigm is apparent in the

Lucan Jesus's claim that his Passion was prophetically blueprinted (Lk. 24:25-27, 44-47). With this said, Paul's biblical arguments in Galatians cannot be said to 'work' except that Jesus's death and resurrection act as a functional prism by which Paul understands the divine economy of salvation. It would be unthinkable, for example, that Paul could conclude that Abraham's seed is the Messiah (Gal. 3:16) or that crucifixion invited God's curse upon the Messiah, in order to redeem a third party from a curse, but for Paul's experience of the crucified and risen Jesus.

Readers must ultimately decide just how plausibly Galatians serves to defend a Torah-independent pathway for gentiles into God's covenant family at one level, and how robustly Paul's recourse to scripture buttresses such a rationale at another. Though his arguments rarely ought to be seen as wildly outside the parameters of known rabbinic exegetical creativity, Paul's use of the Old Testament remains innovative, complex, poetic and still utterly individualist for one essential reason – this thoroughly Jewish apologetic, based on a thoroughly Jewish ancient narrative, culminating in the events surrounding the Jewish Messiah, had at its heart the creation of social space for 'non-Jews' within God's eschatological community.

The argument presented in this chapter has effectively assumed the point made earlier – that Paul's interpretation of the Hebrew Bible has been refracted through his experience of the risen Christ. The literary residue of this encounter is seen in how Paul argues his case in Galatians, especially how he quotes scripture (for the theological questions raised by the Damascus Road Christophany, see Sim 2006: 1–12). The appeal Paul makes to the Bible is ultimately to corroborate his key thesis, stated in Gal. 2:16, and substantiated by a quotation from Ps. 143:2. The Psalm aims to root redemption within divine justice, as the first and penultimate lines depict (Keesmaat 2004: 158–9). Galatians 2:16 is a pivotal moment in the letter, in which Paul explains, by way of a theoretical chastisement of Peter's actions in Antioch, his appraisal of justification. Works of the Law, which identified Israel, were not the identifying mark of the Jesus communities, so Peter's refusal to eat with gentiles in the presence of conservative Jewish believers was a grave offence. Thus, Paul makes a corresponding point to the Psalmist – that justification is divinely instigated and nothing, not even the works of the Law, could provide an alternative basis. The LXX of Ps. 142:2 (MT Ps. 143:2) literally reads: 'And do not enter into judgement with your servant, because no living being will be justified before you.' Paul quotes the second line, adding the phrase 'works of the Law' to drive home the point that Law-keepers are among those Ps. 143:2 refers to.

The biblical citations in the rest of the letter aim to demonstrate that the true insignia of the Jesus communities was the presence of the Spirit, who, on the basis of *pistis* (faith or trust) manifested the 'life' of the new age in the believers. This miraculous and liberating 'life' was originally experienced by the patriarch Abraham, when his own *pistis* in God's promise of a son, despite impossible embryological odds, was rewarded in the birth of Isaac. In Paul's reckoning, Abraham's experience foreshadowed a future generation, whose *pistis* in a corresponding manifestation of miraculous life – the resurrection of the Messiah – would be the foundation for establishing the people of God. (The association of Abraham and Isaac's relationship with the premonition of Christ's resurrection is also evident in Heb. 11:17-19.) The Spirit gives birth to the true children of Abraham (Williams 1988: 714), and the Spirit derives from *pistis* and not Torah. As ought to be apparent, Paul's appeals to the scriptures tell a story of life, faith and blessing prevailing over death, Law and curse. In the next chapter, the centrality of this 'death-overwhelmed-by-life' narrative to the argument of Galatians will be explored.

CHAPTER 4
DEATH, LIFE AND RIGHTEOUSNESS
Andrew K. Boakye

In his controversial book *Beyond the Pleasure Principle* (1922; first published 1920), Sigmund Freud outlined his theory of 'instincts', in which he believed lay the origins of all human behaviour. He resolved them into two principal categories: *eros* (literally love, which he rendered 'life') and *thanatos* (death). Life instincts were those which established and preserved human relationships, sustained the species through procreation and developed familial unity. On the other hand, there was a contrasting human tendency marked by sadism, aggression, self-destruction and the hidden desire to die (only offset by the life instinct) which he deemed the 'death instinct'. Indeed, he concluded that 'the goal of all life is death' (78). Whatever one may think of Freudian psychoanalytic theory, to bookend the human experience with the terms 'life' and 'death' has an almost innate rectitude. These terms in depicting the span of mortality spell out the boundaries of human possibilities, the scope for achievement, potential and self-actualization and the most fundamental way of articulating the substance of human evolution. Even anecdotally, when we say that something is a 'matter of life and death', we mean that it is of grave (no pun intended) seriousness. From the story of Horus dying, merging with the sun god Re and being 'resurrected' with every sunrise, to the awakening of *Sleeping Beauty* from a curse-induced coma by the prince's magical kiss, or the wizard Gandalf dying on Zirak Zigil and being transfigured as Gandalf the White in Tolkien's *Lord of the Rings*, life emerging from death is an essential human narrative (Booker 2004: 193–214). Poets, prophets and philosophers alike have routinely juxtaposed these expressions in a broad range of contexts to denote origin, finality and the essential beauty and horror of everything in between.

It was not uncommon for ancient writers, religious and secular, to employ this very imagery of life emerging from death to depict profound transformations. Jews in the first century CE knew of one such transformation story particularly well. The biblical prophet Ezekiel was a young priest among those Judeans carried off into Babylonian captivity in 579 BCE. While in exile, he exercised a ministry to the Judean captives and predicted the days when they would be liberated following the deportation to Babylon. The prediction took the form of a dramatic vision he received, with which later generations of Jews became well acquainted. In the vision, Ezekiel witnessed a valley laden with decaying skeletons and was divinely instructed to prophesy over them. He obeyed the divine mandate, at which the skeletons were miraculously embodied with flesh, skin, ligaments and muscles; they were then filled with breath (or 'spirit' – in both Hebrew and Greek it is the same word as for breath) and leapt to their feet (Ezek. 37:1-14).

In subsequent Jewish thought, the vision fuelled eschatological speculation about the final resurrection. There are many examples of this; for instance, the author of the *Sibylline Oracles* writes:

> But when at last everything shall have been reduced to dust and ashes and God shall quench the giant fire, even as he kindled it, then God Himself shall fashion again the bones and ashes of men and shall raise up mortals once more as they were before. (*Sib. Or.* 4:179-182)

Ezekiel's vision, however, did not in the immediate instance refer to the final resurrection at the Judgement. The dead bones were a portrait of Judah in captivity; their re-embodiment and reanimation were a liberation metaphor (for more on the influence of Ezekiel 37 on Pauline thought, see Fee 1994: 132; Hafemann 2005: 156–74; Beale 2011: 249–97).

Paul had a curiously corresponding experience; he did not encounter a metaphorical resurrection (like Ezekiel's vision) which pointed to an actual historical event (like Judah's restoration to their homeland). Paul experienced an actual resurrection, when he was confronted by the risen Jesus as he travelled to Damascus, and there are hints throughout Paul's letters – some subtler than others – of the impact it had on his thought. What we find in Paul's letters are frequent uses of the metaphor of new life coming from a state of deadness to narrate episodes of radical transformation (Gualtieri 1982: 177–83; Kreitzer 1993: 808). On occasion, these are in contexts explicitly associated with the resurrection of Jesus (e.g. Rom. 6:3-7), but often they draw upon the language of resurrection or reanimation to address issues in contexts quite unrelated to the actual event of Christ being raised. Two simple examples illustrate the point. In describing deliverance from a traumatic incident during his missionary exploits, Paul writes:

> To an excessive degree we were weighed down beyond our power so as to despair even of life. Indeed, we had the judgment of death

in our very selves in order that we might not be putting confidence in ourselves, but in the God raising the dead, who rescued us from so terrible a death and will continually rescue us – in whom also we have put our hope that he will still rescue us. (2 Cor. 1:8b-10; Boakye's translation)

In this instance, the reversal of this 'deadly peril' was so profound that Paul relates it as a 'resurrection'. He and his co-missionaries were discouraged to the point of thinking they would not live through the trial. Paul interpreted his feelings of imminent death as an arena from which the God who raises the dead would 'resurrect' him.

In Rom. 6:13, Paul employs the death-life contrast as a transformational metaphor separating those body parts serving God as weapons for righteous activity from those members which, as weapons for unrighteous behaviour, are ineffectual for divine purposes. Paul states:

Nor present your body parts as weapons of unrighteousness but present yourselves to God like those who have moved from death to life, and your body parts as weapons of righteousness at God's disposal. (Rom. 6:13, Boakye's translation)

The importance of the conceptualization of life emerging from death is evident both in the frequency with which the relevant terms appear in proximity to each other in Paul's letters and in how the resultant formulations advance the apostle's polemics. Paul's arguments in Galatians about how someone is justified, or attains 'righteousness', take their cue from the paradigm of life emerging from death.

The argument of Galatians describes this 'righting' as an act of reanimation. In Romans, the idea is comprehensively developed (Bird 2003: 41–6). Paul, in Romans 5, embarks on an involved foray into how death came to hold sway over mankind; drawing on the biblical story of Adam, sin was the entry point for death into the world (Rom. 5:12) and the remedy for this was the one righteous act (*dikaiōmatos*) of Christ by which people could experience a 'justification of life' (*dikaiōsin zōēs*), as outlined in Rom. 5:18 (though the term ought not to be understood too restrictively, the contrast between the one deviation and the one act of righteousness points to an epexegetic genitive, i.e., the justification which is life). For Paul, much like the author of the canonical book of Proverbs, life and death are not merely the physical indices of existence versus non-existence (Medina

2010: 199–211). In Proverbs, they operate in ethical and religious spheres, and symbolize inner, emotional dispositions; for example, Prov. 12:28 reads:

> In the path of righteousness there is life, in walking its path there is no death.

In Paul's epistles, most notably Galatians, Romans and 2 Corinthians, the terms are central to the broader soteriological discourse regarding man's relation to God. This chapter will argue that in Galatians, justification is a soteriological expression of 'revivification'.

In Paul's experience, the life-from-death drama par excellence (event and not metaphor – why that matters will become clear shortly) was the resurrection of Jesus. There is only one unambiguous reference to it in the epistle to the Galatians, and even then, it functions as a divine designation much like Rom. 4:24b. Readers should, however, resist marginalizing the importance of life and death formulae in Galatians on this basis, 'for it is these formulae that allow us to see how pivotal the resurrection is to Galatians'. A brief glance at scholarly positions surrounding the issue shows that the trap of marginalizing resurrection in Galatians may not be so easy to avoid.

1. Scholarship on resurrection in Galatians

Although Pauline scholarship is unsurprisingly replete with investigations into resurrection, particularly as it pertains to Paul's apprehension of the Christ event, the influences of Paul's resurrection ideology on his responses to issues in the communities he writes to are given less scholarly attention (Bird 2003: 31–2). Paul often harnesses Jesus's death as an index by which he contextualizes and corrects misdemeanours among the believers (e.g. Rom. 14:15; 1 Cor. 8:11). The immediate explanation for this would seem to be the more natural link between the crucifixion of Christ and Paul's soteriological ideas (e.g. Rom. 3:23-25 or, as he makes explicit in 1 Cor. 15:3b, 'Christ died for our sins according to the Scriptures'). Yet, as Kenneth Grayston observed (despite being criticized for his somewhat over-ambitious claims: Hays 1993: 246), when Paul expounds upon the Christ event as a whole, the weight of Paul's arguments rests on the resurrection (1990: 337). Alternatively, Callan thinks it is unwise to see the two elements of the Christ event as divisible in any simplistic terms (2006: 85).

However, there is no clear 'expounding' of the resurrection of Jesus in Galatians. There is also a broad absence of Paul's standard resurrection lexicon, and Jesus's resurrection only features explicitly in the letter's opening line. Consequently, most commentators routinely treat the resurrection as background noise in Galatians, albeit inescapably essential background noise (Witherington 1998: 76; Wright 2003: 219; 2013: 860). Even Grayston mentioned earlier, while acknowledging the polemical significance of the resurrection, determines not to funnel the Christ event into support of an atonement theory; rather, he suggests the only key question is how the event affects the community.

Others, such as Martyn and Dunn, while not directly minimizing the significance of the resurrection in Galatians, are content to conclude that Paul had no substantial dispute with his interlocutors regarding the resurrection (Dunn 1993: 28–9; Martyn 1997: 85). While there is undoubtedly some truth to this, the implications of the risen Christ's presence on the politics of Israel's identity are profound in certain things Paul says in Galatians. Several scholars, including M. Bird and D. Campbell, having rightly accentuated the profile of resurrection within 'New Perspective' readings of justification, allowed their works to lean heavily on Romans and, to a lesser extent, the Corinthian correspondences, offering only minimal comment on Galatians (Bird 2007: 40; Campbell 2009: 672). Bird in particular has made significant inroads in reemphasizing the substantial functionality of Christ's death and resurrection in Romans. He quite rightly asserts that

> we must not think of Jesus' resurrection solely in terms of his vindication, but concurrently recognize that the resurrection possesses a genuine soteriological function in relation to producing justification. (Bird 2003: 44)

Michael Gorman correctly understands justification in Galatians within a crucifixion-resurrection paradigm, though he reads the attendant lifestyle largely through the eyes of the former (2009: 43–4). R. A. Bryant (2001) attempted a far more thoroughgoing analysis of the significance of resurrection in Galatians, but rather than grapple with the actual presence of the motif, investigated resurrection under the wider rubric of 'apocalyptic'. Thus, the places he sees the risen Christ as crucial to the argument of the letter rely on its apocalyptic elements like the incidence of the ἀποκάλυπ-cognates in 1:11–2:10 or the dawn of the new age in 3:6–4:7 (143). Grayston does not tie the death and life language with resurrection in Galatians though, exegetically, his reading is insightful, particularly in how he contextualizes justification in Gal. 2:11-14 (1990: 68–85).

2. Death and life language in Paul

There are thirty-seven occurrences of the noun *zoē* (life) in the Pauline texts; in ten of these, 'life' appears as part of the composite phrase 'eternal life' (*zōēn aiōnion*), a term pointing to the life of eschatological salvation. In the remaining twenty-seven occasions of *zoē*, nineteen are 'in direct, coterminous juxtaposition with "death" language'. A consideration of the corresponding verb *zaō* (to live) uncovers an essentially equivalent pattern. Of fifty-nine instances of *zaō* in Paul, in its various grammatical incarnations, again, a sizeable thirty-four are directly conjoined to death motifs. For a fuller discussion of the semantic landscape of death-life language in the Pauline corpus, its frequency and the implications of the diffuse dispersion of the terms, see Boakye (2017: 26–30). The following will exemplify how the death-life lexicon serves to advance a Pauline polemic. The two earlier examples from 2 Corinthians 1 and Romans 6 demonstrate how revivification imagery can symbolize ethical and theological paradigms. In the following brief sketch of some of the key arguments in Romans 1–8, it will become clear that the interplay of death and life vocabulary can be central to how Paul explains his position. This is, of course, what I will go on to explain is happening in Galatians.

The proceeding sketch will not attempt to address any of the numerous difficult questions which arise in Romans – it will merely show how revivification, death and life are at the nucleus of its argumentative trajectory – so excuse the size of some of the hermeneutic leaps attempted in what follows.

There is broad agreement that Romans 1–3 is, among other things, Paul's attempt to demonstrate that all humankind, irrespective of ethnic distinction, is equally adrift of right standing with God and equally culpable for so being. Nobody can claim exemption – neither the gentile world (Rom. 1:18-32) nor the Jewish world (Rom. 2:1–3:8). Indeed, Rom. 3:9-20 forms a summative indictment of the very human failure estranging people from their creator, and why the creator's judgement is utterly warranted (Barth 1968: 55–6; Käsemann 1980: 33–6; Fitzmyer 1993: 98; Morgan 1997: 22–9; Jewett 2007: 148). Having denounced impotent 'human' righteousness, the key section in Rom. 3:21-26 announces that the saving 'righteousness of

God', first mentioned in 1:17 and 3:5, is freely available to all, irrespective of ethnic classification, through faith in Christ, whose sacrifice God permitted in an act of undeserved grace. The closing section of Romans 3 summarizes the supremacy of faith, stipulating how one God presides over all humanity, and so this faith opens the door of his righteousness to all humanity; the playing field is level, and nobody has bragging rights in front of God.

The incisive next question must now ask after the nature of this faith; significantly, the transition from Rom. 3:31 to 4:1 is similar to the rhetorical move from Gal. 3:5 to 3:6, the connection between faith and righteousness being resolved by recourse to Abraham. The scholarly impasse over how Abraham resolves the question, beginning with the very translation of Rom. 4:1, cannot be broached here. For our purposes, what seems clear is that Abrahamic faith centres upon his response to a promise made to him by God and originally recorded in Gen. 15:6, and which Paul recalls three times in Romans 4 (4:3, 9, 22). This is the promise that the aged Abraham and his wife Sarah would conceive a male child and heir, despite the near impossible biological odds. Abraham's faith in this promise, God treated (reckoned) as righteousness. How Paul unpacks this faith in Romans 4 is pivotal for the next stage of the argument of Romans and for the point being stressed here:

17 καθὼς γέγραπται ὅτι Πατέρα πολλῶν ἐθνῶν τέθεικά σε, κατέναντι οὗ ἐπίστευσεν θεοῦ τοῦ ζῳοποιοῦντος τοὺς νεκροὺς καὶ καλοῦντος τὰ μὴ ὄντα ὡς ὄντα. 18 ὃς παρ᾽ ἐλπίδα ἐπ᾽ ἐλπίδι ἐπίστευσεν εἰς τὸ γενέσθαι αὐτὸν πατέρα πολλῶν ἐθνῶν κατὰ τὸ εἰρημένον· Οὕτως ἔσται τὸ σπέρμα σου. (Rom. 4:17-18)

[Just as it has been written that 'I have established you as a father of many nations', in the sight of God whom he trusted, the one who causes life to reanimate the dead and calls into being the non-existent things, and whom he trusted in hope against hope, so as to himself become a father of many nations according to what was spoken: 'in this way shall your seed be'.] (Boakye's translation)

Abraham's faith was 'resurrection faith' (see earlier on Gal. 3:6 – Abraham and the Spirit). From the deadness of Abraham and Sarah's reproductive apparatus (Rom. 4:19) life came forth in the form of their son Isaac – the God who reanimates the dead, called Isaac, who did not and by all odds could not exist, into being. It was 'because of this' (Gk. *dio*, Rom. 4:22) that it was reckoned to him as righteousness. Abraham's trust in the God that can resurrect the dead was actualized as righteousness. However, this paradigm was not the exclusive dispensation of Abraham (Rom. 4:23); rather,

24 ἀλλὰ καὶ δι᾽ ἡμᾶς, οἷς μέλλει λογίζεσθαι, τοῖς πιστεύουσιν ἐπὶ τὸν ἐγείραντα Ἰησοῦν τὸν κύριον ἡμῶν ἐκ νεκρῶν, 25 ὃς παρεδόθη διὰ τὰ παραπτώματα ἡμῶν καὶ ἠγέρθη διὰ τὴν δικαίωσιν ἡμῶν. (Rom. 4:24-25)

[But also on our account, to whom it is about to be reckoned, those trusting in the one having raised Jesus from among the dead, who was delivered up on account of our transgressions and was raised for our justification.] (Boakye's translation)

The logic seems unarguable; the believer's faith in the risen Jesus demonstrates his or her trust in the God by whose energy Jesus was raised. The believer has thus mimicked the resurrection faith of Abraham and consequently has that faith actualized as righteousness. What Paul's argument has highlighted to this point is how justification is dependent upon the resurrection of Jesus and how the birth of Isaac was a type of the resurrection of Jesus. (There remains a fair amount of debate regarding whether Abraham, Isaac 'or the ram' in the *Aqedah* story are actually a type of Christ. The Fathers tended to see Isaac as type, for example, Clement of Alexandria, *Paedagogus* 1.5.23:1–2; Melito of Sardis, *Catena on Genesis* V; in John Chrysostom's sermons on Genesis, he saw Isaac and the ram as types (*Hom. Gen.* 47). Von Rad argues that neither should be so perceived ([1959] 1977: 39).) So then, to be justified requires the exhibition of 'faith' or 'trust' that Yahweh can make life emerge from death. Faith language has dominated Romans 1–4; *pistis* appears again in 5:1 and 5:2 (some mss omit the *pistis* in v. 2) which recapitulate the basic argument of Romans 4, before the various blessings of justification are outlined in 5:3-11. After Rom. 5:1-2, the language of faith all but disappears until Romans 9; the noun is absent altogether and the verb appears once in Rom. 6:8. Romans 5–8 is dominated by the language of death and life.

What seems apparent, though given minimal profile in most scholarship, is that the transition of the lexicon of 'faith' to that of 'death and life' is predicated on the death-to-life narrative at the end of Romans 4. God is defined superlatively as 'The Resurrector' (Rom. 4:17, 24; cf. Gal. 1:1), and Abraham's faith, the prototype of the believer in Jesus, defined as trust in the divine power to resurrect. The outworking of this is embedded in the arguments of Romans 5–8.

In Rom. 5:12-21, Paul depicts the reign of death, having been inaugurated by the Adamic trespass in Eden, as being both overwhelmed and terminated by the life of Christ. Life emerges from death such that

> [17] …if by the transgression of one, death ruled through the one, then much more will the recipients of the overflowing of grace and the free donation of righteousness rule in life through the one Jesus, the Messiah. [18] As a result, then, as through one transgression condemnation came upon all humanity, so also through one act of righteousness, a *justification of life* comes upon all humanity. (Rom. 5:17-18; Boakye's translation; emphasis added)

Then in Rom. 6:1-14 comes what has been described as an intensely complex treatment of the relationship between sin and death in Paul, made only more so by the presiding metaphor of baptism (Black 1984: 421). In these verses, the baptismal waters symbolize the burial place (Rom. 6:4) of the 'crucified' former self (Rom. 6:6). Here, the baptizand shares in the death of the Messiah, who having been clothed with the 'likeness of sinful flesh' (Rom. 8:3) opened the doorway to a new sphere of existence – the risen life. The emergence of the baptized one from the 'grave' of the baptismal water corresponds to their raising into the new sphere after the manner of the Messiah's resurrection (Rom. 6:4). This death and new order of life has twin effects – the believer is 'dead' to the lordship of sin (Rom. 6:10-11) and is a candidate for eternal life (Rom. 6:22).

For Paul's believing Jewish hearers a quandary remained. They had lived under the lordship of Torah – how could Paul claim that the Christ event ended the reign of death and sin, without simultaneously suggesting that Torah's reign had also come to an end (something he specifically states in Rom. 10:4)? The somewhat lurid relationship between sin, death and the Law is the subject of Romans 7 and again is partially resolved through a series of death-life contrasts. Like a widow is released from matrimonial obligations upon her husband's death and is free to belong to another man (Rom. 7:1-3), so a Jew must share in death in order to belong to Christ:

> So then my brothers, you also were put to death to the Law through the body of the Messiah, so that you might come to belong to another – that is, to the one having been raised from among the dead, in order that you might produce fruit for God. (Rom. 7:4; Boakye's translation)

The release from the jurisdiction of Torah was a necessary step because of how sin manipulated the Law. The Law ought to have been a path to life but proved a path to death (Rom. 7:10) because sin took advantage of the tension between the deep-seated desire to covet (to cite the example Paul employs) and the command not to covet, thus turning it into actual covetousness and 'killing' the transgressor (Rom. 7:11). Sin, thereby, turns the holy Law (Rom. 7:12) into a virtual slave-master (Rom. 7:15-24) from which only Jesus could liberate (Rom. 7:25). In Romans 8, this freedom is elaborated – it is brought about by the:

νόμος τοῦ πνεύματος τῆς ζωῆς ἐν Χριστῷ Ἰησοῦ. (Rom. 8:2a)

[law of the Spirit of life in Christ Jesus.] (Boakye's translation)

and

10 εἰ δὲ Χριστὸς ἐν ὑμῖν, τὸ μὲν σῶμα νεκρὸν διὰ ἁμαρτίαν τὸ δὲ πνεῦμα ζωὴ διὰ δικαιοσύνην. 11 εἰ δὲ τὸ πνεῦμα τοῦ ἐγείραντος τὸν Ἰησοῦν ἐκ νεκρῶν οἰκεῖ ἐν ὑμῖν, ὁ ἐγείρας Χριστὸν ἐκ νεκρῶν ζωοποιήσει καὶ τὰ θνητὰ σώματα ὑμῶν διὰ τοῦ ἐνοικοῦντος αὐτοῦ πνεύματος ἐν ὑμῖν. (Rom. 8:10-11)

[If Messiah is in you, then on the one hand the body is dead on account of sin, but on the other, the Spirit is life on account of righteousness; and if the Spirit of the one having raised Jesus from among the dead is housed in you, the one having raised Messiah from among the dead will also bring to life your deathly bodies through the indwelling of his Spirit in you.] (Boakye's translation)

There is no condemnation for anyone, Jew or gentile, in Christ (Rom. 8:1), because the Spirit of life has freed them, by reanimating their 'deathly bodies' (Rom. 8:11) – recall the story of Ezek. 37:1-14 – the narrative of Spirit, life and liberation will feature in Galatians below. Again, while it is worth reiterating that this very brief sketch has sidestepped several issues, it ought to demonstrate an important key in Pauline exegesis. The motif of death and life in contrast to one another goes beyond symbolism, imagery or metaphor; as is apparent in Rom. 4:16–8:39, both the substance and dynamics of Paul's arguments hinge upon this contrast. Note the critical relationship between the birth of Isaac, the resurrection of Jesus and the reversal of the Adamic lapse through which death reigned – all have at their heart 'death being exhausted by life'. One might say that in a Pauline vernacular, this is code for divine action in the world – for God to undo the effects of sin and reconcile humanity to himself is to cause life to emerge from death. In the next section, it will become clear that such a view of things was by no means uniquely Pauline – he clearly draws upon a well-travelled paradigm.

3. Life, death and revivification in Jewish texts

No Jew, ancient or modern, would dispute that God is the architect and originator of all life. It is embedded in Jewish thought from man's inception as outlined in the biblical creation myths:

> καὶ ἔπλασεν ὁ θεὸς τὸν ἄνθρωπον χοῦν ἀπὸ τῆς γῆς καὶ ἐνεφύσησεν εἰς τὸ πρόσωπον αὐτοῦ *πνοὴν ζωῆς*, καὶ ἐγένετο ὁ ἄνθρωπος εἰς ψυχὴν *ζῶσαν*.

> [And God formed the man with dust from the ground and he blew into his face a *breath of life* and the man became as a *living* soul.] (Gen. 2:7, LXX; Boakye's translation; emphases added)

As such, when, in the Exodus narratives, Egyptian sorcerers attempted to mimic God's wonders by their esoteric arts, they scored some successes until God commanded Aaron to extend his staff and create live gnats from the dust of the earth (Exod. 8:16-17). The author narrates the magicians' failure to simulate the miracle (Exod. 8:18), reasoning that it was because 'this is the finger of God' (Exod. 8:19a). Evidently then, the creation of life, the animation of dead matter and resurrection all witness to God's presence and activity. Behind these narratives of death and life lie not only the fundamental Jewish conviction that all life originates from God, as we have already seen in Gen. 2:7, but furthermore that all life is under his ultimate control, as captured by Deut. 32:39:

> See now that I, even I, am he; there is no god besides me. I kill and I make alive; I wound and I heal; and no one can deliver from my hand. (cf. 1 Sam. 2:6)

The author of the *Wisdom of Solomon* states in corresponding fashion:

For you have power over life and death;
> You lead mortals down to the gates of Hades and back again.
(*Wisdom of Solomon* 16:13)

The early Jesus communities later ascribed similar language to Jesus (Jn 5:21, 24, 26; 1 Cor. 15:45; Rev. 1:17-18).

Jewish writers further exemplified the magnitude of the divine prerogative over death and life by conceptualizing divine acts as the metaphorical transaction of life emerging from death. The Psalmists routinely articulate deliverance from affliction and danger with such revivification imagery, as in Pss. 71:20, 80:18 and 138:7. In Psalm 16, which Luke places on the lips of Peter in his Pentecost sermon to interpret the resurrection of Jesus, the author writes:

> [10] For you do not give me up to Sheol or let your faithful one see the Pit.
> [11] You show me the path of life. In your presence there is fullness of joy; in your right hand are pleasures forevermore. (Ps. 16:10-11; cf. Acts 2:27-28)

The metaphor is applied in an array of other contexts. In the Jewish romance designated *Joseph and Aseneth*, the author quite beautifully depicts the young Egyptian maiden's 'conversion' to Yahwism as a process of revivification. He writes,

> O Lord, the God of my father Israel, the Most High, the Mighty One, Who *quickens* all things, and calls *them* from darkness into light. And from error into truth, and from *death into life*; O Lord, quicken and bless this virgin. And renew her by thy spirit, and re-mould her by thy secret hand, *And quicken her with your life. And may she eat the bread of thy life,* And may she drink the cup of your blessing, She whom you chose before she was begotten, And may she enter into thy rest, which you have prepared for your elect. (*Joseph and Aseneth* 8:10-11; emphasis added; cf. Kim 2004: 70)

Although there is no unanimous scholarly position regarding what the Qumran community believed about resurrection, some literature from the Qumran library contain resurrection portraits. In Hippolytus's account of resurrection belief at Qumran, he states that 'the doctrine of the resurrection has also derived support among these; for they acknowledge both that the flesh will rise again, and that it will be immortal, in the same manner as the soul is already imperishable' (*Haer.* 9.22). The *Messianic Apocalypse* (4Q521) interpolates passages from Psalm 146 and Isaiah 61 (indeed it appears to be dependent on the former), both of which contain explicit resurrection imagery. Elsewhere in the community's literature, pictures of resurrection are employed to express other ideas. In the *Hodayot* the author uses the motif of being 'raised up' to describe the purification of a sinner who joins the group:

> For the sake of Thy glory Thou hast purified man of sin that he may be made holy for Thee, with no abominable uncleanness and no guilty wickedness; that he may be one [with] the children of Thy truth and partake of the lot of Thy Holy Ones; that bodies gnawed by worms may be raised from the dust to the counsel [of Thy truth]. (1QH^a 11:10-13; Vermes' translation; cf. 1QH^a 6:34)

The death-life metaphor is particularly indicative of the divine presence and work in episodes of personal, political or national disaster in Israel's history. Jewish writers often narrated such adversities as 'deaths' and the remedy, rehabilitation or liberation from turmoil as 'new life', 'rebirth' or 'resurrection'. The import of the metaphor lies precisely in the author's assumption that, just as God alone can re-enliven the dead, only divine intervention could mitigate whatever calamity had befallen the nation, community or individual. In the Hebrew Bible, such episodes also very likely fuelled developing eschatological speculations about final resurrection; passages like Isa. 26:16-21, Dan. 12:1-3 and Hos. 6:1-3 (cf. *1 Enoch* 91:10; 93:2). Almost certainly, though, the supreme divine intervention-expressed-in-revivification-metaphor – and the text which most influenced subsequent Second Temple eschatology – is Ezekiel's vision of Judah's liberation from Babylonian captivity, with which we began the chapter (for a fuller picture of Ezekiel's influence on Judeo-Christian afterlife ideology, see Block 1992: 113–42). So influential was Ezekiel's resurrection narrative that it served as an intertext for other writers confronting the immediacy of death and/or the fragility of life. The author of *4 Maccabees*, in relating the struggle for Jewish autonomy amid the Hellenizing pressure of Antiochus IV 'Epiphanes', records the speech of the righteous mother whose seven sons are condemned to death for their commitment to Torah. In her moving address, she recounts the stories that their father used to tell them, saying:

[15] He sang to you songs of the psalmist David, who said, 'Many are the afflictions of the righteous'. [16] He recounted to you Solomon's proverb, 'There is a tree of life for those who do his will'. [17] *He confirmed the query of Ezekiel, 'Shall these dry bones live?'* [18] For he did not forget to teach you the song that Moses taught, which says, [19] *'I kill and I make alive: this is your life and the length of your days'*. (*4 Macc.* 18:15-19; emphasis added)

In this instance, it is interesting to observe how the writer of *4 Maccabees* associates the 'kill/make alive' motif of Deut. 32:39 (*4 Macc.* 18:19) with the query of Ezek. 37:3 (*4 Macc.* 18:17). In the *Pseudo-Ezekiel* Qumran manuscripts, the composer adopts the first-person stance of the biblical Ezekiel and addresses the vexing question (even of modern interpretation) of whether the dry bones vision was simply a restoration metaphor or indeed had eschatological ramifications (see further Dimant 2000: 527–48). He asks, 'When will [th]ese things come to pass? How shall their faithfulness be rewarded?' (4Q385 2 3). *Pseudo-Ezekiel* gives a twofold response, the first being addressed to the community regarding their liberation, the second to later readers about God resurrecting those who remain faithful to Torah (for a review of the interpretation of resurrection in Ezekiel 37 in this and other Second Temple texts, see Tromp 2007: 61–78). Gary T. Manning sees Ezekiel's language of 'life-giving breath' providing literary impetus to the Johannine 'mini-Pentecost' of Jn. 20:22 (2004: 171). Wright's contention that the parable of the lost son has at its nucleus a basic rehearsal of the story of Judah's restoration from Babylonian captivity is essentially correct (1996: 126–7). Luke's story ends with the father giving the older, more responsible son a reason for his overt rejoicing at the rebel son's return: 'We had to celebrate and rejoice, because this brother of yours *was dead and has come to life*; he was lost and has been found' (Lk. 15:32; emphasis added). There may well be a resonance of Ezekiel's restoration drama in Luke 15 – and while considering how life emerging from death acts in the story of the lost son as a liberation metaphor, we may turn our attention directly to Galatians.

As will be clear, Ezekiel's story almost certainly looms large in the argumentative foreground of Paul's letter (Boakye 2017: 114). It is of a Spirit-instigated movement from death to life, portraying freedom from slavery, and predicting an internalization of the Spirit which would instantiate in God's people an unprecedented way of engaging with God's Law and will. Paul's response to the socio-theological fiasco in the Galatian Jesus communities is a contextually nuanced rehearsal of the same story; it is framed so as to affirm that justification by faith in the risen Jesus, and its associated effects, are the ultimate realization of the Ezekielian vision.

4. Resurrection and the death-life paradigm in Galatians

The use of life and death/crucifixion language in Galatians is not just widespread but, typically, strategic. The employment of the terms reveals a pervasive soteriological framework upon which key elements of the argument rest.

The noun 'life' (*zōē*) appears once in Galatians, in the compound term 'eternal life' (Gal. 6:8). The corresponding verb 'to live' (*zaō*) appears ten times, in six verses (2:14; 2:19; 2:20 (x5); 3:11; 3:12; 5:25). The compound verb 'to make alive' (*zōopoieō*) appears in 3:21. On the other side of the coin: the verb 'to die' (*apothnēskō*) appears at 2:19 and 2:21, and the noun 'dead' (*nekros*) appears in 1:1. The various cognates of the Greek term for 'crucify' (*stauroō*) appear four times in Galatians (2:20; 3:1; 5:24; 6:14). The collocation of these terms in context reveals a pivotal component of the salvation rhetoric of the epistle, and, as in the earlier examples of Jewish texts, the presence and activity of God. In essence, Paul treats justification, the principal soteriological term in the letter, as something divinely engineered, actualized by faith in the risen Christ and manifest in a process of revivification.

We see this distribution of revivification imagery and terminology at key moments in Galatians, as outlined here. The first instance, and the only explicit mention of the resurrection of Jesus in the epistle, is the divine title in the opening line. God is there defined as the 'one having raised Jesus from among the dead'. The next significant concentration of revivification imagery is in Gal. 2:19-20, which forms part of Paul's autobiographical narrative and which Gaventa quite rightly states 'forms the basis for Paul's later exhortation' (1986: 313). Both the language and contextualization of the oft-called 'scriptural section' of Paul's defence is revivification-centric. The contrast between the 'life' that originates from faith (Hab. 2:4, cited in Gal. 3:11) and the 'life' of performing Torah (Lev. 18:5, cited in Gal. 3:12) is played out within the matrix of Pauline 'curse' language in Galatians 3. Accordingly, some commentators see great significance in the Deuteronomic contextualization of the section Gal. 3:10-14; as is argued in the chapter on Paul's use of scripture, the Apostle seems to effectively equate the curse with 'death', as many have rightly observed (e.g. Wright 1991: 137–56; Ciampa 1998: 209; Morales 2010: 106; see further Scott 1993a: 212–16). Others, while invoking the Deuteronomic landscape of Gal. 3:10-14, draw very different conclusions about the curse. In Kahl's innovative rereading, the curse represents the current life realities of conquered nations under Roman rule (2010: 255–6). It is important to observe that the writer of Deuteronomy makes the original association of death with curse throughout Deuteronomy 30, and it is this which Paul draws upon.

Paul's declaration in Gal. 3:21 forms a pivotal element of the revivification rhetoric. The Law's incapacity in Gal. 3:21 is its inability to produce life (see the discussion in Macchia 2017: 639–42). This resonates with Paul's broader association of Torah with death (Gal. 2:19-20; Rom. 7:4-5; 8:2; 1 Cor. 15:56; 2 Cor. 3:6-7). It further corroborates the notion of curse as death (Gal. 3:9-10).

In two of three more key images, Paul juxtaposes the lexis of 'crucifixion' with life (Gal. 5:24-25) and new creation (6:14-15). In the remaining death-life motif, the eternal life reaped by those sowing to the Spirit stands against the corruption (*phthora*) that will be harvested by those sowing to the flesh (Gal. 6:8). It is the profusion of and interaction between the above death and life imagery in Galatians which illustrates how intricately revivification and justification are intertwined in Paul's argument, and this is explored in detail here. As with the example of the reading of Romans 1–8 earlier, the death-life formulations are the impetus of Paul's argument in Galatians. The coherence of these formulations clarifies how conceptualizing justification in revivification terms counteracts the opposition thesis that gentiles must embrace Torah to be fully inducted into the people of God.

The first notable concentration of life-death contrasts occurs in the section Gal. 2:19-20, which rounds off the section offering perhaps the most explicit précis of the challenge to which Galatians is riposte. Having related the debacle at the Antioch meal table in Gal. 2:11-14, where Peter, Barnabas and other Christ-believing Jews deserted the mixed gathering upon the arrival of colleagues of James, Paul sets out his thesis statement (see Chapter 6, 'Unity in Diversity in Christ'). In Gal. 2:15-21, some pivotal terminology is introduced. Paul uses terms like *dikaioō* (justify), *erga nomou* (works of Law), *pistis Christou* (faith in Christ/faithfulness of Christ) and 'life' and 'death' language to address the ethnic marginalization of gentiles at the Antiochene meal celebration, which was clearly indicative of a wider quandary – the basis for defining the identity of the people of God.

The fundamental thesis is in 2:15-16; even Jewish believers like Paul and Peter (to whom the first-person plural at the beginning of 2:15 most directly relates), schooled in Torah, know that to be justified in the sight of God requires one to trust in Jesus – it cannot come from performing the works of the Law. For Paul to allow this to go unchecked would mean reconstructing a structure rightly dismantled according to God's eschatological calendar (2:17-18). Then come two verses with a fivefold instantiation of *zaō* by which Paul uses himself as a test case for how God justifies Jews through Christ:

ἐγὼ γὰρ διὰ νόμου νόμῳ ἀπέθανον, ἵνα θεῷ ζήσω. Χριστῷ συνεσταύρωμαι·

ζῶ δὲ οὐκέτι ἐγώ,

ζῇ δὲ ἐν ἐμοὶ Χριστός·

ὃ δὲ νῦν ζῶ ἐν σαρκί, ἐν πίστει ζῶ τῇ τοῦ υἱοῦ τοῦ θεοῦ τοῦ ἀγαπήσαντός με καὶ παραδόντος ἑαυτὸν ὑπὲρ ἐμοῦ.

[For I through the Law *died* to the Law, in order that I might *live* to God. I have been *co-crucified* with Christ

And I *live* no longer

But Messiah *lives* in me

And that which I now *live* in flesh, I *live* by faith in the Son of God, the one having loved me and *given himself over* on my behalf.] (Gal. 2:19-20; Boakye's translation; emphases added)

In two steps, Paul sets up a 'revivification framework' which elucidates his own transformative experience. The assertion that 'I died to the Law *in order that* I might live to God', which would have outraged Paul's Jewish contemporaries, demonstrates life overcoming death; in Pauline thought, new life emerging from death did not only happen to Jesus, but was now happening through him. Paul elaborates the ontological reality of being re-enlivened with a unique potency, by which he became conscious of a newly created cosmos (cf. Hubing 2015: 229–45). So completely had Paul been transformed that even how he spoke of this emergent order was imbued with Christ consciousness – the old order had been 'crucified' (Gal. 6:14) as had the framework of his own self-identity (Gal. 2:19) and that frail element of the human constitution that was susceptible to the self-destructive consequences of un-curtailed lust (Gal. 5:24). Paul's fury at the situation in Antioch was predicated on this self-awareness – his inner metamorphosis was exemplary of 'Israel in Christ'. The behaviour of Peter, Barnabas and the other Jewish believers told a very different and very regressive story in Paul's mind. Only by reaffirming the former strictures could one legitimize the ostracization of non-Jews. Where the risen Christ was the energy of one's existence, he alone became the primal insignia of identity – to deny this was to turn back the eschatological clock (Hafemann 1997: 352).

Paul explicates his experience by equating 'death to Law' with 'co-crucifixion with Christ'. In so doing, he positions himself with the aforementioned Jewish writers, employing the death-life motif to describe emergence into a new arena. Having experienced the risen Christ 'in himself' (Gal. 1:16), the apostle reasoned that he had experienced an about-turn of self-identity of the highest order imaginable, and as writers before him surmised, such a reversal could only have been divinely instigated (the notion of reconfigured identity within the context of resurrection most likely lies behind Phil. 3:3-11). Consequently, he too articulated the transformation as revivification, a movement from death to life.

However, the events of the Damascus Road provided Paul with a unique analogue: unlike those writers before him, Paul did not encounter an event which he described and interpreted in terms of resurrection – he encountered a resurrection by which he interpreted and described an event – specifically the reconfiguration of his own self-identity. So, this was not just a death, but a death 'to Law' – death to one sphere of identity (Law) and new birth to another (the risen Christ). It is co-crucifixion with Christ because Christ was the template – he underwent a transformation of identity by death and recreation, and anyone 'in Christ', resultantly experiences the same (Lewis 2005: 162–4; Kahl 2010: 280–1; Turley 2015: 127–9). As earlier stated, however, Jesus's transformation narrative differed from the reversal dramas of other Jewish texts because it was not a metaphor. Similarly, Paul's change should not be read as a transformation allegory, but an 'eschatological participation' in the Christ event. That is to say, Paul is 'newly created' because he now exists in the sphere of the risen Christ or, in Paul's shorthand, is 'in Christ' (hence, Gal. 2:20; being a 'new creation in Christ' is explicit in 2 Cor. 5:17). Within this sphere of identity those with faith have a new disposition. Just as Christ himself died and was recreated with an unprecedented identity categorization (the substance of 1 Cor. 15:35-49), so are all who are in Christ.

Having 'suffered' crucifixion, Paul can say 'I no longer live', which seems consistent until one considers the very last clause in 2:20 – 'and that which I now *live* in the flesh, I *live* by faith in the son of God' (emphases added). At this point, readers may wish that Paul would make up his mind – is he, in his own estimations, alive or dead (!)? It is the conjoining phrase that makes the verse rational – 'Messiah lives in me'. Paul is not confused; rather, he is acutely aware that he is 'alive' in a renewed and exceptional way (an argument elaborated in Rom. 7:1-12). In Romans, Paul acknowledges the life he had before his Torah-education ('and I was once alive apart from the Law; Rom. 7:9a) and how that ended when sin manipulated Torah and he 'died' (Rom. 7:9c). It is this 'death' which Paul describes as 'through Law' in Gal. 2:19 (for other autobiographical readings of Rom. 7:9, see Mounce 1995: 164–5; Matera 2010: 174–5). Faith, however, instigates a new mode of existence – 'life to God' (cf. Rom. 6:10; *4 Macc.* 7:19; 16:25, which all use the phrase 'live to God' in the context of a risen existence) – or, as Paul also has it, the presence of the risen Christ in him. The risen Christ is an animating agent, a 'life-giving spirit' as Paul renders the thought elsewhere (1 Cor. 15:45; cf. Rom. 5:10b). The soteriological significance of Jesus's risen life is evident from how Paul depicts Jesus's work formulaically and autobiographically. For Jesus is variously

> τοῦ δόντος ἑαυτὸν ὑπὲρ τῶν ἁμαρτιῶν ἡμῶν, ὅπως ἐξέληται ἡμᾶς ἐκ τοῦ αἰῶνος τοῦ ἐνεστῶτος πονηροῦ.

> [*the one having given himself over on behalf of* our sins, so that he might rescue us from the age of the present evil.] (Gal. 1:4a, b; Boakye's translation; emphasis added)

and

> τοῦ υἱοῦ τοῦ θεοῦ τοῦ ἀγαπήσαντός με καὶ *παραδόντος ἑαυτὸν ὑπὲρ ἐμοῦ*.

> [the son of God, the one having loved me and *given himself over on my behalf*.] (Gal. 2:20c; Boakye's translation; emphasis added).

It seems that Jesus's vicarious self-giving and concomitant enlivening of Paul (2:20) was, in Paul's own thinking, directly equivalent to Jesus rescuing (him) from the age of the present evil (1:4). Jesus made Paul alive following his death to Law – 'the Law itself could not generate life' as Paul goes on to relate in Gal. 3:21b:

> εἰ γὰρ ἐδόθη νόμος ὁ δυνάμενος ζῳοποιῆσαι, ὄντως ἐκ νόμου ἂν ἦν ἡ δικαιοσύνη·

> [for if a law was given which was able to produce life, certainly righteousness would derive from law.] (Boakye's translation)

Note that the semantic proximity with the final clause in the thesis statement, Gal. 2:21, strengthens the point:

εἰ γὰρ διὰ νόμου δικαιοσύνη, ἄρα Χριστὸς δωρεὰν ἀπέθανεν.

[for if righteousness (is) through law, then Christ died needlessly.] (Boakye's translation)

Both clauses make equivalent and mutually interpretive claims. First, both imply that 'righteousness' (*dikaiosunē*) does not derive from Law. Second, the immediacy with which Gal. 3:21 associates justification with making alive corresponds with 2:21; for Paul says that Jesus need not have died if the Law could secure righteousness. Clearly it could not – Jesus needed to die in order to bring the life of the new age into the present experience (cf. Mohrmann 2009: 164–6). This brings us to one final issue.

The different spheres of 'life' which Paul has expounded by way of autobiography in Gal. 2:19-20 recur in the so-called scriptural polemic of 3:10-13:

ὅτι δὲ ἐν νόμῳ οὐδεὶς δικαιοῦται παρὰ τῷ θεῷ δῆλον, ὅτι ὁ δίκαιος ἐκ πίστεως ζήσεται·

[And that in Law no one is justified before God (is) self-evident, because the righteous from faith will live.] (Gal. 3:11; Boakye's translation)

ὁ δὲ νόμος οὐκ ἔστιν ἐκ πίστεως, ἀλλ᾽ ὁ ποιήσας αὐτὰ ζήσεται ἐν αὐτοῖς.

[And the Law is not of faith, but the one doing these things will live in them.] (Gal. 3:12; Boakye's translation)

Paul's utilization of Hab. 2:4 in Gal. 3:11 rehearses that it is clear no one will be justified before God by virtue of the Law, because the justified one 'will live' (*zēsetai*) by faith. Once more, this tallies with 3:21 and the critical correlation between 'life' and justification. (The citation of Hab. 2:4 in the thesis statement of Romans – Rom. 1:17 – serves the same function, as Taylor (2004: 337–48); contra Hays (2002: 279–81), where Hab. 2:4 is interpreted Christologically. In Rom. 1:17, Hab. 2:4 is employed to illustrate the relationship between faith as response to the gospel, justification and life, pre-empting the Abraham argument in Romans 4.) The Law, not being grounded on faith (*ek pisteōs*), could not be the source of this 'justification life'. However, as was the case with the newly freed slaves addressed by the author of Lev. 18:5 (cited in Gal. 3:12), those observing the Law 'will live' (*zēsetai*) in the sense of being preserved or sustained. Two quite different categorizations of 'life' are under consideration. One is a life that amounts to the individual's commitment to the practice of Torah – the life is 'in the doing' of the Law (Wakefield insists that the 'life' of Gal. 3:10-13 is not to be understood soteriologically, but ethically; that is, how 'life' is lived, not attained. See Wakefield 2003: 131–84).

On this basis, there is a correspondence between the *poiēsas auta* (doing these things) of Lev. 18:5 quoted in Gal. 3:12 and the slightly awkward sounding *tou poiēsai auta* (so as to do them) of Deut. 27:26 quoted in Gal. 3:10. Both indicate a life to be simply equated with the doing of the Law – not a life that the Law itself generates. The other sphere of life is that which originates from 'Christ', which requires faith (*pistis*). That is, it is not a life that the believers themselves produce, but one that is 'activated' by faith. So once more, the reader may infer that the Law cannot generate life (3:21).

Furthermore, if Christ is the 'source' of life, the Spirit is the 'vehicle' of life, as seen initially by the predicament at the heart of the interrogation immediately following Gal. 2:15-21 in 3:1-5. (The functional closeness of the risen Christ and the Spirit in Pauline theologizing is evident in a number of formulations. These include the use of the term 'the Spirit of his son' in Gal. 4:6, the depiction of Jesus as 'life giving spirit' in 1 Cor. 15:45 and the effectual equation of Jesus and the Spirit in 2 Cor. 3:17-18.) This is then given further shape in Gal. 5:24-25:

οἱ δὲ τοῦ Χριστοῦ τὴν σάρκα ἐσταύρωσαν σὺν τοῖς παθήμασιν καὶ ταῖς ἐπιθυμίαις. Εἰ ζῶμεν πνεύματι, πνεύματι καὶ στοιχῶμεν.

[And those of Christ crucified the flesh with its associated passions and lusts. If we live by virtue of Spirit, let us order our steps by Spirit.] (Boakye's translation)

Gentiles need not be said to have 'died to the Law' (contra McKnight 2000: 279) but have suffered crucifixion in a fashion that parallels Paul's own journey. Paul's transformation should be understood as normative for 'Jews in Christ'. Gentiles have crucified the flesh and the associated self-indulgent practices. Like their Jewish counterparts, they have experienced 'death by crucifixion', modelled on the Christ event. At this, Paul may assert that the

Gentiles live by Spirit (5:25a). 'Live' here cannot denote 'act according to', which is captured by *stoicheō* in 5:25b. It is thus to be understood as the 'justified life'. The only association of 'life' with the Spirit in Galatians is in 6:8, where it is from the Spirit that the faithful will procure eternal life. However, the association between Spirit, life and Christ is made explicit in Romans – as we have already outlined, the language of 'faith' which dominates Romans 1–4 effectively disappears and paves the way for the language of life and death in Romans 5–8. Paul writes in Rom. 8:2 that

> the law of the Spirit of life in Christ Jesus has set you free from the law of sin and of death. (NRSV).

In view of how the transformative component of justification in Gal. 2:19-20 and 5:24-25 is depicted as crucifixion and new life, the epistle's finale is fascinating (Weima 1995: 198). Paul depicts an agonizing rupture between himself and the present cosmos by employing one final use of 'crucify' (*stauroō*); in so doing the apostle narrates what has happened to himself with respect to the world, and indeed to the world with respect to himself (Gal. 6:14). In these closing convictions, what emerges from this eschatological 'crucifixion' is described in Gal. 6:15 as 'new creation' (*kainē ktisis*). Although Moo correctly flags the complexities of the use of 'new creation' in the context of ancient Jewish apocalyptic (2010: 44–7), the term seems fitting in Gal. 6:15. It is unlikely, though not unthinkable, that the phrase draws upon a pre-established maxim known to the Galatians (Betz 1979: 319–20; Longenecker 1990: 295–7). Rather, the term ought to be understood within the realms, first, of Paul's other use of the term in 2 Cor. 5:17 and, second, the broader use of the term in Second Temple Jewish thought.

Whilst debate persists regarding whether *kainē ktisis* in 2 Cor. 5:17 should be read anthropologically (the new creation refers to an individual Christ believer), municipally (the new creation refers to a renewed community) or cosmologically (the new creation refers to a newly created order), three factors mitigate against overconfidence in any one position over against the other. Initially, Paul's cumbersome syntax is unhelpful – the verse is literally 'so if someone in Christ, new creation'. Furthermore, all three positions receive some support from the ancient literature. Aseneth's 'conversion' is in view when the author of *Joseph and Aseneth* writes, 'Behold, from today, you will be renewed and formed anew and made alive again, and you will eat blessed bread of life, and drink a blessed cup of immortality, and anoint yourself with blessed ointment of incorruptibility' (*Joseph and Aseneth* 15:4).

In the closing chapters of Isaiah, the prophet's vision of the eschatological renewal of the world is linked with the reconfigured holy city: 'For I am about to create new heavens and a new earth; the former things shall not be remembered or come to mind. But be glad and rejoice forever in what I am creating; for I am about to create Jerusalem as a joy, and its people as a delight' (Isa. 65:17-18; cf. Levison 1993: 189). Other writers saw in the great remaking of the earth a restoration of Edenic conditions; for instance, the author of *2 Baruch*, foresees a time when

> health will descend in dew, and illness will vanish, and fear and tribulation and lamentation will pass away from among men, and joy will encompass the earth. And nobody will again die untimely, nor will any adversity take place suddenly. (*2 Bar.* 73:2-3)

Finally, the three ideas are not so contextually disparate that any of them should be screened out altogether, although the cosmological reading is most consistent with the broader Pauline witness.

What is most interesting is that, like in *Joseph and Aseneth*, in Isa. 66:22-23, Gal. 6:15 and a corresponding passage in Eph. 2:15 (to which we will return) the new creation is associated with gentile induction into the people of God. The community language in the build-up to 2 Cor. 5:17, especially in view of the nature of Paul's opposition in 2 Corinthians (2 Cor. 3:4-18), implies it is consistent:

> [14] For the love of Christ urges us on, because we are convinced that one has died for *all*; therefore, *all* have died. [15] And he died for *all*, so that those who live might live no longer for themselves, but for him who died and was raised for them. [16] From now on, therefore, we regard *no one* from a human point of view; even though we once knew Christ from a human point of view, we know him no longer in that way. [17] So if *anyone* is in Christ, there is a new creation: everything old has passed away; see, everything has become new! (2 Cor. 5:14-17, NRSV; emphases added)

For the Apostle, the Christ event was the pivotal watershed in cosmic history; after this, Paul could not view humanity through 'fleshly' lenses (NRSV's 'from a human point of view'). He certainly could no longer see Christ this way, though he once did (2 Cor. 5:16; contra Bultmann 1976: 155). Paul's determination of Christ's death is no longer reliant on the sociopolitical circumstances that led to it, but the eschatological purposes of God in reconciliation. So, if anyone is in Christ, they have died by virtue of Christ's own death (2 Cor. 5:14), a notion which is soteriologically proximal to the 'co-crucifixion' in Gal. 2:19, 5:24 and 6:14. As such those who 'live', might live to the one who died and was raised for them (ἵνα οἱ ζῶντες μηκέτι ἑαυτοῖς ζῶσιν ἀλλὰ τῷ ὑπὲρ αὐτῶν ἀποθανόντι καὶ ἐγερθέντι) – dying in order to reveal a new order of life has direct analogues in the same three pericopae in Galatians (2:20; 5:25; 6:15). All people, with no ethnic particularity, may identify with the risen Christ and be engulfed within the new order.

Second, however, Gal. 6:15 fits with the broader Second Temple witness to the objective of the new creation; God's good world has been corrupted by the ravages of sin and death, and disenchanted Jewish writers speculated about a glorious reordering of the cosmos, using the language of new creation:

> [75] I answered and said, 'If I have found favour in your sight, O Lord, show this also to your servant: whether after death, as soon as everyone of us yields up the soul, we shall be kept in rest until those times come when you will renew the creation, or whether we shall be tormented at once?' (*4 Ezra* 7:75)

> [29] And the angel of the presence, who went before the camp of Israel, took the tablets of the division of years from the time of the creation of the law and testimony according to their weeks (of years), according to the jubilees, year by year throughout the full number of jubilees, from [the day of creation until] the day of the new creation when the heaven and earth and all of their creatures shall be renewed according to the powers of heaven and according to the whole nature of earth, until the sanctuary of the Lord is created in Jerusalem upon Mount Zion. (*Jub.* 1:29; cf. 4:26)

> And the work of . . . and they shall recount Thy glory throughout all Thy dominion For Thou hast shown them that which they had not [seen by removing all] ancient things and creating new ones, by breaking asunder things anciently established, and raising up the things of eternity. (*1QH^a* 13:11-12; Vermes' translation)

As already noted, Paul understands his own death and life transformation within the context of Christ's apocalyptic deliverance of humanity from the present age (correspondence of Gal. 2:20 with Gal. 1:4). In Gal. 6:14, Paul elaborates the idea, which he understands as the initial in-breaking of the eschatological finalities the authors mentioned earlier narrate. He has been severed from the world, resting as it does on a characteristic platform of binary polarities now rendered defunct by the cross. These polarities include the circumcised-uncircumcised distinction, the irrelevance of which is outlined in 6:15 and in equivalent fashion in 5:6 (cf. Gal. 3:28). In the former world, boasting about the external emblems of ethnicity and the associated, self-pioneered hierarchy of pedigree might be worthwhile. The cross has, however, established a new order, in which the experience of those with faith is governed by a new 'canon' (Gal. 6:16a). The verb detailing this 'governance' is the same verb used in 5:25 to articulate conduct instigated by the Spirit and, moreover, is the only other use of the verb in the epistle (*stoicheō*); thus, it makes sense to comprehend the 'canon' or 'rule' (Gk. *kanōn*) of 6:16a as Spirit. In asserting this canon, the strong implication is that it is followed over and against another canon, which logically, textually (e.g. Gal. 5:18) and contextually, is the Law.

5. Righteousness

Having appraised the breadth of revivification language in Galatians, that is, the narrative framework of life emerging from death, we may now return to where we began and what this has to do with 'righteousness', a term which can be overinvested with notions of moral correctness (Martyn 2000: 249). For the sake of clarity, a very brief pointer about the term is in order. In Greek, quite unlike English, the cognate terms associated with the noun 'righteousness' all look like they come from the same lexical family, as the following table shows in a simple manner (for more in-depth semantic and linguistic analysis of the terms, see Cosgrove 1987: 653–70; Popkes 2005: 129–46; Harink 2013: 40–65):

Greek term	Corresponding English term
δικαιοσύνη	Righteousness
δίκαιος	Righteous
δικαιόω	Justify

As ought to be clear, the difficulty in English is with the verb. This could be solved by using the English terms 'justice', 'just' and 'justify', but owing to how the English language has developed, this might (and in some arenas does) introduce all manner of ideas into our study of Paul, which he never intended. Some have even opted to reintroduce the Middle English term 'rightwise' to convey the meaning of the verb because terms like 'justify' or 'declare righteous' may not be accurate enough renderings of Paul's intended meaning (e.g. Hooker 2008: 359). This is significant for a whole host of related reasons, but for current purposes, it is important to bear in mind while we explore how the apostle describes righteousness in terms of death and life. Whatever Paul means exactly by 'justify', it ought to be understood within the semantic context of something being 'right'.

Consider the four uses of 'righteousness' in Galatians:

[21] I do not nullify the grace of God; for if *righteousness* comes through the law, then Christ died for nothing. (Gal. 2:21; the NRSV misleadingly has 'justification' instead of 'righteousness' here)

[6] Just as Abraham believed God, and it was reckoned to him as *righteousness*. (Gal. 3:6)

[21] Is the law then opposed to the promises of God? Certainly not! For if a law had been given that could make alive, then *righteousness* would indeed come through the law. (Gal. 3:21)

[5] For through the Spirit, by faith, we eagerly wait for the hope of *righteousness*. (Gal. 5:5; emphases added)

Contextually, all the instantiations of 'righteousness' in Galatians essentially make one broad point, which is only indirectly linked to moral propriety. In 'dying to the Law in order to live to God' (Gal. 2:19), Paul did not negate God's grace (2:21a). Rather, he lives by faith in the Son of God who delivered himself up (2:20), so Christ's death was a necessary step in the divine plan (inferred from 2:21b). The implication of the conditional clause in 2:21 is that righteousness does not emerge from Law, so the key question becomes 'what links life on the basis of faith and the death of Christ?'

The next section clarifies that faith and not (works of) Law is the origin of the Spirit – 'neither righteousness nor Spirit originate in the Law', but in faith which is the basis of life (Gal. 3:1-5). The conclusion is then underscored insofar as Abraham attained righteousness because he exercised faith, independently of Law, that God could produce life. This life was manifest in the form of his son Isaac, with his wife Sarah, and, thus, Paul later tells readers that Isaac was born according to Spirit (Gal. 4:29). God can make life emerge from death, as is exemplified in Isaac's birth and the resurrection of Jesus. The Law cannot make life emerge from death and, hence, once more, righteousness is not from Law (Gal. 3:21). Thus, the link between life on the basis of faith and the death of Christ is as follows: *God raised the crucified Christ from the dead (Gal. 1:1); God calls people to trust in his life-giving power in the same way he called Abraham to. Those who respond with trust, or faith, will be true sons of Abraham (Gal. 3:7-9) – that is, they will be brought into new life as Isaac was. This new life is birth according to Spirit, which, in the new age, refers to that revolutionary sphere of existence energized by the risen Christ, conveyed into the faithful by the Spirit (Gal. 4:28).* Thus, it is by the Spirit that the faithful 'eagerly wait for the hope of righteousness' (Gal. 5:5); it is from the Spirit, received through faith, that God's people may have confidence about being in the right before God in the end time (cf. Gal. 6:8).

Galatians highlights a strong link between righteousness and 'life', a position which is substantiated by Romans (cf. Rom. 5:17-18). The initial incidence of justification language in Galatians (and, therefore, in Paul) is contextually grounded in the dynamics of interethnic social mixing prompted by the divided fellowship at Antioch. Thus, the 'life' language, and associated lexicon of 'death' and 'crucifixion', within the broader contextual matrix of forming an ethnically unified believing fellowship, is a vehicle by which Paul describes how someone is justified. It is this paradigm he designates the 'truth of the gospel' (Gal. 2:5, 14) – the establishment of a family with an unprecedented identity, one which is not organized by whether one is 'Jew or Greek' (Gal. 3:28; cf. 1 Cor. 10:32). Rather, this family is identified by a 'life' which both emerges from crucifixion (Gal. 2:19; 5:24-25) and is triggered by faith (Gal. 2:20; 3:11). To possess this life is to 'live to God' (2:19) or to 'live by Spirit' (5:25). It is to be 'in Christ' (3:26, 28; 5:6; 6:15) and thus to be immersed in the experience of Christ, who was raised to new life by God the Father (1:1).

With this in mind, 'righteousness' in Galatians ought to be understood as a 'right status' (Das 2014: 320–1; Boakye 2017: 20–1). The right status before God is 'revivified status'. There are strong echoes of these Pauline ideas of revivification, faith, Spirit, the culmination of Law and interethnic cohesion in the Deutero-Pauline material:

> You were *dead* through the trespasses and sins . . . But God, who is rich in mercy, out of the great love with which he loved us [5] even when we were dead through our trespasses, *made us alive* together with Christ – by grace you have been saved – [6] and *raised us up* with him . . . For by grace you have been saved through *faith* . . . [15] He has abolished the *law* with its commandments and ordinances, that he might create

in himself *one new humanity* in place of the two, thus making peace, [16] and might reconcile both groups to God in one body through the cross, thus putting to death that hostility through it. [17] So he came and proclaimed peace to you who were far off and peace to those who were near; [18] for through him both of us have access in one *Spirit* to the Father. (Eph. 2:1, 4-6, 8, 15-18; emphases added).

Of course, from within this right status is the Spirit-empowered proclivity to exhibit both moral restraint and community-oriented *agape* love (Gal. 5:16-26). Two more corroborative ideas require mention in closing.

First, there are hints elsewhere in Paul of a pivotal link between revivification and righteousness. The rather troublesome, albeit deeply significant, phrase 'the righteousness of God' (for a thorough history of reception of the term in Christian thought from the Greek Fathers to the New Perspective, see Irons 2015: 9–60) appears eight times in Paul (Rom. 1:17; 3:5, 21, 22; 10:3 (x 2); 2 Cor. 5:21; Phil. 3:9). Luther, taking up the Augustinian mantle of undeserved divine grace, and tormented by the inability to reconcile his vocation as pious monk with his constitution as perennial sinner, found respite in Paul. He concluded that God communicated his righteousness as a gift, imputing forensic acquittal on those with faith. Later interpreters, however, remain divided on its meaning; two prevalent positions suggest that it either refers to God's retributive judgement upon the sinful (Bultmann 1964: 13; Irons 2015: 272–336) or God's fidelity to the covenants he made with Israel, principally the one with Abraham (Käsemann 1969: 168–82; Wright 1997: 96–8).

A lesser reiterated observation is the revivification context in which the term frequently appears. In Rom. 1:17, which many scholars read as the thesis statement (Morgan 1997: 18–22) of the whole letter, 2 Cor. 5:21 and Phil. 3:9, such a contextual matrix is clearly discernible. It is the revelation of the righteousness of God in Rom. 1:17 that substantiates Paul's refusal to be embarrassed by the Gospel (presumably because it revolves around a crucified Messiah). The term is then legitimized by the intertext from Hab. 2:4 – the righteous 'will live' by faith. The claim of 2 Cor. 5:21 that 'for our sake he (God) made him (Jesus) to be sin who knew no sin, so that in him (Jesus) we might become the righteousness of God' concludes a pericope about how Jesus is the conduit by which mankind is reconciled to God. To be reconciled in this way requires one to be newly created in Christ (2 Cor. 5:17), which is predicated on a person's death and rebirth in Christ, because 'one has died for all, therefore, all have died . . . and he died for all, so that those who live might live no longer for themselves, but for him who died and was raised for them' (2 Cor. 5:14b-15). In Phil. 3:9, Paul depicts the relativization of all the markers of his social and ethnocultural pedigree (listed in Phil. 3:4-5) in view of his knowledge of Christ. In this new sphere, that is, 'in Christ', Paul rendered all the credentials of his former pedigree null and void. Within this 'in Christ' status, Paul stood in the right before God on the basis of faith and not Torah, so that he might 'know Christ and the power of his resurrection and the sharing of his sufferings by becoming like him in his death, if somehow I may attain the resurrection from the dead' (Phil 3:10-11). This resurrection power, we may assume, is what lies behind this momentous transformation, by which Paul goes from exemplary Law-abiding Pharisee to sharer in the sufferings of Christ.

Whatever Paul intends to convey by the righteousness of God, it is on display in the resurrection of Jesus, but, furthermore, in how the faithful participate in the risen Messiah and experience a newly reanimated existence themselves. In similar fashion, 'righteousness', as it pertains to the argument of Galatians, points to that reconfigured status, modelled by Abraham, by which relation to God is predicated on trusting that life emerges from and subsumes death. Paul, like many writers before and since, treated the tropes of life and death as much more than just descriptions of existence versus non-existence. In apposition, life and death spoke of the divine work of rescue, reconciliation and rehabilitation both in Paul's experiences of ministry and in his soteriological formulations. However, Paul is not in the initial instance being poetic; there was an exceptional dimension to his writing, borne of a remoulded outlook. Many Jews believed that there would be a physical resurrection at the end of time as, say, the author of the *Apocalypse of Moses* writes:

> [3] Then all flesh from Adam up to that great day shall be raised, such as shall be the holy people; [4] then to them shall be given every joy of Paradise and God shall be in their midst. (*Apoc. Mos.* 13:3-4)

What no Jewish group foresaw was one individual undergoing the end-time, recreative resurrection in the present time. So completely had the script been rewritten on account of Jesus's resurrection that Paul felt impelled to speak of God's salvific and transformative work in terms prescribed by the event. Paul's God was the one having raised Jesus from the dead (Gal. 1:1). God's people were those in Christ; not a people primarily defined by ethnic, social or gender categories (Gal. 3:28), but rather by rebirth (Gal. 2:19; 5:24-25) by virtue of being in Christ.

Second, and following on from the first idea, several scholars have pointed to the back narratives Paul has inherited, and to which his polemical strategizing is beholden (e.g. Hays 1989: 21–2; Wright 1992: 405). M. Harmon recently made a most impressive case for the influence of Deutero-Isaiah in Galatians, most notably the influence of the Servant Songs in Galatians 1–2 and the Isaianic slant on the Law that he reads in Galatians 3–4 (2010: 47–202). Yet even Harmon is aware that, shy of specific citations, the influence of any element of Israel's narrative history has a speculative component (33). Das analyses the following 'grand narrative themes' in Galatians proposed by an array of interpreters:

1. The Influx of the Nations into Zion (Gal. 3:13-14; 22-26; 4:1-7), as proposed by Terence Donaldson and N. T. Wright

2. Covenant (Gal. 3:16-18; 4:21-31), especially as represented by N. T. Wright

3. The Aqedah: Isaac's Near Sacrifice (Gal. 3:13), as argued by Scott Hahn and the late Alan Segal

4. The Exodus from Egypt (Gal. 4:1-7), as articulated by James Scott and Sylvia Keesmat

5. The Spirit as the Exodus/Wilderness Cloud (Gal. 5:18), proposed by William N. Wilder

6. The Emperor Cult (Gal. 6:12-13), as represented by Bruce Winter, N. T. Wright, and Justin Hardin (2016: 30).

Like Harmon's offering, each of these will have their strengths and weaknesses – as no doubt will the proposal suggested later. I would add to Das's list and suggest that the predominant meta-narrative standing over Galatians, evidenced by the Pauline emphasis on death-life motifs as outlined in this chapter, is 'Liberation by Spirit-initiated life: the Valley of the Dry Bones' (Gal. 3:6-29; 4:21-31). There are, to be sure, no citations from Ezekiel 37 in Galatians, but that their core stories are shared seems undeniable. A moment of liberation (restoration in Ezekiel and justification in Galatians) is conceptualized and experienced in a transformative revivification event under the auspices of the Spirit. This is a moment when new covenant and new creation intertwine (Dunn 1993: 343; Wright 2005: 34–9; Bird 2016: 160–6) and a renewed people of God comes into being with a newfound aptitude to engage with God's commandments. In summary, see Table 4.1 (Boakye 2017: 114).

Table 4.1 The Narrative Core of Restoration in Ezekiel and Justification in Galatians

Motif	Ezekiel	Galatians
People are in a state of 'death'	37:1-2	2:19a; 5:24
This death is the curse incurred as punishment for sin, so . . .	37:23	3:10; 4:8
God intervenes . . .	37:4-5	4:4
. . . through his Spirit.	37:14	3:1-5, 14; 4:6
The Spirit revivifies the dead . . .	37:10	5:25
. . . representing freedom from slavery	37:11-12	4:6-9
A new community is birthed	37:21-26	3:26-29
. . . which engages with God's Law(s) in an unprecedented way	37:24	5:16-18

Ezekiel's story is Paul's story – the creator God is the God of resurrection – he restores, rehabilitates and rectifies by imbuing arenas of death with the energy of new life. If the Galatian believers asked plainly why Torah is soteriologically inert and why gentiles have no need of embracing it, this story would be the core of the answer. In the deadness of sin and estrangement from God, no law, not even Torah, can bring someone back to life – this can only be accomplished by faith in the risen Messiah.

CHAPTER 5
LAW AND SPIRIT
Andrew K. Boakye

Scholars have correctly, but somewhat narrowly, over-focused on the contrast between the Law and 'faith' or Law and 'Spirit' when navigating Paul's messianic soteriology, but by and large, they have circumvented its third component – 'life' (Gal. 2:19; 3:11, 12; cf. Rom. 8:2; 10:5). As has been argued in the previous chapters, the introduction of Abraham into the argument of Galatians is far more bespoke than the instantiation of an example of faith from Israelite history. Receiving the Spirit and entering into the right covenant status before God represented the same eschatological moment (Gal. 3:1-6) and were predicated on the same eschatological foundation – that trust leads to justification life. The associated legal corollary of this is expanded in Galatians; trust leads to justification life but observing the Law does not. It is within this paradigm that we may ask what the problems in Galatia tell us about Paul, and the roles of both the Torah and the Spirit.

The critical appeal to revivification imagery in Galatians is no more acutely significant than when attempting to disambiguate this most thorny of quandaries in Pauline studies – how did Paul appropriate and evaluate the Torah following his association with the Jesus movement? Though Romans 7 is perhaps Paul's most sustained treatment of the place of the Law (twenty-three of the seventy-seven occurrences of *nomos* in Romans are in chapter 7 alone), perhaps the direct (albeit not unambiguous) answer to why the Law was not apt to justify comes in Gal. 3:21 – 'the Law cannot generate life'; the argument of this chapter launches from here.

The account of Paul's rendition of the Torah presented in this chapter propels from three related observations. The first issue is the statement in Gal. 3:21. Whilst Pauline scholarship has bemoaned the obscurity of Paul's 'post-Jesus movement' relationship with the Law of Moses, the saying in question strikes me as the nearest readers will come to a clear answer. If the Law has a soteriological limitation, then what is it? According to Gal. 3:21, it is the Law's incapacity to produce life. Bruce acknowledges the connection between 'making alive' and being 'justified', noting that ζῳοποιέω is practically synonymous with δικαιόω – to be justified (by faith) is to receive life (by faith) (1982: 180). Betz suggests that Paul is contradicting the traditional Rabbinic stance that the Torah was a source of eternal life (e.g. Hillel's statement in *m. 'Abot* 2:8: 'the more Torah, the more life'; or the claim of *Sir.* 17:11: 'He endowed them with the life-giving law' (νόμον ζωῆς); see further *Pss. Sol.* 14:2; *2 Esd.* 14:30) while avoiding the excesses of Marcion in utterly severing the promises to Abraham from Torah (1979: 173–4). Burton (1920) reads Law and promise as occupying different forensic 'spheres'. The Law condemns – it does not convey God's relationship with mankind – and the promise pardons; the contrast is to counter the opponents' position that the Law 'could' pardon (192–4). Lull offers an interesting outworking of the contrast between Law and promise by relating Gal. 3:21 to the references to Law as 'pedagogue' in 3:24-25:

> The Law's task, however, was not to produce righteousness and new life any more than it was the duty of the pedagogue to create in a child the stage of life in which 'virtue' might be achieved. (1984: 497)

Mohrmann writes that ζωοποιέω in Gal. 3:21 is a 'synonym for resurrection and, by extension, eternal life' (2009: 166). D. Campbell rightly points to the contrast of two different types of life on the basis of the juxtaposition of Hab. 2:4 and Lev 18:5, noting how the former elucidates the equation of 'justification and life' (2013: 859–60). Lewis (2005), more broadly, sees Paul applying the motifs of spatial, temporal and ethical dualism to contrast experiences of life in Christ (God's new age/new creation) with life in the present evil age/this world. He helpfully sees both eternal life and current experience of the new life conveyed in Gal. 3:21 (146, 173–4). Despite the telling assertions of many commentators on the passage, its ramifications need to be pressed with far greater rigour.

The second issue is the exegetical puzzle which emerges from Gal. 3:14 (Williams 1988: 712). This text makes two associated assertions, both of which require unpacking with respect to the co-text. The first of these is the effective equation of the blessing of Abraham with the promise of the Spirit. The second of these is the use of the term 'Spirit' in any fashion to describe the content of the Abrahamic promises. Nowhere in the scriptures does God promise 'the Spirit' to Abraham. This becomes significant because the co-text refers to the curse of the Law. There is no corresponding blessing of the 'Law'; rather the blessing of 'Abraham'. The third and final issue is the New Covenant context of the letter as a whole. A bird's eye view of Galatians reveals two fairly unambiguous rubrics – the presence and activity of the

Spirit (Gal. 3:2-5, 14; 4:6, 29; 5:5, 13-25) and the role of the Law (2:15-21; 3:2-5, 17-24). Both headlines emerge from pivotal questions raised in the text itself; the question of the origin of the Spirit in 3:2 and the question of why the Law was given in the first place in 3:19. The restoration eschatology of Jeremiah and the associated prophetic utterances in Ezekiel reveal that the phenomenon of 'internalization' is the unique moment of New Covenant fulfilment – the internalization of 'Law' in Jeremiah and of 'Spirit' in Ezekiel. The experience of the Galatian gentiles and Paul's response to their socio-religious dilemma evidence that the Apostle reckoned the New Covenant prophecies to be taking shape within this beleaguered community.

Paul's understanding of the Law in Galatians must ultimately be resolved within the context of the pneumatological ethics of the New Covenant mandate amid the newly birthed community. There is a critical distinction emerging from Gal. 3:21; the Law cannot generate life, for this is the exclusive dispensation of the risen Christ whom the Spirit mediates into the faithful, as I have argued elsewhere (Boakye 2017: 148). The prophetic assurances of Ezekiel and Jeremiah intertwine in Galatians in a moment of internalization – the internalization of the Law and the Spirit. As Ezekiel foresaw, the Spirit would liberate God's people by an act of resurrection, and Jeremiah predicted that the Law would be inscribed on the hearts of the people, and these twin actions would mark their restoration from exile and reconciliation with Yahweh. Paul deduced that justification, that is, being brought into right covenant status with Yahweh by being revivified from the deadness of sin, was the ultimate restoration and ultimate reconciliation the people awaited, beyond geographical or political relocation (Wright 1992: 268–72; Boakye 2017: 153).

1. No one will be justified by works of Law

No simple attempt to summarize the evolution of Paul's understanding of the Jewish Law will do it justice, as the scholarly landscape suggests. Ever since E. P. Sanders's critique of the predominant Lutheran hermeneutics, scholarly readings of Paul's apprehension of Torah have led in a plethora of directions. Heikki Räisänen despairs of any genuine continuity in Paul (1987: 106–8). In Hans Hübner's (1984) view, Paul deems the Law to have demonic origin, leading to aberrant behaviour among the Galatian gentiles. The betrayal Paul feels at the hands of the Galatians accounts for his caustic-sounding statements, but by the time he writes Romans, he has had time to process his thoughts and develop a less antagonistic position on Torah (27, 54; from the English translation of the 1975 German original). A position originally popularized by Franz Rosenzweig in the years following the First World War, and later taken up most forcefully by Krister Stendahl and Lloyd Gaston, suggests Paul taught that Israel and the church are to coexist side by side. Israel was to continue in submission to the original covenants made with the patriarchs, and the latter, made up of a gentile contingent, introduced into the fold by the ministry of Jesus. The work of Stendahl and Gaston intimates that a collective guilt about the church's moral apathy (and even complicity) during the Holocaust and the anti-Semitic undercurrents of much 'replacement theology' inform this 'two-covenant' line of thinking. Mark Nanos (1996) holds that Paul's letters reflect intra-Jewish debate about the hermeneutics of the Law and how gentiles interacting with the Jewish community ought to conduct themselves. The departure point of his reading of Galatians is that Paul's opponents are not Jewish Christian missionaries but local synagogues trying to mitigate the compromises expected of non-Jews by Rome. This can be avoided and the benefits of a *religio licita* afforded if the gentiles would be circumcised and come under the umbrella of Judaism (Nanos 2002). Caroline Johnson Hodge (2007) is among those reading the seemingly pejorative things Paul says about the Law strictly because he writes to gentile audiences. As such, Paul's polemics are not an internal critique of Jews or Judaism. She radically opposes the collapsing of ethno-racial categories to explain Paul, arguing (along with Kimber Buell) that 'there is no ethnically neutral "Christianity" implied in Gal. 3:28' (2004: 250). Alternatively, Daniel Boyarin argues that Paul is quite specifically embroiled in a critique of Judaism (something which many argue Boyarin himself is engaged in; e.g. Bird 2016: 25) and of the particularity of Jewish cultural practices which of themselves were incapable of embracing all humanity in an existential oneness. In Boyarin's (1997) reckoning, Paul attempts to collapse Jewish ethno-distinctiveness by allegorizing key elements of the Law, spiritualizing and, therefore, universalizing their meaning. Boyarin's Paul was motivated by a passionate desire for human unity and the erasure of differences and hierarchies between human beings (106; cf. Boyarin 1993: 47–80).

Not all commentators were convinced by E. P. Sanders's findings, even if his appraisal of ancient Judaism could not be ignored (Barclay 1986: 8). Some writers have been critical of his over-selective choice of Rabbinic evidence (Thomas 2005: 295–7). The essays in the volume edited by D. A. Carson et al., *Justification and Variegated Nomism Volume I: The Complexities of Second Temple Judaism* (2001), went some way to demonstrating that Sanders's portrait was not nearly as neat as he proposed. Key Jewish texts in fact did evidence a soteriological meritocracy of works, and others implied far more ambiguous positions. I suggest that we remain mindful of Sanders's inferences and their limitations. What we know for certain is that Paul does not utterly reject the Torah and, in fact, frequently describes it as good (Rom. 7:12), uses it to buttress his ethical demands (e.g. 1 Cor. 6:16) and celebrates it as a divine gift to Israel (Rom. 9:4). Yet within the economy of salvation, and most notably in the argument of Galatians, he drew a pronounced line in the sand – gentiles were not to be subjected to the demands and dictates of the Law, and even for Israel, the Law had temporal limits and a remit which was not, in the initial instance, soteriological. The following survey of Law in Galatians will position the argument of this chapter.

The Greek term for 'Law', *nomos*, appears for the first of thirty-three times in Galatians at 2:16, in the composite term 'works of Law'. We previously considered how the key terms in Gal. 2:15-21 most likely emerged from the context of the Gentile believers being ostracized by Jewish believers at a community meal in Antioch (Gal. 2:11-14). Consequently, Paul states in Gal. 2:16:

> And knowing that a man is not justified from the works of the law except through faith in Jesus Christ. And we believed in Christ Jesus, in order that we might be justified from faith in Christ, and not from the works of the law, because no human being will be justified by the works of the law. (Boakye's translation)

Sanders prompted commentators to ask how exactly the term 'works of Law' (Gk. *erga nomou*) functions in 2:16 and elsewhere in Galatians. What is the correct context within which to comprehend Paul's revisionist attitude towards the Law? How did Paul's view of the Law impact debates about Jewish ethnicity? Our consideration of the Law in Pauline thought in Galatians will begin by briefly asking how *erga nomou* functions in Gal. 2:16. Schreiner provides a useful summary of the diverse renditions of *erga nomou* (1993: 975–7).

Of the scholars who were influenced by Sanders's emphasis on the covenantal nature of ancient Judaism, one of the most frequently cited is James D. G. Dunn, who claimed that Sanders did not go far enough in connecting Paul's theology with covenantal nomism (1983: 100). Dunn, unlike Sanders, did not adjudge Paul to be repudiating key pillars of covenantal nomism, like election, covenant and Law, but rather of those aspects of Jewish religious praxis that separated Jews from Gentiles. Paul's problem was not with Judaism as such, but with the exclusivist hubris of those Jews for whom practices like circumcision, Sabbath observance and Kashrut (the Jewish dietary code) separated and elevated the Jew above the non-Jew. According to Dunn, 'works of the Law' referred to these practices (for an account and defence of the position, see Dunn 1992: 99–117). Dunn even saw an analogue for Paul's use of *erga nomou* in the Qumran text *Miqsat Ma'ase Ha-Torah* (4QMMT[a]), which the Dead Sea community employed to depict intra-sectarian ritual observances (see Dunn 1997: 151; for a response to Dunn, see Abegg 1999: 139–47).

A number of scholars have rejected Dunn's reductionism and posited that the works of the Law refer to all the demands of Torah, and not just those with nationalistic exceptionality (Westerholm 1988: 121; Schreiner 1991: 217–44; 2010: 161; de Boer 2011: 148). There are certain parallel phrases in Jewish literature approximately contemporary with Paul which might well support such a position, notably 4QFlor 1:7 which contains the near identical phrase in Hebrew, and also 1QS 5:21; 6:18; 1QpHab 7:11; and CD XIII:11. The problem with the comparison (e.g. Byrne 1996: 117–21; Martyn 1997: 260–3) is the six highly context-specific ways Paul uses *erga nomou* in Galatians (2:16 (x 3); 3:2, 5, 10). They all relate to 'justification' and stand in contrast with the motif of *pistis* – paradigms which as we have already noted emerged from the crisis at the Antiochene supper related in Gal. 2:11-14. This is language which emerged in Paul's polemic as a direct result of ethnic marginalization of gentiles at the behest of the circumcision contingent associated with the apostle James. Even if, as the likes of R. Longenecker argue, contra Dunn et al., that *erga nomou* summarizes the 'legalistic complex of ideas having to do with winning God's favour by a merit-amassing observance of Torah' (Longenecker 1990: 82), it is difficult not to submit that, contextually, the key ways of 'amassing merit' are as Dunn describes.

Some opposing Dunn's general scheme tend to draw upon the use of *erga* (works) in Romans without *nomou* and suggest that when Paul speaks of the futility of 'works', it goes beyond the dictates of Torah and applies to any form of human striving. As such, no one is justified by humanly driven initiative of any kind. This was the position held by the Reformers, most notably Martin Luther, who wrote in his treatise on Christian freedom:

A bad or good house does not make a bad or good builder, but a good or bad builder makes a good or bad house. And in general no work makes the workman such as it is itself; but the workman makes the work such as he is himself. Such is the case, too, with the works of men. Such as the man himself is, whether in faith or in unbelief, such is his work: good if it be done in faith; bad if in unbelief. For as works do not make a believing man, so neither do they make a justified man; but faith, as it makes a man a believer and justified, so also it makes his works good. Since then works justify no man, but a man must be justified before he can do any good work, it is most evident that it is faith alone which, by the mere mercy of God through Christ, and by means of His word, can worthily and sufficiently justify and save the person; and that a Christian man needs no work, no law, for his salvation. (1520; English translation, 2007: 48–9)

However, it is widely held that Luther quite likely read his personal conflicts with what he saw as a corrupt Catholic hierarchy into Galatians, seeing those clerics who 'sold' forgiveness to the wealthy in the same light as Paul's opponents who were demanding a 'righteousness of works' from gentiles. Thesis 32 of Luther's ninety-five challenges to the Catholic hierarchy read: 'Those who suppose that on account of their letters of indulgence they are sure of salvation will be eternally damned along with their teachers'; thesis 81 stated: 'This shameless preaching of pardons makes it hard even for learned men to defend the pope's honour against calumny or to answer the indubitably shrewd questions of the laity.'

In whatever way readers judge Paul to understand the works of the Law, what is unambiguous is that his evaluation of them is profoundly negative, as in Gal. 2:16 earlier and the other three occurrences of the phrase in the epistle:

The only thing I want to learn from you is this: Did you receive the Spirit by doing the works of the law or by believing what you heard? (Gal. 3:2)

Well then, does God supply you with the Spirit and work miracles among you by your doing the works of the law, or by your believing what you heard? (Gal. 3:5)

For all who rely on the works of the law are under a curse; for it is written, 'Cursed is everyone who does not observe and obey all the things written in the book of the law.' (Gal. 3:10)

The works of the Law cannot procure justification (2:16), they are not the origin of the Spirit (the clear implication of the interrogation in 3:2-5) and those identified by the works of Law are even under a divine curse (3:10). A consideration of the remaining uses of *nomos* in Galatians up to the inevitable question posed in 3:19 reveals a similar pessimism. However, in addressing that very question of the Law giving, Paul uncovers key aspects of how his 'pneumatology' interrelates with the function of the Law. At its heart, the relationship between the Law and the Spirit in Galatians (and in Paul more broadly) is antithetical unless it is rationalized in light of Christ's death and resurrection. It is this very rationalization which emerges from the theology of the 'New Covenant', and which this chapter argues illustrates some degree of consistency between how Paul apprehended Torah after he accepted Jesus as the Christ.

In assessing Paul's outlook as 'negative', one must always bear in mind the highly polemical and adversarial tenor of Galatians. Paul is not pessimistic about the Law as such, but about his opponents' warped appropriation of it, which introduced all manner of discordant notes in God's eschatological agenda. For example, demanding gentile adherence to Torah unnaturally prolonged the role of Torah, distorting how the divine sequence of end-time events unfolded.

2. Why then the Law?

If readers had followed and understood Paul's argument up to Gal. 3:19, then the enquiry contained in the verse was a natural corollary. If the Law had no soteriological value, then why did God give the Law in the first place? Having made certain assertions concerning the Law, Paul could not sidestep the question, which the following survey of *nomos* language in Galatians will examine. The following texts all render the Law decidedly secondary, consigning its operational significance to a yester-age, distancing it from the decisive issues in the salvation futures of God's end-time people and depicting it as culminating in the principal thing to which it ultimately had always pointed to – Christ.

In Gal. 2:19, Paul makes the shocking claim that through the Law, he died to the Law, in order that he might live to God. The phrase 'live to God' (associated in Chapter 4, 'Death, Life and Righteousness', with a mode of 'risen existence') within Second Temple texts often refers to a renewed life resulting from commitment to God, especially resurrection following martyrdom. This is evident in the Lucan version of the 'marriage at the resurrection' dispute, where Abraham and his progeny are also said to 'live to God'. We also read in *4 Maccabees* 7:

> But as many as attend to religion with a whole heart, these alone are able to control the passions of the flesh, since they believe that they, like our patriarchs Abraham and Isaac and Jacob, do not die to God, but live to God. (*4 Macc.* 7:18-19)

In Gal. 2:21, the redundancy of the Law in connection with justification is reiterated in a conditional clause that resembles 3:18 and 3:21c:

> *For if* righteousness is through *Law, then* Christ died without cause. (Gal. 2:21; literal translation)

> *For if* the inheritance is of *Law, it is no more* of promise. (Gal. 3:18b; literal translation)

> *For if* a *law* had been given which had been able to make alive, indeed righteousness *would have been* out of Law. (Gal. 3:21c; literal translation)

These conditional clauses suggest that (1) righteousness before God flows from Jesus's crucifixion and not the Law; (2) the covenant promises God made to the patriarch Abraham are inherited solely by Christ and those in Christ (Gal. 3:16-17) – conditions which the introduction of the Law did not alter; (3) attaining righteousness before God is related to being made alive and neither Torah nor any other law could bring this about.

A biblical rationale for the inadequacy of the Torah to justify is proposed in Gal. 3:11-13. In 3:11, it is obvious that the Law cannot justify, for Habakkuk's experience (Hab. 2:4) was that the righteous would live (in Habakkuk's context, this meant not be killed by Babylonians) on the basis of faith. The stance is corroborated by the citation in the next verse, Gal. 3:12. The Law does not function on the basis of faith – rather, if practitioners did what the Law demanded, they would reap the associated benefits of so doing. To drive the point home, consider how Gal. 3:11-12 functions to pre-announce and corroborate Gal. 3:21:

ὅτι δὲ ἐν νόμῳ οὐδεὶς δικαιοῦται παρὰ τῷ θεῷ δῆλον,
ὅτι

Ὁ δίκαιος ἐκ πίστεως ζήσεται·
ὁ δὲ νόμος οὐκ ἔστιν ἐκ πίστεως,
ἀλλ᾽
Ὁ ποιήσας αὐτὰ ζήσεται ἐν αὐτοῖς.

Galatians 3:21 is pre-empted by the scriptural logic of Gal. 3:11-12 – the instantiation of eschatological life is predicated upon faith and not Law. This paradigm, made explicit in 3:21, is initially spelled out in that:

1. It is obvious that no one will be justified before God by Law
2. because . . .
3. The righteous ἐκ πίστεως ζήσεται
4. And the Law is not ἐκ πίστεως
5. BUT
6. Those doing these [things] (i.e. the things demanded by Torah) ζήσεται by them.

Justification life emerges from faith (ἐκ πίστεως); faith generates this life. The Law operates in an alternate sphere – it is not ἐκ πίστεως, that is, it is not from a domain by which it can generate life. The domain of the Law is such that doing it (Ὁ ποιήσας αὐτὰ) permits the practitioner to exist and be kept safe within that domain (ζήσεται ἐν αὐτοῖς). The benefits and procurements of Torah are available if one does what Torah insists upon – the life is the effective output of the practitioners themselves and not something actually produced by the Torah. The life Paul himself experiences – life to God (Gal. 2:19) – which he explicitly distinguishes from his previous mode of existence ('and I no longer live', in Gal. 2:20a) and identifies as a life enlivened by the risen Christ ('and Messiah lives in me', in Gal. 2:20b) is produced by faith ('that which I now live in flesh, I live by faith in the son of God who loved me and gave himself up on my behalf', in Gal. 2:20c). This is the critical distinction – a life produced by legal observance and thus existentially restricted by the dictates of Torah on one hand and the presence of the risen Messiah, mediated by the Spirit to those who trust in Messiah, on the other.

The curse of the Law, set out in 3:10, is remedied by Christ in 3:13, a clear implication of which being that Israel had indeed incurred the curse.

Knowing, then, the Law's secondary nature as an additive to the economy of salvation and all that the Law was not apt to achieve, Paul pursues the obvious question – what was the Law's God-given purpose (Gal. 3:19)?

Unpacking the answer in the rest of 3:19 sheds further light on Paul's stance on the Law in Galatians:

It was added – implying, again, that it had a secondary, unoriginal character. (Lull 1986: 482)

Because of transgressions – transgression suggests breaking of a rule; it seems the Law specified moral lapses as infractions of divine codes. (For surveys on the meaning of this phrase, see Lull 1986: 482–6; Hong 1993: 149–56)

Until the offspring would come – 'until' sets temporal limits upon the Law's role; the 'offspring' or 'seed' is Christ. (3:16)

To whom the promise had been made – the promise was, of course, made to Abraham, but in some way realised in Christ.

And it was ordained through angels by a mediator – the angels and the intermediary, clearly intended to be Moses, further underscore the indirect, secondary nature of the Law giving. Indeed, referring to Moses as the mediator seems intended to lay stress on the nature of the giving of the Law rather than its content. (Gaston asserts that Paul was not referring to the Jewish tradition that the Law giving was in the presence of angels (e.g. Acts 7:53; Heb. 2:2), but rather the tradition of the giving of a law (not Torah) to the gentiles by seventy angels; see Gaston 1982: 65–75)

These ideas are given further profile in Gal. 3:21-25. Once more pre-empting the predictable question, 3:21a rules out the possibility that the Law and the promises to Abraham – both of which hailed from the one God – were at odds. It was simply that the promise to Abraham involved the instantiation of life, specifically the birth of Isaac (cf. Gal. 4:22-29; Rom. 4:17-19), and God did not give a Law that could make life; life could never emerge from anything a person did – even 'doing' the Law (Gal. 3:21b; this may explain the indefiniteness of the verse; if any law were given with the ability to revivify, righteousness would emerge from it, but God gave no such law, not even the Law of Moses). Galatians 3:22-24 uses two verbs that depict detention or confinement to show that Israel was 'locked up' under sin by the Law. Notice in 3:22 the Law is referred to as 'the Scripture' (Gk. ἡ γραφὴ), literally the 'writing' – there is a significance to this which will become clear momentarily. Israel's 'incarceration' by the Law persisted until the one moment of the coming of faith (3:23) and Christ (3:24) and to this end the Law acted as a 'pedagogue' (Gk. *paidagōgos*), a term depicting a tutor whose office is training in maturity (for fuller details, see Lull 1986: 481–98). This role was critical; the Law was given to an Israel newly freed from captivity in Egypt, and Paul sees this Israel as a naïve juvenile in need of close micromanagement (Gal. 4:1-3). The termination of the Law's role was the advent of Christ, sent by God to 'redeem' Israel (Gal. 4:4-5). There are two more components signifying the end of the Law's role – the adoption of Israel as God's children and the marking of this new relationship by the coming of the Spirit into the hearts of the people. The first of these concepts is controversial for a few reasons.

Initially, there is some linguistic dispute regarding whether *huiothesia* ought to be understood as 'adoption' specifically or as 'sonship' more generally. The weight of literary evidence contemporary with Paul favours the former, though ideas contained within 'sonship' are exegetically proximal to 'adoption'. However, even if the term is understood as a reference to adoption, debate remains regarding the context of adoption. It may reflect the legal process within Hellenistic Law (Lührmann 1992: 79) or be an allusion to adoption in the Hebrew Bible (Scott 1993a: 216–17). The strong Exodus imagery behind Gal. 4:1-7 points to the latter (Scott 1992: 126–45). Another tension is sparked by Paul's seemingly arbitrary alternation of personal pronouns in 4:3-7 (first-person plural in 4:3, 5; second-person plural in 4:6; second-person singular in 4:7). It is generally held that when Paul speaks in the first person in Galatians, he includes himself and fellow Jews or Jewish Christ believers, and second-person references are addressed to the Galatian gentiles. This distinction is not neat by any means; Martyn is among those who argue that both groups are in purview throughout Gal. 4:3.7 regardless of the pronoun (1995: 17). Greater specificity seems warranted here, though, and the logic is not tremendously complex.

Paul has established that since faith has arrived (Gal. 3:23, 25), all (i.e. Jew and gentile) are sons of God through faith in Christ (3:26). For those believing in Christ, there is a spiritual oneness that transcends any form of social 'othering' (3:28). The closing verse of Galatians 3 declares that those who are of Christ are Abraham's true descendants and heirs (*klēronomoi*) according to promise; the opening *legō de* of Gal. 4:1 ('But I say to you') suggests a contrast drawing on the conclusion of chapter 3. This is confirmed with the repetition of 'heir' (*klēronomos*) – 'for as much time as the heir is an infant, despite being lord of all, there is no difference from a slave' (Gal. 4:1; Boakye's translation); Gal. 4:1-7 aims to elaborate the character and conditions of the inheritance. The logic is that Jew and gentile will ultimately become coequal heirs, having both endured a period of immaturity in slavery before entering 'spiritual adulthood' in freedom. Even though God adopted the Exodus community (Exod. 4:22-23; Deut. 32:5-6; Hos. 11:1; cf. Rom. 9:4), their inheritance rights were not granted as a privilege. When it came to actually receiving their share of the estate, it was, in real terms, as if they had not been adopted – they were like slaves, with no inheritance rights, still needing to be steered by the Law. In other words, they were no more apt to receive the inheritance than gentiles – only together in Christ were both groups jointly ready (Gal. 3:26-29). So then, Gal. 4:3 denotes that 'in the same way, when we (the Jews) were infants, we were enslaved under the elemental forces of the cosmos'. Then God sent his son (4:4) in order that the ones under the Law might be redeemed (again, clearly the Jews) in order that we (the Jews) might receive the adoption as sons (4:5). With Paul's reasoning for equal inheritance rights in place, Gal. 4:6 can be understood as a reference to Jew and gentile – because 'you' (i.e. you all) are sons, God sent the Spirit of his son into 'our' hearts. (Interestingly, some later mss have 'your' hearts in 4:6). The change in personal pronouns here thus aims to clarify which communities Paul has in mind. It is most likely because the 'slavery' of Israel and the inclusion of Torah under the *stoicheia* (elemental forces of the cosmos) was a more complex issue that it was spelled out first and with such precision; Israel did not just need redemption from pagan hegemonies, but from Torah. That the gentiles were formerly slaves to idols, from which they needed freeing, was a given in Paul's mind (Gal. 4:8-9; cf. 2:15). Once both groups were free, and 'grown up' having ditched the emblems of their spiritual adolescence (Law and idols), they became sons and recipients of the Spirit.

This idea of Israel's redemption expressed in Gal. 4:4-6 (a theme which is central to the biblical narrative, e.g., Ps. 130:8; Hos. 13:14; Mic. 4:10; Lk. 1:68; 24:21) forms an important structural parallel with Gal. 3:13-14; in 3:14a, that the blessing of Abraham might be to the 'nations' permits the first-person plural in 3:14b to address both Jew and gentile, much like the second-person plurals in 4:6:

> *Christ redeemed* us *from* the curse of *the Law*, having become a curse for us; for it has been written, 'Cursed *is* everyone having been hung on a tree'; that the blessing of Abraham might be to the nations in Christ Jesus, *that we might receive* the *promise of the Spirit through faith*. (Gal. 3:13-14; emphases added)

> But when the fullness of the time came, God sent forth his son, having come into being out of a woman, having come under Law, that *he*

might redeem the ones *under Law, that we might receive the adoption of sons.* And because you are sons, God sent forth *the Spirit* of his son into your hearts, crying, Abba! Father! (Gal. 4:4-6; emphases added)

The passages express that: Christ . . . redeemed us . . . from the Law . . . in order that . . . we might receive (something). In the former passage, it is the promise of the Spirit we (i.e. Israel) receive; the latter passage has Israel receive adoption, which is then qualified by the presence of the Spirit in the people's hearts. So far, this is clearly not a linear answer to what sounds like a straightforward question – so if one were to articulate Paul's response to the question of why God gave the Law, it might go something like this.

The Law was given to diagnose, identify and codify sin as transgression, thus hemming the people of Israel in on all sides with the realization that their moral failures were not just internal infractions, but violations of the divine design for human living (Gal. 3:22-23). This, in Pauline thought, amounts to a state of 'death' (i.e. the curse of the Law) which the Law showed up, but was powerless to reverse (3:10, 21). Israel's liberation from this state of death meant to die to the very Law which had highlighted its own inadequacy as a remedy for sin – that is, 'through the Law, Israel had to die to the Law' (2:19). To be freed from the cycle of slavery to sin, in other words to be brought to life again, required faith in Christ (2:20; 3:11-12, 22-24). Indeed, Paul often links Law with death in a fashion that points forward to life (Rom. 7:5, 10-13; 8:2; 1 Cor. 15:56; 2 Cor. 3:6). R. Longenecker acutely and meaningfully observes that the Law's purpose was to work itself out of a job and point beyond itself to a fuller relationship with God (1990: 91). What Longenecker depicts as the 'fuller relationship' approximates to that new sphere of existence after having been rescued from the age of the present evil (Gal. 1:4), where one lives by faith in the son of God (2:20). However, in Galatians, there is one motif above all which characterizes and supervises the new era of life to God – 'Spirit'.

3. The end of the Law and the dawn of the Spirit

Whether one adopts the position of Dunn, Wright et al. in reading the 'works of the Law' as those specific practices which act as ethnic boundary markers between Jew and gentile or follow Luther's ideological heirs in viewing them as the totality of the mandates of the Law, the substantial difference between the two is minimized in Galatians. For even if Paul intended the works of the Law to include all the Law's decrees and fiats, the ones at the heart of the polemic in Galatians are those very ethno-distinctive rites with the potential to socially cordon off non-Jews from full community participation. Specifically, these are Sabbath observance (Gal. 4:10), Kashrut (Gal. 2:12) and primarily circumcision (2:3; 5:2, 6, 11; 6:12-15). Indeed, in Gal. 5:3, Paul asserts that anyone who submits to circumcision underwrites a de facto self-imposed obligation to the entire Law.

With this in mind, and with the shortcomings of the Law being hinted at throughout the letter and specified in 3:21, we must return briefly to the pivotal interrogation in the opening of Galatians 3. Having established that Jesus's death was unwarranted if the Law could set someone right before God (Gal. 2:21), Paul asks in infuriated fashion if the Galatians had been hoodwinked into missing Jesus's death – was Jesus not clearly crucified (3:1)? The next part of the interrogation contains a note of the significance Paul affords it – 'this only I want to learn from you' (3:2). This one thing Paul determined to discover was the origin of the Spirit. Paul asks, 'Did you receive the Spirit from works of Law or the hearing of faith' (ἐξ ἔργων νόμου τὸ πνεῦμα ἐλάβετε ἢ ἐξ ἀκοῆς πίστεως)? He then poses a related question in Gal. 3:5: 'Therefore, the one supplying to you the Spirit and working powers among you [is it] from works of the Law or the hearing of faith' (ὁ οὖν ἐπιχορηγῶν ὑμῖν τὸ πνεῦμα καὶ ἐνεργῶν δυνάμεις ἐν ὑμῖν, ἐξ ἔργων νόμου ἢ ἐξ ἀκοῆς πίστεως)? He answers these questions in slightly oblique, albeit unambiguous style, in a way that will set up an unexpected, unsettling but powerful conclusion about the place of the Torah and concomitant emergence of the Spirit.

Paul responds to his rhetorical questions by outlining how Abraham came into right relation to God – in the 'faith-versus-works-of-Law' quandary, Paul responds by asserting that 'you received the Spirit in the same way Abraham was counted as righteous before God – by faith' (paraphrasing Gal. 3:6). Second Temple Jews routinely celebrated Abraham as an exemplar of trust in God; however, in their texts, Abraham was usually recognized as faithful because of his 'obedience' (i.e. things he did – recall the earlier contrast). This is seen dramatically in Abraham's endurance of ten trials (*m. 'Abot* 5:3 for Abraham's endurance in Second Temple tradition, see Noegel 2003: 73–83) and supremely in the binding of Isaac (Gen. 22:12; cf. Heb. 11:17; Jas 2:26; *1 Macc.* 2:52; *Jud.* 8:26; *Sir.* 44:20; *Jub.* 17:17–18:16). Yet Paul has more far-reaching reasons for citing the Abraham tradition from Gen. 15:6 to express the idea that faith and not works of Law bring forth the Spirit. Evaluating Paul's thesis begins with recognizing the soteriological significance most Jewish groups attached to being 'physical' descendants of Abraham. For example, the author of 4 *Maccabees* writes:

> Never may we, the children of Abraham, think so basely that out of cowardice we feign a role unbecoming to us . . . Therefore, O children of Abraham, die nobly for your religion! (*4 Macc.* 6:17, 22)

The prophet Isaiah declares:

> But you, Israel, my servant, Jacob, whom I have chosen, the offspring of Abraham, my friend; [9] you whom I took from the ends of the earth, and called from its farthest corners, saying to you, 'You are my servant, I have chosen you and not cast you off'; [10] do not fear, for I am with you, do not be afraid, for I am your God; I will strengthen you, I will help you, I will uphold you with my victorious right hand. (Isa. 41:8-10; cf. Lk. 3:8; 19:9; Jn 8:33; Justin, *Dial.*, 140)

At this point we will re-rehearse some of the material from Chapter 3, 'Scripture and Promise', to specify how Law functions in Galatians. As we have already noted, Paul attempts to cut across the traditional view and suggest that the 'true' descendants of Abraham are not his physical, genetic progeny, but those who have faith as he did (Gal. 3:7-9). The context of Gen. 15:6 is crucial for the effectiveness of Paul's argument. Abraham believed that God would give him a son with his wife Sarah, despite the embryological unlikelihood of conceiving, given that both he and Sarah were well advanced in age. This son would be the progenitor of a vast nation; Abraham believed this irrespective of anything he did (leaving Haran, etc.). Purely on the basis of Abraham's trust in God's pledge, God accepted the patriarch into a covenant relationship. Paul will reiterate this point in Gal. 3:15-18, where he argues that Moses's Law did not even emerge till 430 years after God made the covenant promises to Abraham and, as such, could not alter the terms of the covenant. A number of Jewish writers attempted to circumvent the notion that Abraham could not technically have been a Law keeper as the Law did not appear until several generations after his death. In Philo's *De Abrahamo*, for example, the Law is depicted as the codification of that which Abraham did by virtue of obeying the laws of nature (*De Abrahamo* 275–6). Alternatively, the author of *Jubilees* has Abraham celebrating First-fruits (15:1-2) and Tabernacles (16:20-31), feasts historically instituted by

Moses much later. If Abraham could be accepted into right relation to God on the grounds of faith irrespective of the Law, this would be no less true for his real descendants. However, this is not faith in some generic sense – it is faith that God is able to make life emanate from death (Rom. 4:17). This is specified positively in Gal. 3:11 (the ones in the right are those who 'live' because of faith, citing Hab. 2:4) and negatively in Gal. 3:12 (this life will not come from the Law, citing Lev. 18:5). The argument has a couple more key steps.

The Law pronounced a curse on Israel for her stubborn refusal to resist worshipping the idols of the nations (Gal. 3:10; cf. Deut. 30:11-20), a curse which was lifted when Jesus was crucified (Gal. 3:13). The effect of the expunging of the curse on Israel was that, in Christ, Abraham might finally become the blessing to the gentiles God had promised (Gen. 18:18; 22:18; 26:4) which meant all people would receive 'the promise of the Spirit' (Gal. 3:14).

The enigmatic and pivotal conclusion of Gal. 3:14 has led to much speculation, as the promises to Abraham in Genesis never mention the Spirit. Paul provides the essential commentary in Gal. 4:21-31, an allegory about the birth of his first two sons. His first son Ishmael was born to the slave woman Hagar because Abraham and Sarah decided to short circuit the promise and give Abraham a son 'by hook or by crook'. Isaac, Abraham's son by his aged wife Sarah, was born against all gynaecological probabilities, simply because God promised it would happen (Gal. 4:23). Paul, therefore, designates Isaac as born *di' epangelias* (through a promise) in Gal. 4:23 and 'born according to Spirit' in Gal. 4:29; those gentiles in Galatia trusting solely in Christ to be justified were children of promise according to Isaac (4:28). The rationale seems clear.

The promise of Spirit is a direct reference to the conception and birth of Isaac; Abraham had faith that God could make life where death lingered, and this was manifested in Isaac coming to life against the odds (Boakye 2017: 136–9). The association with Spirit and new life originates from the creation texts themselves, where, in Gen. 2:7, the Lord God formed man from the dust of the ground and breathed into his nostrils the 'breath of life'; and the man became a 'living' being (Yates 2008: 24–7). Isaac's birth, then, acts as a model for justification – the movement from death to life on the basis of faith. This rationale allows us to exegetically reaffirm the puzzling statement of Gal. 3:16, expanded in Chapter 3 (see earlier). The promise is made to Abraham and Christ in that in both their respective experiences, there is a supernatural materialization of life. The Spirit conveys the life of Christ into the faithful (Gal. 5:25), and Isaac was born according to the Spirit (Gal. 4:29); hence, the promise may rightly be designated the promise of Spirit (Gal. 3:14).

Paul's argument has come full circle – it is by the presence and power of the Spirit that Israel and the nations are justified before God – and this relies on faith, not the Torah, bringing us to one final important element of the juxtaposition of Law and Spirit.

4. Spirit, flesh and the ethics of the New Covenant

The prophet Jeremiah predicted a day of great renewal, when God would draw up a new contract with his people, by which the errors of the past would be erased and God himself would reinvigorate the people's ability to submit to his commands and decrees. In this well-known prophetic utterance, Jeremiah declares:

> The days are surely coming, says the Lord, when I will make a *new covenant* with the house of Israel and the house of Judah. It will not be like the covenant that I made with their ancestors when I took them by the hand to bring them out of the land of Egypt – a covenant that they broke, though I was their husband, says the Lord. But this is the covenant that I will make with the house of Israel after those days, says the Lord: *I will put my law within them, and I will write it on their hearts; and I will be their God, and they shall be my people.* No longer shall they teach one another, or say to each other, 'Know the Lord', for they shall all know me, from the least of them to the greatest, says the Lord; for I will forgive their iniquity, and remember their sin no more. (Jer. 31:31-34; emphasis added)

In a corresponding prophecy, Ezekiel spoke of national and political renewal and restoration, writing:

> I will take you from the nations, and gather you from all the countries, and bring you into your own land. I will sprinkle clean water upon you, and you shall be clean from all your uncleannesses, and from all your idols I will cleanse you. A new heart I will give you, and a new spirit I will put within you; and I will remove from your body the heart of stone and give you a heart of flesh. I will put my spirit within

you, and make you follow my statutes and be careful to observe my ordinances. (Ezek. 36:24-27)

As already noted, commentators are generally agreed that the two prophets are speaking of the same event (Wallis 1969: 107; Block 1989: 39; Laney 1990: 41; Allen 2008: 356). Certainly, both prophets are concerned with the notion of 'internalization' at the heart level – internalization of the Law in the case of Jeremiah and of Spirit in Ezekiel's context. In one of only two occasions where Paul mentions the New Covenant, he implies that the true destination of God's commands is the hearts of the people, and not stone tablets as when Moses first received the Decalogue:

> [2] You yourselves are our letter, written on our hearts, to be known and read by all; [3] and you show that you are a letter of Christ, prepared by us, written not with ink but with the Spirit of the living God, not on tablets of stone but on tablets of human hearts. [4] Such is the confidence that we have through Christ toward God. [5] Not that we are competent of ourselves to claim anything as coming from us; our competence is from God, [6] who has made us competent to be ministers of a new covenant, not of letter but of spirit; for the letter kills, but the Spirit gives life. (2 Cor. 3:2-6)

These texts have important resonances with the context of Galatians. For if the Law played a role in dealing with the sin of God's people before the coming of the Messiah, what would be the people's ethical barometer after Messiah's coming? Having marginalized the place of the Law in the age of the Messiah, did Paul create a moral vacuum in the Galatian Jesus communities? Were Paul to have posed this question himself in his usual pre-emptive manner, he would answer with a standard 'may it never be'!

For Paul previously stated, using patently 'Exodus'-style vocabulary, that Israel needed to be stewarded by the Law, which acted as a custodian until the people reached a level of maturity (Gal. 4:1-2). At this time Israel would receive their rights as adopted sons of God and be redeemed from the supervision of the Law by Messiah, whereby

> because you are children, God has sent the Spirit of his Son into our hearts, crying, 'Abba! Father!' (Gal. 4:6)

The term 'Spirit of his son', a reference to the Holy Spirit, need not be cause for confusion; a number of Pauline texts treat the Holy Spirit and the Spirit of

Christ as effectively interchangeable (e.g. Rom. 8:9; 1 Cor. 15:45; 2 Cor. 3:17-18; Phil. 1:19). The designation may be to acknowledge that the sonship of the people is a derivative of the sonship of Christ to God (Boakye 2017: 91). Mark, in his Gospel, places the Aramaic phrase 'Abba' (an affectionate term for 'father') on the lips of Jesus in Gethsemane. Paul may have been cognizant of a tradition of invoking the term in contexts of submission to the divine will; as in Mk 14:36, here in Gal. 4:6 and Rom. 8:15, the term is a faithful cry of a child placing confidence in a loving parent.

At this stage of the life of God's renewed people, their ethical direction would not be governed by a written Law – recall the earlier comment regarding Paul's depiction of the Law as the 'writing' (ἡ γραφὴ) in Gal. 3:22; it seems that Paul wants to draw a distinction between Law as written code and the new engagement with the Law corresponding to the inception of the New Covenant. This distinction likely lies beneath the Spirit-letter dichotomy seen in Paul (Rom. 2:29; 7:6; 2 Cor. 3:6; e.g. see Richardson 1973: 210–12; Westerholm 1984: 229–48). This new engagement with the Law would be governed by the Spirit of God in the hearts of the people. Through the Spirit, God himself would stimulate in his people a hitherto unprecedented proclivity to obey his decrees. As Barclay writes, justification is not a morally barren doctrine (1988: 223). By the internalization of the Spirit, the demands of the Law and the broader desires and wishes of God became an internalized reality, as jointly foreseen by Jeremiah and Ezekiel. As Greenberg nicely summarizes:

> God will no longer gamble with Israel as he did in old times, and Israel rebelled against him; in the future – no more experiments! God will put his spirit into them, he will alter their hearts (their minds) and make it impossible for them to be anything but obedient to his rules and his commandments. (1990: 375)

There are certain key corollaries of the new ethical direction that Paul maps out which are germane to the function of the Spirit in Galatians.

First, Paul is unambiguously negative about those gentiles who dare to be circumcised, for so doing will sever them from Christ and bind them to all the Law's commands (Gal. 5:1-4). Second, Paul summates the entire Law in the command to love one's neighbour (although this is another insurmountable tension in Räisänen (1987: 113–18); others do not see a summation of Torah at all, but rather a way to communicate that for Jewish Christ believers, loving uncircumcised Gentiles as brothers is the eschatological fulfilment of God's design to include Gentiles in the Kingdom; e.g. Chandler 2013: 40–7). Indeed, he speaks of the Law being 'fulfilled' by such love; if liberation from the supervision of the Law and the coming of the Spirit are coterminous events (Gal. 4:5-6), Paul likely reckoned this love to be an outworking of the Spirit's power (Gal. 5:14). In this regard, it is probably not a coincidence that the first 'fruit of the Spirit' is love (ἀγάπη; Gal. 5:22). Third, Paul is unequivocal in his determination that life possessed by the Spirit is independent of life beholden to the Law (Gal. 5:18). To walk in the Spirit is the pathway to avoiding the indulgence of lustful human desire, or 'flesh' as Paul has it (Gal. 5:16-17). To be possessed by the Spirit is to manifest the fruit of the Spirit (Gal. 5:22-23) and cast off the works of the flesh (Gal. 5:19-21), many of which are the very crimes of disunity and partisan politics threatening the cohesion of the Galatian Jesus assemblies (making enemies, rivalry, resentments, outbursts of anger, jealous disputes, divisions, cabals and envy are eight of the seventeen listed works of flesh). Fourth, and perhaps most interestingly, Paul speaks of the fulfilment of a 'Law of Christ'. As discussed in an earlier chapter, conjoining 'Christ' and 'Law' seems baffling given the context of Galatians, but there is an inherent logic, especially in light of Gal. 5:14.

When we considered the use of Lev. 19:18 in Gal. 5:14, the 'Law of Christ' was shown to be a summative term for how the pivotal love command could be brought to bear within the Galatian community. This idea may be extended by considering how the Spirit fits into the picture. A potential schism in the Galatian churches is strongly implied throughout the letter; the most natural fault-line along which the divisions existed separated those loyal to Paul's Law-free rendition of the Gospel and those persuaded by the rhetoric of Paul's opponents. It is most likely within this context that Paul writes:

My friends, if anyone is detected in a transgression, *you who have received the Spirit* should restore such a one in a spirit of gentleness. Take care that you yourselves are not tempted. ² Bear one another's burdens, and in this way you will *fulfil* the *law of Christ*. (Gal. 6:1-2, NRSV; emphasis added)

The NRSV has awkwardly, though contextually correctly, paraphrased *hoi pneumatikoi* (literally, the spiritual ones) as 'the ones having the Spirit'. The term 'fulfil' translates *anaplēroō* (literally, fill up, or completely fulfil), which is a cognate of the term used in 5:14 to denote love for one's neighbour as fulfilment of Torah (*plēroō*), and strongly implies that the realization of Christ's law is some manner of definitive example of 'loving neighbour as self'. There are numerous analytical quandaries associated with the phrase 'Law of Christ', including whether 'law' should be understood as something other than Torah and how exactly it 'belongs' to Christ. Adeyemi, for example, argues that the 'Law' in the case of the 'Law of Christ' does not relate to Torah (2006: 438–52). Bayes proposes that the 'Law of Christ' refers to the Law 'having originated' with Christ (2000: 171–2); Hays treats the phrase as exemplary – it is Christ's example of burden-bearing and a template for relationships between believers (1987: 287).

If the division in the community is as described here, the 'spiritual ones' are likely to be those who have accepted Paul's rendition of the Gospel and are being commissioned to gently restore those seduced by the rival message. As such, the former party is asked to 'bear the burdens' of the latter, and 'in this way' (Gk. *houtōs*) completely fulfil the 'Law of Christ' (Gal. 6:2). Contextually, and with Gal. 5:14 in the interpretive backdrop, the spiritual ones are those who acknowledge and experience the Torah as an inner reality impressed upon the hearts under the auspices of the Spirit, as per the prophecies of Jeremiah and Ezekiel. The 'Law of Christ' is the Spirit-directed fulfilment of the Law's true destination – the hearts of God's New Covenant people. As such, those restoring their wayward brethren have shown they love their neighbour as themselves, they exhibit the fruit of the Spirit and intuitively know the demands of God (cf. Jer. 31:34).

5. Concluding thoughts

Despite the numerous complexities Galatians raises regarding Paul's stance on Torah, what does seem certain is summed up by Kruse:

> Whilst the apostle Paul had many positive things to say about the Law, nevertheless, a very significant change took place in his understanding of its role with the advent of Christ, his death, resurrection and sending of the Holy Spirit. (2014: 29)

Paul was a zealous guardian of the Law (Gal. 1:14) in the tradition of Phinehas (Num. 25:5-9) and Mattathias (*1 Macc.* 2:24-27) and serially harassed the fledgling Jesus movement as potentially dangerous compromisers. Then

Paul received a mystifying call as he travelled to Damascus (Gal. 1:15; cf. Jer. 1:5; Isa. 6:1-8), at which point, God was pleased:

ἀποκαλύψαι τὸν υἱὸν αὐτοῦ ἐν ἐμοί, ἵνα εὐαγγελίζωμαι αὐτὸν ἐν τοῖς ἔθνεσιν.

[To reveal his son in me, in order that I might proclaim him among the gentiles.] (Gal. 1:16; Boakye's translation)

When Paul depicts his transformation using the language of death and reanimation (Gal. 2:19) and elaborates this using the language of cosmic rescue and participation (Gal. 2:20; cf. Gal. 1:4), the reasoning seems to be this: The God who raised Jesus from the dead (Gal. 1:1) revealed the risen Jesus in Paul such that Paul experienced death and rebirth in himself. This signified the dawning of the new era; Paul and all believers had been delivered from the 'age of the present evil' (Gal. 1:4) into that realm where the new canon of Spirit operated (Gal. 6:16), the terms of which were inscribed in their hearts as foreseen by Jeremiah and Ezekiel (the New Covenant). The gentiles would experience the same death and rebirth (Gal. 5:24-25) as would the cosmos itself (Gal. 6:14-15). As such, the resurrection of Christ, and not the Torah, was now the context within which to navigate and interpret the divine will. God was reconfiguring humanity by birthing them anew; through his Spirit, God was bringing his New Covenant people into being as he had brought Isaac into being. This narrative was latent in the written Law (especially Genesis and Deuteronomy) and in Israel's prophetic corpus, which routinely employed visualizations of death and rebirth to portray deliverance (Ps. 116; Isa. 26:19; Ezek. 37:1-14; Hos. 6:1-3; etc.). The Law, then, pointed beyond itself, ahead to a time of an 'actual', not a 'symbolic', manifestation of new life. This would correspond to the actual new life episode of Isaac's birth, and in this way, the subject of this manifestation of new life would be the true and sole heir of the promise made to Abraham: the true seed, and that seed is Messiah (Gal. 3:16). At this juncture, the Law's purpose as a written code would expire and first Israel's and then the world's interaction with it would change irrevocably. In Galatians, Paul argues that this time was marked by the presence and activity of God's Spirit (Gal. 3:3, 5; 4:6), doing among the community, from the seat of the hearts of God's people, what the Law could only point to from tablets of stone.

CHAPTER 6
UNITY IN DIVERSITY IN CHRIST
Peter Oakes

The key direction of Paul's letter to the Galatians is towards unity, oneness. Faced with an issue about some Galatian gentiles thinking of practising circumcision, Paul responds with an argument driving towards a theology of oneness in Christ and an ethic of love, the key virtue for unity. More specifically, the drive is towards unity in diversity. In particular this is unity in communities which diverge between practising and not practising circumcision. However, at the climax of his theological argument, Paul suddenly broadens the unity out widely, to encompass not only ethnic unity between Jew and gentile, but unity between slave and free, and gender unity. Whatever diversity is produced by birth (or later enslavement), in Christ there is to be unity in that diversity, a unity carried out in practice through love. Paul's opponents were a threat to both unity and diversity. In Paul's view, they brought division and their only solution to division was erasure of difference: all gentiles must act as Jews. Paradoxically, Paul's conclusion that there is no Jew or Greek, since both are one in Christ, sustains the diversity of the lives of Jews and Greeks in the body of Christ, the broad Christian community.

An assertion that unity in diversity in Christ is the key direction of argument in Galatians is likely to meet with one or more of three types of reaction. Some will argue that it is not true, or is far from central, or that the formulation is problematic. Others will suspect that this reading of the text is just what one would expect from me (Oakes), a white academic, shocked by the polarities revealed in events such as the 2016 Brexit referendum and the election of President Trump. Moreover, they will suspect that, as a Christian writer, the attribution of my politically favoured attitudes is part of a strategy to make Paul and Christianity appear superior to other religious views. Finally, some will suggest that, whether or not unity in diversity in Christ is the most prominent direction of Galatians, it is so obviously an element of the letter that most scholars of the past couple of centuries have argued for it in one way or another, so my argument is nothing new.

The objections, though not overthrowing the argument of this chapter, do draw attention to some cautions as to how far we should take it. The degree of correspondence between this reading of Paul and my own identity and views also merits comment. The prior scholarship on unity in diversity offers both some important steps for the current argument but also a significant number of lines of thought that should probably not be followed. After tackling each of these issues, we will work our way through the key sections of the letter that function together to show the centrality of unity in diversity in Christ in the thought of Galatians.

1. Objections to seeing unity in diversity in Christ as a central theme of Galatians

One objection to this is lexical. In Galatians, there is a scarcity of explicit unity vocabulary. For instance, words from the *koinōnia* (fellowship) word group occur only twice (2:9; 6:6). The term *heis* (one) occurs in only three verses in a significant way (3:16, 20, 28). Even words from the *agapē* (love) word group occur only five times (2:20; 5:6, 13, 14, 22). This contrasts with the high frequency of terms such as those in the *nomos* (law) and *pistis* (trust, loyalty) word groups, which occur thirty-three and twenty-seven times, respectively. Related to the lexical objection is a structural one. In particular, the issue of unity is not raised in Galatians 1. Paul describes his calling without setting it up in unity terms. The unity narrative gets going only in Galatians 2.

The lexical objection should caution us against viewing Paul's unity argument in overly abstract terms. Paul develops his theological argument as being about unity specifically in relation to diversity in practice of Jewish law. His reference to slave/free and male/female polarities in 3:28 is a startling surprise, albeit a very significant one. Also, even though the call for love in Galatians 5 is not described as being specifically between Jews and gentiles – it appears to encompass all in the community – the letter ends back on the circumcision/uncircumcision issue, with an assertion that it is that divide that has disappeared (6:15). However, the broadening of the categories, seen in 3:28, does fit Paul's argument. Looking back from 3:28 we can see that Paul's argument for oneness in Christ can apply to many social polarities.

The structural objection is less pressing. One way or another, Paul clearly perceives his teaching as being under threat; so a passage defending his authority to speak is clearly an important precursor to further argument. He also does introduce the topic of his call to preach to gentiles (1:16), which will be important for what follows in regard to unity. A more substantial structural objection to the degree of centrality of the unity in diversity argument would be if there were a very sharp division between the argument of Galatians 2–4 and Gal. 5:1–6:10, with the 'theological' and 'ethical' sections of the letter being seen as addressing very different issues. This dichotomy has often been a feature of studies of Galatians. For instance, Richard Longenecker sees Paul combating two problems in the Galatian churches, a 'proposed acceptance of Jewish nomism' and ethical failure, including 'certain libertine tendencies', with Paul switching to address the second problem in 5:13–6:10 (1990: 238). However, the 'unity in diversity' theme is one which, if it is seen as applying to Galatians 2–4, is relatively straightforward to find in the subsequent 'ethical' part of the letter.

A further type of objection is seen in the work of scholars such as Elizabeth Castelli (1991) and Joseph Marchal (2006, on Philippians). They would accept that Paul has a forceful rhetoric of unity but would disagree that this is supportive of diversity. They see Paul as inscribing a theology of domination, based on submission to his authority and that of a divine lord seen as supportive of his authority. Castelli and Marchal are right in seeing Paul as not being a generalized libertarian. As Louis Martyn (1985) argues, if one does see Christ, for Paul, as in some sense doing away with various polarities, such as Jew and Greek, the other side of that coin is that he introduces fresh ones. Unity in diversity, for Paul, is unity in diversity in Christ. The diversity in question is bounded by the Christian community. It is also clear that Paul is not at all tolerant of some types of diversity of Christian teaching (esp. Gal. 1:6-9). As Marchal argues, Paul rapidly moves from 3:28 to argument that calls for imitation of him (2012: 222–3). Marchal also points out that almost everywhere in the text, including just after 3:28, Paul bases his rhetoric on assumptions about often-oppressive societal structures, such as patriarchal ones and that of servitude, for example, sons inherit, slaves do not (Gal. 4:1-5), albeit with occasionally disruptive use of imagery, such as that of himself as mother (Gal. 4:19; Marchal 2012: 220–1).

The diversity in view in the present chapter is social diversity of people in the Christian communities. Marchal is right that Paul has not escaped the hierarchical language game of his time: Paul does still construct text by use of language that is often based on stereotyped and asymmetric structures such as monarchy. He is also insistent on major elements of his own teaching, rejecting diverse alternative views. However, in Galatians, Paul's own teaching that he is insisting on is that diverse people should be able to eat together. He rejects a diversity of view that denies communal sharing to those different from the dominant group, unless they change and become like the dominant group. That reading of Paul does not solve every Foucauldian conundrum but, in the present day, it feels an important goal to pursue.

2. A white Christian academic finding his own views in Paul

This was sharply enunciated by David Horrell (2017) in relation to me and others, but I have long been aware of it. The issue is not even just about my own views. I expect these views to be shared by much of the core audience of my 2015 Galatians commentary, as can be seen by my decision to begin the Preface thus: 'Unity in diversity in Christ. People of all kinds eating together through common relation to Christ' (Oakes 2015: xi). However, the words are also at the head of the book because I think that, despite the survey of scholarship that we will shortly come to, the foregrounding of this issue is a distinctive of the commentary. More particularly, the words are there because, notwithstanding my earlier comment, I expect most of the book's audience not to think of the headline issues of Galatians in those terms. I expect most ministerial and church readers to think of the headline issues as being about justification, faith, law and so on. The opening words of the book are an initial attempt to change the reading frame with which many (predominantly white Christian) readers approach Galatians.

I don't think I have an agenda of trying to prove the superiority of Paul's ideas over Judaism. Apart from being white and Christian, a key part of my location is that I am part of the Department of Religions and Theology at the University of Manchester, one of Europe's main hubs for Jewish studies. Very aware of the complexities on both sides of the comparison of ancient ideas, I would not think of trying to construct some sort of overall evaluation of their relative merits. (I was disappointed that Horrell did not make reference to my indicating of limits to the diversity that Paul legitimates in Galatians; Oakes 2015: 129).

Having said that, the terms in which I set up the debate in the present chapter are, as I will discuss again later, morally loaded. 'Unity' and 'diversity' are morally positive terms in most current forms of discourse. If, even just in the spaces of Christian meetings, Paul's teaching got slaves and owners eating together and, consequently, the owners behaving better towards their slaves, that would be a better situation than it not happening – even though it is clearly far from the best situation, which would be abolition of slavery or, at least, freeing of all slaves by all Christian owners. It is often morally better for certain things to happen than not happen. However, that is far from saying that we can, in practice, make a judgement on the overall moral goodness of two systems of ideas and practices, whether that is (some current form of) Christianity and (some current form of) Judaism or some other pair of systems. A person within a system can seek to evaluate where they think they should be. An academic outside the system would have great difficulty in helpfully doing that for them. Some academic studies are important for uncovering problematic aspects of systems, including some aspects of which members may not be aware. However, biblical scholars are unlikely to be among the academics achieving that in relation to anything beyond the dynamics of particular biblical texts or of communities using biblical texts in particular ways.

Anyway, I can be open about some aims of my own work on unity in diversity in Galatians. One is for readers to understand Galatians better, because I do think that the unity in diversity issue is really present there and that there are significant things to learn about the way in which Paul configures it in the text. A second is to encourage an increased degree of unity in diversity within many church communities. My hope is also that the experience and visibility of unity in diversity within those groups will have positive ramifications within wider society that interacts with those groups. Churches that act as centres of prejudice and division certainly have a deadening effect beyond their doors. My belief is that, conversely, Christian communities of unity in diversity can have an enlivening effect in their area.

A brief extra comment that I would make on this issue is that identity is a very complex matter of history. I am a white male Christian but my scholarly identity is shaped not only by having spent all my career among Jewish studies scholars but also by my core approaches being decisively affected by women's scholarship, especially Lilian Portefaix's *Sisters Rejoice: Paul's Letter to the Philippians and Luke-Acts as Received by First Century Philippian Women* (1988). To quite an extent my scholarly identity is as an advocate of reading texts as being written for the full range of their diverse expected audience.

3. Previous scholarship on unity in diversity as a theme of Galatians

Any number of scholars could be considered here. We will pick out six whose approaches are particularly significant for understanding the current landscape of thought: F. C. Baur's nineteenth-century appeal to the issue of 'higher consciousness'; James Dunn's New Perspective approach; N. T. Wright's 'one family' idea; Bruce Hansen's use of an 'apocalyptic' approach; Brigitte Kahl's political approach; John Barclay's recent work on gift.

F. C. Baur's classic understanding of Paul exercised a considerable influence on scholarship through the twentieth century and still has echoes today. For Baur, what he saw as the universalism of Paul's gospel was one of its defining features. Writing on Romans, but expressing his overall view on Paul, Baur comments,

> In the Epistle to the Romans his task is to remove the last remnants of Jewish particularism, by showing that it is but a stage, a stepping-stone to the universalism of Christianity, in which all nations would be embraced. (1876: 253)

This developmental idea is elaborated in a comment on the opposition that Paul faced.

> We must allow so much to the Apostle's opponents, that the chief reason why their Judaistic position was so narrow was just their natural incapacity to raise themselves from a lower state of religious consciousness to a higher and freer one. (253)

Baur's concept is evolutionary, seeing Judaism as a stage towards the development of the higher ideas of Christianity. The upward progress is from particularism to universalism. Whereas Judaism related to a specific national group, Christianity embraced all nations. Unity in Christ could encompass international diversity.

Baur's concept of 'higher' 'religious consciousness' drew on influences such as Hegel's idea of human progress. Effectively, Baur represented an idea of the progress of thought towards a nineteenth-century north-European academic Protestant post-Enlightenment culture! Baur was probably right that Paul's thought was an important step on the way to that culture. However, there are all sorts of problems with the evaluative nature of the term 'higher', the related idea of progress and the historical judgements that underlie the use of these ideas by Baur.

Even within a nineteenth-century context there are major questions over how 'universalistic' the culture really was. One only has to think of European treatment of various minorities and of populations beyond Europe. Within a first-century context, the issues are even sharper. It is not really historically viable to seek to demonstrate that Pauline Christianity represented a 'higher consciousness' than non-Christian Judaism of his day. It is also questionable how far one could see Pauline Christianity as being more universalistic than first-century Judaism. Although Judaism was bounded by being a way of life generally linked to a particular ethnicity, Pauline Christianity was a way of life that was linked to membership of even more sharply bounded communities. It was probably some way from what nineteenth-century German thinkers would actually have regarded as universalism.

James Dunn (1993) comes at the issue of unity in diversity in Galatians through the New Perspective lens of seeing covenant and law as ethnic markers. On 'grace' in Gal. 2:21, he comments,

> It was of the essence of that grace, in Paul's experience and understanding, that it was to be freely extended to the Gentiles as well. So any retreat back into a Judaism, or Jewish Christianity, which insisted that Jew and Gentile should eat separately, was to render invalid the whole gospel. (147–8)

More broadly, he writes that

> what Paul was concerned about was the fact that covenant promise and law had become too inextricably identified with ethnic Israel as such, with the Jewish people marked out in their national distinctiveness by the practices of circumcision, food laws, and sabbath in particular (Wright appropriately coins the phrase 'national righteousness'). They would recognize that what Paul was endeavoring to do was to free both promise and law for a wider range of recipients, freed from the ethnic constraints which he saw to be narrowing the grace of God and diverting the saving purpose of God out of its main channel – Christ. (1988a: lxxvi–vii)

For Dunn, Paul's problem is not with Jewish law as such, but with certain characteristic law practices as 'ethnic constraints' to the scope of God's grace.

Dunn is probably right that 'grace' in 2:21 relates to ethnic inclusiveness: the bringing of gentiles into the covenant alongside Jews (see argument later). However, it is far from clear that the range of points that Paul makes about limitations of the law or of 'works of the law' in Galatians (and in Romans) is generally of the law specifically as ethnic marker. Paul says many key things about the law other than on the subject of ethnic marking. For Paul, the issues of sin and righteousness are not purely about group definition. Dunn has also recently been criticized for effectively smuggling in Baur-type evaluations of the relative merits of inclusive Pauline Christianity and less inclusive Judaism (e.g. Horrell 2017: 127–8). Dunn is not pursuing inherently evaluative ideas of 'higher consciousness' but, for good or ill, he clearly does effectively operate with some idea of relative merits of the two sets of ideas and practices. However, as noted earlier, there is an extent to which any attempt to discuss unity, diversity, particularity and related terms will carry some implicit evaluation even in the choice of terms itself.

N. T. Wright, as Dunn notes, also sees the law issues in Galatians in New Perspective terms of identity marking. However, Wright takes this in a distinctive way with his key idea of God's intention to create 'a single family'. Wright's focus on identity issues is seen when, commenting on Gal. 2:15-16a, he writes,

> At a stroke, Paul has told us what it means to be 'declared righteous'. It means to have God himself acknowledge that you are a member of 'Israel', a 'Jew', one of the 'covenant family': the 'righteous' in that sense. Yes, 'righteous' means all sorts of other things as well. But unless it means at least that, and centrally, then verse 16 is a massive non sequitur . . . What matters is not now Torah, but Messiah. *Justification is all about being declared to be a member of God's people*; and this people is defined in relation to the Messiah himself. (2013: 856; his emphasis)

Wright narrows Israel to the Messiah, which then provides a route to making the scope of 'Israel' universal through the possibility of people being 'in' the Messiah. A key element of this is the idea that when Gal. 3:15-18 argues that the Abrahamic promise was directed to 'one *sperma*', usually translated as 'one seed', this should be taken in the sense of 'one family'. He unpacks the key points of this text as:

> (a) the creator and covenant God intended a single family, and promised it to Abraham; (b) he has now created it in the Messiah; (c) Torah would create a plurality; therefore (d) to go back to Torah would be to go against the original intention, now accomplished in the Messiah. Torah, in other words, cannot annul the promise made to Abraham nearly half a millennium earlier (3.17). (869)

Wright's point about Torah here is that, as it mandates practices such as Jews and gentiles eating separately from each other, it creates two families, contrary to God's intention to create a single family.

It is reasonable to argue that Paul has in mind the topic of membership of God's people when he writes 2:16. However, it is harder to demonstrate that, in Galatians, the most central meaning of righteousness/justification language is about covenant membership. 'Righteousness' language in Galatians is not tightly specified. We can see it coordinated with a range of ideas: life, blessing, relationship to the Spirit. The term probably also includes both some ethical component and some idea of a verdict by God.

Wright is clearly correct that Paul is using the 'one *sperma*' argument in 3:16 to set up the argument that incorporation in Christ means his people are a single group. However, Paul does not appear to bring this argument home until 3:28. In his *Paul for Everyone* commentary, Wright translates 3:16 as,

> It doesn't say 'his seeds', as though referring to several families, but indicates a single family by saying 'and to your seed', meaning the Messiah. (2002: 35)

As Wright demonstrates in *Climax of Covenant*, 'family' is indeed a possible sense of *sperma* (1991: chapter 8). However, Martin de Boer's demonstration of usage by Jewish texts of the term *sperma*, in relation to specific persons (2011: 222–3), provides a sense which fits much more easily with the ending of 3:16, ὅς ἐστιν Χριστός (which is Christ).

A major recent development which, to an extent, builds on the New Perspective approach is the use of apocalyptic ideas by J. Louis Martyn (esp. 1985, 1997) and a number of others such as de Boer (2011). Bruce Hansen links apocalyptic thinking with 'ethnic reasoning' to produce a new framing of the unity in diversity issue in his 2010 monograph, *All of You Are One*. A string of quotations from his book shows a major arc of Hansen's thought.

> Martyn's innovation has been to recognize that in Galatians, Paul has brought the primary apocalyptic motifs to bear not on the parousia but on the crucifixion . . . [This is shown by] 'The motif of the triple crucifixion – that of Christ, that of the cosmos, that of Paul'. (2010: 83, quoting Martyn 1985: 420)
>
> The binary social divisions expressed by the formula ['neither circumcision is anything, nor uncircumcision'; Gal. 6:15] fall on the

cosmos side of the Christ-versus-cosmos duality. Conversely, 'all of you are one in Christ Jesus' (3.28d) corresponds to the new creation.

A chief characteristic of 'the present evil age' (1.4) from which Christ gave himself to rescue believers is the division of the world into privileged versus marginalized statuses. (Hansen 2010: 85–6)

In wresting the rhetoric of Abrahamic descent from his opponents in Galatia, Paul produces an alternate ethnic rhetoric that trumped their claims. Paul's reflections on the apocalyptic implications of the cross of Christ and his modulation of the theme of faith support his construction of a new ethnic identity in Christ. (102)

In his chapter on Galatians, Hansen makes many convincing exegetical points in his argument demonstrating the importance of unity in the letter. However, Martyn's idea that the main effect of Christ's action, as described in Galatians, is on the cosmos is unconvincing. In Galatians, the main effect of Christ's action is clearly on people (see Oakes 2015: 190–1). This problematizes Hansen's appeal to Martyn's ideas.

On the 'ethnic reasoning' aspect of Hansen's work, he does provide convincing evidence that many of Paul's arguments are cast in terms such as genealogy, that is, in terms related to ethnic discourse. However, there are problems in seeing this as producing 'a new ethnic identity'. Hansen argues, rightly, that the new identity does not eradicate prior ethnic identities such as Jewish identity (2010: 104–5, 202). Since this is the case, and despite the various theorists who Hansen cites in support of his approach, describing the new identity in Christ as being 'ethnic' seems to me to muddy the waters, creating a tendency to underplay the distinctive retained ethnic identities.

The theme of unity in diversity is essential to many recent political readings of Galatians. These range from historically focused readings to readings centred on current issues of gender or sexuality. Brigitte Kahl argues for a counter-imperial reading in which Galatians offers 'an uncompromising embrace of the other', in contrast to Caesar (2010: 284). She writes,

The theological backbone of Paul's argument is a discourse of law and oneness that draws on the oneness of God as core-commandment of Torah (Exod. 20:1–5; Deut. 6:4). Oneness in the Messiah (3:28), however, is not the absence of diversity, but the contestation of an enslaving uniformity imposed by Caesar as the supreme 'mediator' of the law, including Torah. (2014: 514)

The one gospel of Christ is only intact so long as it comprises *both* gospels, the 'gospel of circumcision' *and* the 'gospel of the foreskin' (2:7) . . . If oneness in Christ turns into oneness without the other, or against the other, it mutates back into the likeness of the imperial *euangelion* ['gospel/good news announcement']. (2010: 275; emphasis added)

Much of what Kahl argues on unity in diversity is compelling. She is also right in arguing, contrary to Baur, that Paul is not against Judaism (2014: 504–5). However, like Baur, Kahl seems inclined to describe Paul's stance in overly sweeping philosophical terms, attributing to him a degree of philosophical systematization that he probably does not have. Also, although it is right that Paul is arguing against a range of norms of the culture of the first-century Roman Empire, Kahl probably pushes the links with Caesar rather too far. Paul's opponents are likely to have motives, other than those related to the Roman imperial programme, for encouraging Judaizing uniformity.

A final comment is needed on the way in which a number of alternative views of what are central issues in Galatians involve conclusions relating to unity. A prominent recent example is the work of John Barclay on the theme of 'gift'. For him, communal unity is a key outworking of the gift. He reassesses his reading of the 'ethical' section of Galatians. Whereas, in *Obeying the Truth* (1988), he connected Galatians 5–6 to the rest of the letter by seeing it as dealing with ethical issues raised as a result of the challenge of Paul's opponents on matters of law, Barclay now sees the ethics as flowing from the gift.

Returning to Galatians 5–6 after many years, I now offer a new reading of its focus and function, based on a fresh analysis of the letter as a whole . . . My argument [on 6:1-6] amounts to the claim that social practice is, for Paul, the necessary expression of the Christ-gift, and that noncompetitive communities, ordered by a new calibration of worth, articulate and, in a certain sense, define the character of the Christ-event as unconditional gift. (2014: 307)

For Barclay, non-competitive communal unity is the ethical expression of a life shaped by gift. There is considerable strength in this idea. In terms of shape of argument, the main difference between that and the current chapter is that I am seeing unity in diversity as Paul's aim, with the theological argument being brought in by him to make the case for that, whereas Barclay sees Paul seeking to present the theology of gift, then expressing the effects of that theology. There must, however, be a limit to the extent to which these directions of thought differ. In Barclay's view, Paul is responding to the occasion of Galatians (e.g. 2015: 333), so the deployment of gift theology does have a communal aim. Conversely, I do not think that Paul creates theology ex nihilo to use in argument for unity in diversity. Undoubtedly, what he writes is generally an expression of theological views that he already held prior to beginning the composition of the letter. The conclusions generally flow from prior theological views, rather than the theology being constructed tactically to support the conclusions.

Chapter 2 in this book also argues that, although Barclay's idea of the key role of gift in Paul's thought is generally convincing, his linking of gift so strongly to the past Christ-event underplays the importance of current relationship to the living Christ. The non-competitive communities that Paul strives to sustain stem more from being in Christ than from orientation towards the gift – although clearly the two circumstances are not in competition with each other.

4. Setting up the argument

There are two aspects to Paul's presentation of unity in diversity in Christ in Galatians. One is rhetorical. Paul faces a problem of gentile Christians being encouraged to adopt the practice of circumcision. His key rhetorical move in Galatians is to transpose this into a problem about unity in diversity in Christ. The second aspect is substantive. Paul sees his opponents' message as a substantive threat to unity, especially unity between diverse groups of Christians. He is concerned not only about gentiles avoiding circumcision but also about unity in Christ between gentiles as gentiles and Jews as Jews. He also sees this as part of a wider issue of unity and love. He meets the challenge with arguments which are not just about gentiles and the law but which go beyond into broader issues of unity and love.

We will consider five broad exegetical arguments that build towards seeing unity in diversity in Christ as a central focus of Galatians.

a. Galatians 2:1-10 presents Paul as going to Jerusalem seeking unity in diversity.

b. The Antioch incident of 2:11-14 launches the central argument of the letter.

c. The central argument of the letter runs towards unity in diversity in Christ.

d. The 'ethical' section of the letter (5:13–6:10) focuses on love, the key virtue for unity.

e. The letter ends by returning to the key unity issue, 'neither circumcision nor uncircumcision'.

5. Paul goes to Jerusalem seeking unity in diversity (Gal. 2:1-10)

Faced with the problem enunciated in Gal. 6:11-12 . . .

> See with what large letters I write to you in my own hand. [12] Those who want to make a good showing in flesh, these are the ones who are compelling you to be circumcised

. . . Paul begins the body of his letter by telling three stories. The first of these (Gal. 1:11-24) is about the divine origin of his gospel. The second (2:1-10) recounts a trip to Jerusalem. The third (2:11-14) describes the occurrence of divisions at Antioch. We will focus here on the second.

In Gal. 2:1-10, Paul, at the instigation of God, takes the initiative in seeking to ensure unity with the Jerusalem Christian leaders. His actions in Jerusalem instantiate his gospel's priority for unity. As reported in this passage, his actions are successful.

Why is Paul worried in Gal. 2:2?

> I went up [to Jerusalem] in accordance with a revelation and set out to them the gospel that I preach among the gentiles – privately, to those who seemed to be something – lest I am running, or have run, in vain.

Despite Paul's confidence, emphasized at length in Galatians 1, that his gospel was revealed to him by God (1:11-12, 16), he expresses a worry in 2:2 that led him to a private explanation of his message to the Jerusalem Christian leaders. Despite having spelled out his independence from those leaders in learning his gospel (1:12, 16-17), Paul seeks some kind of reassurance through his meeting with them.

In view of Galatians 1, it looks unlikely that Paul wanted to check that his gospel was correct. What would make more sense is that Paul wants reassurance of unity with the first apostles. Since his gospel places a high value on Christian unity, it would be intrinsically frustrating to his project if there could not be unity between him and the acknowledged leaders of the Jesus movement.

Paul takes with him to Jerusalem a gentile, Titus. In 2:3-5, Paul describes what happens or, rather, does not happen and does so in a way that links it to the Galatian situation. He also uses terms that he will employ to link what happens to Titus both to the Antioch incident and to the actions of Paul's opponents in Galatia.

> 2:3 But not even Titus, who was with me, was compelled to be circumcised (ἠναγκάσθη περιτμηθῆναι), despite being a Greek. 4 This arose on account of the false brothers who had been brought in, who slipped in to spy on our freedom which we have in Christ Jesus, so that they might enslave us. 5 We did not give in to them for a moment in submission, so that the truth of the gospel would remain for you (ἵνα ἡ ἀλήθεια τοῦ εὐαγγελίου διαμείνῃ πρὸς ὑμᾶς).

Paul creates three links here. The most direct is the surprising twist at the end of v. 5. Paul is narrating events in Jerusalem that took place some years prior to the letter, but describes his actions as being for the sake of the Galatians. More specifically, it is to preserve 'the truth of the gospel' for the Galatians. Presumably, Paul could also say the same in relation to other Christian gentiles: his resistance to Titus being circumcised preserved the truth of the gospel for them too. However, Paul particularly applies this to the Galatians because it is crucial to the issue they are currently facing.

There are then two lexical links, each of which Paul uses to point in the same pair of directions. The first is: 'was compelled to be circumcised' (ἠναγκάσθη περιτμηθῆναι; 2:3). At the end of the letter, Paul uses the same phrase for his opponents in Galatia.

> Those who want to make a good showing in flesh, these are the ones who are compelling you to be circumcised (ἀναγκάζουσιν ὑμᾶς περιτέμνεσθαι). (6:12)

Much sooner in the letter, he challenges Peter by use of similar language:

> I said to Cephas [Peter], in front of everyone, 'If you, being a Jew, live in a gentile manner and not a Jewish manner, how can you be compelling the gentiles to Judaize?' (πῶς τὰ ἔθνη ἀναγκάζεις ἰουδαΐζειν). (2:14)

The term *ioudaïzein*, 'to Judaize', has a problematic history of interpretation. It has usually been used to denote the actions of people who try 'to persuade others to adopt Jewish practices' (see, e.g., Bruce 1982: 23). However, this Galatians text is indicative of use elsewhere and means something like 'to adopt Jewish practices' (Oakes 2015: 80, citing Add. Esth. 8:17 = Esther 8:17 LXX; Josephus, *B.J.* 2.454; Dunn 1993, 15, 129). Coming only a few verses after Paul's comment in 2:3 about Titus, it is clear that Paul is somehow tying Peter's actions at Antioch to what happened over Titus in Jerusalem. We will discuss Paul's deployment of the Antioch incident later. The point here is that he connects his Jerusalem trip to the Antioch incident in such a way as to make clear that his Jerusalem trip relates to the same issues.

This connection is made even stronger by the second lexical link, 'the truth of the gospel'.

> We did not give in to them for a moment in submission, so that the truth of the gospel (ἡ ἀλήθεια τοῦ εὐαγγελίου) would remain for you. (2:5)

Paul clearly links back to this in the justification for his challenge to Peter at Antioch.

> But when I saw that they were not walking in line with the truth of the gospel (τὴν ἀλήθειαν τοῦ εὐαγγελίου), I said to Cephas, in front of everyone, ... how can you be compelling the gentiles to Judaize? (2:14)

The term 'the truth' probably also provides another link to Paul's opponents, whom he describes as those who, 'cut in on you to stop you obeying the truth (ἀληθείᾳ)' (5:7).

A third striking feature of Paul's narration of his Jerusalem visit (after his surprising worry of 2:2 and the links made in 2:3-5) is the curious, stuttering delay that Paul puts into the narrative by his comments about 'reputation' (*prosōpon*, literally, face) (2:6). At the start of the verse, he appears about to tell us the Jerusalem leaders' reaction to his gospel, but then surprisingly gets diverted,

> But from those who seemed to be something (τῶν δοκούντων εἶναί τι) – whatever they were makes no difference to me: God does not have regard for a person's reputation (πρόσωπον) – those who seemed to be something added nothing to my message.

The topic of reputation has effectively been set up since 2:2, where Paul describes the Jerusalem leaders as *hoi dokousin* (literally, those seeming, meaning those with a reputation, in this case as prominent leaders). As de Boer argues, this term could be one used by his opponents (2011, 106–7) and Paul's odd focus on the issue in 2:6 could be defensive. However, as with 2:3-5, Paul later describes his opponents using a term related to the vocabulary of 2:6.

> Those who want to make a good showing (εὐπροσωπῆσαι) in flesh, these are the ones who are compelling you to be circumcised. (6:12)

As Bruce Winter argues, they are wanting 'to make a good face', *prosōpon*, the term in 2:6 (1994: 137–9). Since 'God does not have regard for a person's πρόσωπον (face/reputation)', the opponents' mission is futile (on the key role of honour in Galatians, see Harvey 2012, 2018).

There may also be a broader link to the issue of unity in diversity. To characterize God as one who 'does not have regard for a person's reputation' (2:6) makes God the natural sponsor of communities in which reputation is not a basis for distinction between people. Characterizing God in this way provides an important theological resource for a unity in diversity argument. Paul appears to go out of his way to 'shoehorn' this characterization of God into his Jerusalem narrative.

Paul also puts himself on God's side in this matter, 'whatever they were makes no difference to me: God does not have regard for a person's reputation'. This is in line with him as a person to whom 'the world was crucified' (6:14). Paul presents himself as a paradigm and champion of God's way of building communities that are not based on reputation.

In Gal. 2:7-9, we finally reach the point that we have been expecting the narrative to head to: a declaration of unity in Jerusalem:

> Those who seemed to be pillars, gave me and Barnabas the right hand of fellowship, that we might go to the gentiles, and they to the circumcised. (2:9)

One point to note here is that this is unity in diversity. Paul and Peter have two different mission agendas but they, and the other Jerusalem leaders, agree to recognize both. Paul has gone to Jerusalem seeking unity but with a determination not to compromise on the maintenance of diversity, as exemplified by the uncircumcised Titus. This narrative shows Paul achieving unity in diversity in Jerusalem.

6. The Antioch incident (2:11-14) launches the central argument of Galatians

Paul's most significant rhetorical move in composing Galatians is to take an issue about circumcision and transpose it into an issue about unity. He takes an issue about whether Christian gentiles need to live like Jews and turns it into an issue about whether Christian gentiles and Christian Jews can eat together: into an issue about unity in diversity in Christ. This transposition has substantial rhetorical advantages for Paul. Whereas the idea and practice of gentile circumcision sound like things that could be argued for or against, ideas such as unity and practices such as eating together sound inherently valuable. They would probably especially sound positive for Paul's gentile audience, promising an end to exclusion and disadvantage. (As I suggested at the start of this chapter, Paul also saw a practical threat to unity in the teaching of his opponents. Even though Paul's transposition of the topic from circumcision to unity was rhetorically helpful, it was not done merely for rhetorical effect.)

Paul achieves this transposition by constructing a central section of the letter that runs from 2:11 to 3:29 (with a coda extending it to 4:7, see Chapter 1 of this book). It runs from the Antioch incident to the declaration of oneness in Christ, with 'no Jew nor Greek'. The declaration of 3:28-29 completes the solution to the problem, depicted by Paul both as being set up by Peter's actions in Antioch and as being equivalent to what is happening among the Christians in Galatia.

The idea that the account of the Antioch incident launches the central argument of Galatians finds various forms of support. The first of these is inherent in the surprise of the account itself, which lends it particular rhetorical weight. Galatians 2:11 is a shock both in the flow of Galatians and in the history of the early Christian movement. Paul opposes Peter, does so in public and tells the Galatians about it. Christian writings and iconography came to see the two as complementary figures, the two great early missionary apostles. The disagreement is a shock, as is the using of it to launch an argument. It is also a sudden reversal in the flow of Galatians. Peter and Paul are in fellowship in 2:9 and at odds in 2:11. Furthermore, it is awkward for the drive towards unity that Paul has been working towards since 2:1. His success in gaining agreement in 2:7-9 seems quickly to come to nothing when it faces a practical test. It therefore needs Paul to be doing something rhetorically very weighty for it to be worth exposing this apparent failure in his strategy.

Some scholars would respond to this argument by suggesting that the Antioch incident is only referred to by Paul because his opponents have already reported it to the Galatians, using it to support their arguments against Paul (e.g. Moo 2013: 144). It is conceivable that this was the case. However, the weight that Paul puts on the incident, and the way in which he uses it to set his core argument going, makes it look to me more likely that Paul introduced the incident as a deliberate rhetorical move.

Paul handles the account of the Antioch incident in such a way that his main argument flows indistinguishably from the narrative of his challenge to Peter. It is clear that, by the end of Galatians 2, what is being said is very much for the Galatians' benefit, but it is not clear where, if at all, Paul stops addressing Peter. Paul confronts Peter in 2:14. He follows up with, 'We, Jews by nature', clearly referring at least to himself and Peter. This is then the start of a sentence that runs right through 2:16, the key verse about trust/loyalty, Christ, law and righteousness. The terms of that verse then echo repeatedly through the next chapter: a statement apparently made to Peter in Antioch pervades the main argument of the letter. The account of the Antioch incident launches the argument.

As discussed earlier, Paul also makes lexical links between the Antioch incident, Titus's visit to Jerusalem and the situation in Galatia. In 2:14, the terms 'the truth of the gospel' and 'compelling the gentiles to Judaize' link to Titus in 2:3-5 and to the Galatian situation in 6:12 and (less fully) in 5:7. A further conceptual link to the Galatian situation is that Peter and the others who withdrew from eating with gentiles are accused of hypocrisy in 2:13. A charge of hypocrisy is effectively also levelled at Paul's opponents in Galatia in 6:12-13, although without use of the term itself (see later on 6:11-18).

By directly linking the account of the Antioch incident to Titus's visit and the Galatian situation, Paul equates those issues of gentile circumcision with the issue of Christian Jews stopping eating with Christian gentiles. The entry ritual issue is transposed into a social one (how people relate) and a social ritual one: eating together always has a ritual aspect and especially did so for the early Christians (see Uro 2016; DeMaris 2008). As a social ritual, eating together is a central expression of social unity. It also carried, and still carries, other freight such as an expression of the honour attributed to others with whom one does or does not dine (more broadly, on meals in the early Christian movement, see Smith and Taussig 2012).

7. The central argument of Galatians runs towards unity in diversity in Christ

The structure of the central argument can be viewed as follows.

a. The Antioch incident shows that the issue in Galatia is one of unity between Christian Jews and Christian gentiles (2:11-14).

b. Righteousness for Christian Jews comes through trust in Christ (2:15-21).

c. Righteousness for Christian gentiles comes through trust in Christ (3:1-14).

d. Diverse Christians, Jew and gentile, etc., are united in Christ, members of the family of Abraham (3:15-29)

After Gal. 3:29 (and 4:1-7, which combines additional concluding points to 3:2-29 with setting up the exhortation of 4:8-10), a further set of arguments and imperatives approach practical issues in the Galatian situation, such as calendrical observance and circumcision (4:8–5:13a), a key motif in these passages being slavery and the need to avoid a return to it. There is clearly a degree of arbitrariness in seeing what we are calling 'the central argument' as running just to 3:29. However, 3:2-29 is a strongly coherent, extensive and weighty section (held together by the tightly constructed chain of argument about Spirit, promise and Abraham). Once 3:2-29 is seen as a key argumentative unit, 2:15-21 is pulled in by the extensive parallels made between the texts. As noted earlier, 2:15-21 flows uninterruptedly from 2:11. Also, once 2:11-14 is brought in, it becomes clear that the conclusion of 3:28-29 deals with the issue of unity between Christian Jews and Christian gentiles raised in 2:11-14. Once 2:11–3:29 is seen as a complete argument, it becomes central to the reading of the letter. This centrality has, in practice, been evident in the reading of the letter through the centuries. We have considered Gal. 2:11-14, earlier, so we will begin from 2:15.

Galatians 2:15-21 is, rather surprisingly, presented as Paul's response to the Antioch incident. Having castigated Peter for 'compelling the gentiles to Judaize' (2:14), we expect Paul to make an argument about the lack of need for gentiles to do so. The fact that this does not happen directly until 3:2 is one of the indicators that 2:15ff belongs with 3:2ff as part of the same argument. Paul's strategy is to build an argument about Christian Jews' dependence on Christ, with the aim of then showing that the situation for Christian gentiles is equivalent.

Gal 2:15-16a sets out what Christian Jews know about righteousness, trust, Christ and works of the law. Although Paul appears to begin with Jews in general, 'We, Jews by nature', his statement that 'we trusted in Christ Jesus' (2:16) makes it clear that he only has Christian Jews, such as Peter and himself, in mind. He presents Christian Jews as dependent for righteousness on *pistis Iēsou Christou*, irrespective of their possession of the law. As Chapter 2 of this book argues, this *pistis* is a trust and loyalty relationship with Christ. In 2:19-20, Paul's recounts his experience of death, life, law, Christ and trust, probably as a paradigmatic Christian Jew and, apart from 2:19a, also a paradigmatic Christian in general (Oakes 2015: 94–5). In 2:21, Paul argues that, if law is the basis of righteousness, Christ's death was pointless and that, consequently, acting as though law was the basis of righteousness would be a setting aside of God's grace: 'I do not set aside the grace of God, for if there is righteousness through Law, then Christ died for nothing.'

As we saw earlier, for James Dunn, what Paul sees as being at issue in 2:21 are the events of the Antioch incident: insisting 'that Jew and Gentile should eat separately, was to render invalid the whole gospel' (1993: 147–9). For Dunn, the 'grace of God' in 2:21 is a reference to its manifestation in Paul's calling and mission to the gentiles (147, citing Gal. 1:15; 2:9). Dunn's reading of 2:21 is better contextualized than that of E. P. Sanders, for whom the verse expresses the general soteriological principle of dependence on the death of Christ (1977: 443, 489–90; 1983: 152). Sanders's generalized point makes good sense of 2:20-21 but is less well tailored to 2:21 acting as a conclusion to the whole passage from 2:11 (or from 2:1).

In 3:1, Paul switches focus directly to the Galatians, pointing them to the Cross: 'you to whom Jesus Christ was presented before your very eyes as having been crucified'. This is probably a link back to the reference to Christ's death in 2:21. Paul then works his way from the Galatians' experience of the Spirit through both to being part of Abraham's family and to a configuration of trust and righteousness, apart from law, that is made parallel to the situation ascribed to Christian Jews in 2:16.

In 3:2, Paul's starting point for discussing Christian gentiles is similar to and different from that for Christian Jews. Galatians 3:2, like 2:16, appeals to knowledge in relation to 'works of the law'. There is a rhetorical variation in that whereas Paul asserts his and Peter's knowledge, 'we know that' (2:16), Paul says to the Galatians, ironically, 'I would like to learn from you' (3:2). However, in each case, there is an appeal to something being known and, in each case, the thing known is that something does not, or did not, happen 'by works of law'.

> Just this one thing I want to learn from you: Was it by works of law (ἐξ ἔργων νόμου) that you received the Spirit, or by a message of trust (ἐξ ἀκοῆς πίστεως)? (3:2)

The parallels with 2:16 are the appeal to knowledge, the lack of success of action *ex ergōn nomou* (by works of law) and the contrasting success of action *ek pisteōs* (by trust/loyalty). Paul presents the same negative and positive conditions as applying to both Christian Jews and Christian gentiles.

The difference in Paul's discussion of gentiles is that he begins building his argument from their experience of the Spirit, presumably implying some sort of generally agreed on communal experience. He drives the point home in 3:3-5. They have to admit that their experience of the Spirit followed his preaching of trust in/loyalty to Christ, rather than having followed the arrival of his opponents with their message of circumcision. (Alternatively, if the Galatians were familiar with synagogue life, Paul could conceivably be asking them to reflect on whether the manifestations of the Spirit were present in the house churches or in the synagogues.)

Having used the Galatians' experience of the Spirit to establish a basic knowledge/works/trust parallel between Christian gentiles and Christian Jews, Paul moves the argument further by bringing in Abraham and the issue of righteousness. He first puts the Christian gentiles into Abraham's family by declaring as his children all who share Abraham's characteristic of trust/loyalty, seen in Gen. 15:6.

> Just as Abraham 'trusted (ἐπίστευσεν) God and it was reckoned to him as righteousness', know then that those who are of trust (οἱ ἐκ πίστεως), these are sons of Abraham. (Gal. 3:6-7)

Paul then turns the Abraham link into a way of tying the gentiles further into the language of Gal. 2:16 by making their newly declared relationship with Abraham the basis for a declaration of righteousness.

> The Scripture, seeing beforehand that God considers the gentiles righteous on the basis of trust (ἐκ πίστεως δικαιοῖ τὰ ἔθνη ὁ θεός),

proclaimed the gospel in advance to Abraham, 'In you will all the gentiles be blessed' (2:8).

Paul's argument is that gentiles who come to have trust are thereby children of Abraham, which means they are 'in' Abraham. This fulfils a Genesis 'quotation' (probably an amalgam of Gen. 12:3 and 18:8: Oakes 2015: 105) because Paul takes 'blessed' to be equivalent to 'declared righteous'. Gentiles who are 'of trust' are 'sons of Abraham', therefore 'in Abraham', therefore 'blessed', that is, 'declared righteous'. So the process of Gentiles coming to trust in Christ is what the Scripture saw beforehand in Gen. 12:3/18:8!

Further exegetical fireworks ensue. In biblical terms, if there are blessings, there are likely to be curses facing the other way (paradigmatically in Deuteronomy 27–28). Readers who have kept track of the relationship between 3:2-9 and 2:16 should be able to figure out what Paul will do with the idea of curse. Given that 3:6-9 attaches 'blessing' to being 'of trust' and to 'righteousness' language, 2:16 indicates that Paul is likely to attach curse to being 'of works of law'. This is exactly what he does in 3:10.

It still comes as a shock, because we would be expecting it to be Paul's opponents who would be presenting Scripture as putting Paul and the followers of his 'law-free' gospel under a curse such as Deut. 27:26, which Paul quotes – and his opponents quite likely did make this argument. To get out of this bind, Paul returns to the argument of Gal. 2:16 and reinforces it by asserting that its pattern fits a further scriptural text, Hab. 2:4, and that the combination of this text and Lev. 18:5 shows his opponents' law-based approach to be wrong.

[3:10] For as many as are of works of law are under a curse. For it is written, 'Cursed is every person who does not remain in all the things written in the book of the law, to do them.' [11] Because no one is considered righteous before God by means of law, it is clear that, 'The one who is righteous on the basis of trust will live.' [12] The law is not on the basis of trust: instead, 'The one who does these things will live by means of them.'

Paul refers back, in 3:11, to the conclusion that he sees himself as having already proved in 2:16. In 3:11, he argues that, since righteousness is not established through law, it must be as Habakkuk said – that righteousness, and hence life, comes on the basis of trust/loyalty (for this reading of 3:11, see Chapter 2). Paul then uses Lev. 18:5 to argue that a legal basis is not a trust basis: Habakkuk talks of life through trust/loyalty whereas Leviticus talks of life through action (in obedience to law). The implication is that his opponents' law-based route does not lead to righteousness. Significantly for our current argument, Paul has also now tied the Christian gentiles directly into the pattern of trust and righteousness applied to Christian Jews in 2:16. He has also mirrored the linking of this to 'life' language that was seen in 2:19-20.

Paul's argument in 3:11-12 leaves the issue of curse unanswered, a point especially pertinent to gentiles who would be assumed to fall under the curse as law-breakers. To deal with this, Paul, in another astonishing move, appeals to Deut. 21:23.

> Christ redeemed us from the curse of the law, becoming a curse on our behalf, because it is written, 'Cursed is everyone who hangs on a tree'. (Gal. 3:13)

The effect of the curse being dealt with is that blessing can now come to the gentiles. That enables Paul to tie the strands of the argument of 3:2-14 together.

> So that the blessing of Abraham would come to the gentiles in Christ Jesus, so that we would receive the promise of the Spirit through trust. (3:14)

Through incorporation in Christ, the law-breaking gentiles are no longer cursed, so they can be blessed. This was the blessing promised in connection with Abraham, which turns out to be the Spirit, as experienced by Christians. This has come about through trust (in Christ).

Paul then heads towards the key pay-off, arguing in 3:15-29 that all Christians (in particular, Jews and gentiles) are united in Christ, members of the family of Abraham. Paul begins this by apparently heading in the wrong direction in 3:16.

> The promises were spoken to Abraham and to his seed – it does not say 'and to the seeds', as if to many, but as to one: 'and to your seed' (οὐ λέγει· καὶ τοῖς σπέρμασιν, ὡς ἐπὶ πολλῶν ἀλλ᾽ ὡς ἐφ᾽ ἑνός· καὶ τῷ σπέρματί σου), who is Christ.

In 3:7-8, Paul had gone to some lengths to establish that gentile believers in Christ were 'sons of Abraham', were 'in' Abraham. In 3:14, Paul had described the Spirit as 'the promise' and had paralleled it with 'the blessing of Abraham', which the gentiles had now received. Why does Paul turn round in 3:16 and argue that the Abrahamic promise is not for many people, many descendants, but just for Christ?

The acuteness of the paradox is crucial to Paul's argument: if you are not the 'one', you will not inherit the promise. Christ is one. Being in Christ is being one (this is where Paul will get to in 3:28). Unity is inherent to the structure of the promise. Division, as seen at Antioch, contradicts it.

Paul then makes the point that this principle predates the law of Moses, and therefore cannot be set aside by the law (hence by the kind of legal consideration seen at Antioch). The promise came four hundred years before the law (3:17), and the Abrahamic inheritance was declared as coming through promise, and therefore not through law (3:18). In fact, the law was only enacted because of sins and was only needed until 'the seed' arrived (3:19). Now that 'the seed', Christ, trust/loyalty have arrived, people are no longer under the provisions of the law (3:22-25), the kind of provisions seen in action at Antioch.

Everyone(!) is now a 'son of God' by incorporation into Christ through trust and baptism (3:26-27). Although Paul does not make a point of it, baptism is a socially inclusive commitment ritual, in contrast to his opponents' call for circumcision, a ritual which relates especially to some people and not others (Oakes 2015: 130). Paul then moves to his conclusion,

> There is no Jew nor Greek . . . For you are all 'one' in Christ Jesus. If you (ὑμεῖς, plural) are of Christ, then you are Abraham's seed, heirs according to the promise. (3:28-29)

Being in Christ makes people 'one'. They are united in the 'one' seed of Abraham. Hence, paradoxically, Paul sees himself as able to turn around his argument of 3:16 and declare it as fitting the pattern of the many becoming Abraham's seed.

This completes the strand of argument relating to Abraham, begun in 3:6, which was itself a way of carrying forward the argument of 3:2-5. This argument related Christian gentiles to Abraham, which inherently challenged the division between Christian gentiles and Christian Jews. The presentation of the parallel between Christian gentiles and Christian Jews was reinforced by the range of parallel ideas on law, trust, righteousness and life, and by the reference back to the ideas of 2:16. All this leads towards the conclusion of 3:28-29 which makes unity between Christian Jews and Christian gentiles a defining feature of Christian identity. This, in practice, requires an end to the kind of disunity on view and Antioch and now in danger of reappearing in Galatia.

Paul has made his argument. He has dealt with the key Galatian issue of circumcision, and with the Antioch incident. Why does he mention categories beyond Jew and Greek?

There is no Jew or Greek. There is no slave or free. There is no male and female. For you are all 'one' in Christ Jesus. If you are of Christ, then you are Abraham's seed, heirs according to the promise.

Paul chose to declare that the essential oneness in Christ is not only a matter of Jew-gentile relations. The oneness encompasses all aspects of life. Slavery needed (and still needs) abolishing. However, as well as the problem of the slave system itself, there were also many specific evils that were part of that system. Prejudice and division between free and slave was endemic and, in most cases, extreme. Galatians 3:28, among other things, effectively calls for slaves and free to eat together, in an extension of the principle of Paul's opposition to the division over eating in Antioch. As noted earlier, eating together also carries a range of social and cultural effects. Gender prejudice and division was also endemic in the first century. Gender relations varied, of course, but they were all within a strongly patriarchal social structure. Men eating with women in a context of mutual respect was contrary to much that went on.

Paul's few words widening the scope of oneness in Christ beyond the Jew/gentile polarity make a tremendous difference to the force of his argument for readers who use his text in modern times. He makes it clear that, although he is making his argument in the context of Jew/gentile divisions among Christians, his argument is for unity in diversity in Christ across divisions in general. Although scholars of recent decades have been right in bringing the focus of study of Galatians onto the specifics of the historical setting of the letter as centring on Jew/gentile issues, as against previous generations of scholars who had seen the letter in more abstract theological terms, Paul does not permit the unity in diversity issue to be limited solely to the Jew/gentile division. The context may be Jew/gentile but the unity that Paul argues for extends to a far broader range of polarities.

8. The 'ethical' section of Galatians (5:13–6:10) focuses on love, the key virtue for unity

As noted earlier, many past scholars saw the section of Galatians that dealt in an extended way with moral issues, 5:13–6:10, as facing the opposite direction from the rest of the letter: the early chapters argued for freedom over against legalism; the latter ones pulled back from any extreme application of freedom (libertinism), arguing for love and mutual service. Barclay (1988) modified this by arguing that the 5:13–6:10 section responded to criticisms by Paul's opponents of the moral implications of Paul's arguments against the law. Barclay's recent approach is to see the community building of the latter part of Galatians as being an outworking of thinking intrinsic in Paul's theology of the gift. The present chapter, too, argues that, far from facing in the opposite direction from the earlier part of the letter, 5:13–6:10 is an outworking of its theology. However, the chapter is also suggesting that 5:13–6:10 is, to a significant extent, a continuation of the letter's core argumentative aim, in support of unity in diversity in Christ.

A first indicator that Paul is doing this comes in the way that Gal. 5:5-6 links together the discourse of 2:11–3:29 with what will come in 5:13–6:10.

> For we, by the Spirit, by trust, eagerly await the hope of righteousness.
> For in Christ Jesus neither circumcision matters, nor uncircumcision,
> but trust, working through love.

A surprisingly full set of terminology from Galatians 2–3 is brought back in here. The conclusion of 3:28 is restated in terms of a circumcision/uncircumcision difference. The statement leads through to the new term, 'love'. Broadly speaking, 5:6 is a restatement of Paul's call for unity: community members should be united in love, rather than divided by circumcision issues as at Antioch.

After a brief tirade against his opponents for the damage they are causing among the Galatians, Paul develops the theme of love at length, beginning in 5:13.

> Only, do not make freedom an opportunity for the flesh, but through
> love be slaves to one another.

In the subsequent passage, Paul repeatedly puts love in the context of the threat of disunity. In 5:14-15 he directly contrasts love with division.

> 'You shall love your neighbour as yourself.' But if you bite and devour
> one another, watch out in case you are destroyed by one another.

The 'fruit of the Spirit', headed by love (5:22), is set off against the 'works of the flesh' (5:19-21). As de Boer observes, of the fifteen 'works' that are listed, more than half are in the area of 'communal discord' (2011: 358–9).

Enmities, strife, jealousy, angers, selfish ambitions, divisions, sects, envies. (5:20-21)

Having begun this section on love with a warning about division, he ends in a similar way.

Let us not be full of empty glory, provoking one another, envying one another. (5:26)

As well as love being set up in contrast to disunity, there is a more complex set of lexical and conceptual interrelationships that link 5:13–6:10 into the main argument of the letter. These revolve around the way in which the contrast between love and division is enmeshed with a contrast between Spirit and 'flesh', then with the way in which 'works' and 'law' are brought into the passage.

The Spirit represented the distinguishing experience of the Galatian Christians that provided Paul with his route into arguing directly about Christian gentile existence. In 3:2-5, he set up the route to that experience as being through his message of trust/loyalty, in contrast to 'works of law'. He set up the experience itself as a mode of existence in contrast to flesh (3:3). After 5:13–6:10, Paul will also characterize his opponents as seeking 'to make a good showing in flesh' (6:12).

In 5:13, Christians are directed away from 'flesh' towards love. In 5:16-17, life by the Spirit is emphatically contrasted with life oriented towards flesh. 'The works of the flesh' are a list of qualities that would widely have been seen as negative, including the eight connected with division (5:19-21). 'The fruit of the Spirit' is a list of positive qualities headed by love and with several other socially cohesive ones (5:22-23). The flesh has been crucified by Christians, and they are called to live by Spirit (5:24-25), in contrast with provoking each other (5:26). Unexpectedly, in 5:13–6:10, the law is not simply a negative factor paralleled with either flesh or 'works'. Love fulfils 'all the law' (5:14). Life in the Spirit means not being 'under law' (5:18). Bearing each other's burdens fulfils 'the law of Christ' (6:2).

Unity is far from being the only topic of 5:13–6:10. Although many of the extended points and individual sayings do have a tendency towards group cohesion, there is also spread of other topics, ranging from idolatry (5:20) to humility (5:23; 6:1), although none is developed at any length. There is also a drive towards doing good, both to Christians and to those beyond the community, that brings the section to a close.

The way in which 5:13–6:10 reinforces Paul's main argument in the letter is subtle but present. In 5:5-6, those living by the Spirit, trusting, incorporated in Christ – all of which Paul sees as characteristics of Galatians who are faithful to his gospel – are directed towards love, as a contrast to the circumcision/uncircumcision distinction. From 5:13 onwards, their life in the Spirit is presented as producing love and virtue, whereas the life of the 'flesh' – the life to which the Galatians have been drawn by Paul's opponents (3:3) – produces various forms of evil, especially those associated with division. Paul has lined up his gospel and its followers with the Spirit, love, self-control (5:23) and virtue, while lining up his opponents' message with flesh, disunity, passions (5:24) and vices. He has also undercut his opponents' arguments by presenting the Spirit-led outcome of his gospel as a fulfilment of law (this does take us back to Barclay 1988). This rhetoric all works so effectively because, although unity is not the dominant topic of 5:13–6:10, love is particularly prominent, and love lines up especially well as a characteristic of Paul's unity message, as we saw in his use of it in 5:5-6.

We can also read 5:13–6:10 in terms of experience. Just as, in 3:2-5, the Galatians are reminded that Paul's message brought their experience of the Spirit, so, in 5:13-24 in particular, they are reminded that that Spirit-led life, brought about through Paul's message, had actually produced in them a loving communal life, a life that was now being damaged by the effects of the message of Paul's opponents.

9. The letter ends by returning to the key unity in diversity issue: 'neither circumcision nor uncircumcision' (6:15)

The end section of Galatians (6:11-18) returns the focus explicitly onto the situation facing the Galatians. Paul attacks those who are promoting circumcision (6:11-13) and distinguishes his outlook from theirs (6:14). Two points in particular indicate that, in this end section, he is returning to the key issue as being one of unity in diversity.

The first is subtle and has been partly discussed earlier. When Paul characterizes his opponents in 6:12-13, he does so in terms that present them as parallel to Peter in the Antioch incident. Paul's opponents are those who 'are compelling you to be circumcised' (6:12); Peter was 'compelling the gentiles to Judaize' (2:14). Paul's opponents do not 'keep the law themselves' (6:13); Peter 'used to eat together with the gentiles' (2:12) and is characterized alongside Paul as having 'been found to be sinners' (2:17). Paul's opponents promote circumcision 'only so that they would not be persecuted' (6:12); Paul presents the driver for Peter's actions at Antioch as being 'when they [certain people from James] came, he used to draw back and to separate himself, fearing those of circumcision' (2:12). All in all, Paul's opponents are presented in 6:12-13 as being hypocrites, a charge specifically made by Paul about the behaviour of Peter and others at Antioch (2:13).

There has been progression in Paul's argument through the course of the letter. For instance, by the end of it, Paul has shifted his main attacks away from his Galatian hearers and towards his opponents. He has also moved to describing, relatively directly, what his opponents are advocating, whereas earlier in the letter his approach to that was more oblique. However, as well as progression there is also repetition and reinforcement. Paul's opponents and the situation that the Galatians are facing may be more directly described in 6:12-13, but the opponents and situation are still being characterized in terms of the Antioch incident. Galatians 6:12-13 talks about circumcision, but it does so by using patterns from the incident about Christian Jews and Christian gentiles not eating together. The ending of the letter still takes us back to Antioch.

The second indicator is more straightforward. The endpoint of Paul's final burst of argument in 6:12-15 is another restatement of 3:28. Galatians 6:15 essentially restates 5:6 but with a different conclusion. Galatians 5:6 did the same for 3:28. The degree to which unity in diversity in Christ is a central issue for Galatians is indicated here both by the final argument ending with it and by the fact that the letter now contains three statements of the same point, all of which are rhetorically crafted for maximum impact and all of which are placed at rhetorically climactic points.

> There is no Jew nor Greek. There is no slave nor free. There is no male and female. For you are all 'one' in Christ Jesus. (3:28)

> For in Christ Jesus neither circumcision matters, nor uncircumcision, but trust, working through love. (5:6)

> For neither circumcision is anything, nor is uncircumcision, but new creation is. (6:15)

10. Conclusions

Because of all that has intervened since Paul's day, it is very hard for us to imagine his viewpoint. He was a first-century Jew. He believed that the

Messiah had come and that, although the Messiah was now in heaven, he was still present through the action of the Spirit and that people could be incorporated in the Messiah through trust in/loyalty to him. Paul believed that the Messiah had come not only to save Jews from the present evil age but also to do this for the other peoples of the world. Paul believed that incorporation in the Messiah was the way to bring unity between all people. From Paul's perspective, this primarily meant unity between Jew and gentile, but he also believed it to be true of other binaries such as slave/free and male/female.

We live centuries later, at a time when the early Christian movement has evolved into various institutional forms of Christianity, many of which in turn have become linked with other institutions such as nation states. We live at a time after the development of Rabbinic Judaism, as a way of life which, among other things, is defined over against Christianity. We live after generations of Christians persecuting Jews: both Christian Jews and non-Christian Jews. The churches forgot Paul's 'nor uncircumcision'. They made 'uncircumcision' a defining mark of Christianity, misapplying Gal. 5:2 to Jews when it was intended only as a ban on gentile circumcision. The result drove the Jewish voice out of churches, using Paul's text to frustrate Paul's vision of Christian diversity. The term 'Christian Jew' would be seen by most people today, Jews and non-Jews, as an oxymoron.

We live conscious of a world of many religions, aware of the fact that, for most adherents, religious identity is a key component of their identity as a whole and aware of the fact that most of these religious identities are viewed as being incompatible with Christian belief and practice.

All this means that, in most places in the world, it is only in churches that the Pauline vision of unity in diversity in Christ is immediately relevant. However, this sphere is still significant for billions of people. In this sphere, the issue of unity in diversity is crucial, especially in terms of the experience of those who are excluded or marginalized. It is an issue that merits careful consideration and, for those who buy into this vision, action.

CHAPTER 7
CONCLUSION
Andrew K. Boakye

Galatians, unlike its thematic counterpart Romans, provides readers with sufficient internal evidence to construct a reasonably lucid portrait of the *Sitz im Leben*. More subtly, it hints at how Paul's resolution of the issues disrupting the Galatian Jesus assemblies are connected to the broader redemptive-historical narrative of which the death and resurrection of the Messiah are central components. The chapters in this volume are concerned with shedding fresh light on how the issues 'on the ground' are connected to Paul's revised Christocentric salvific scheme and, thus, how the letter as a whole informs his broader vision.

This broader vision, as our subtitle intimates, is captured by a revolutionary oneness which Paul deems possible because people experience a new mode of life, founded upon trust in the risen Jesus. As Kim has suggested, Paul may well have considered himself an apostle, eschatological herald and decisive agent or instrument for God's plan of salvation for gentiles and Jews and even developed the scheme by interpreting the Damascus revelation through Isaiah and other prophetic texts (2012: 24). It was Johannes Munck (1959) who perhaps most famously argued that Paul's evangelization of the non-Jewish world stemmed from a deeper concern for how Israel herself stood before Yahweh. As early as John Chrysostom commenting on Rom. 15:10, writers have tried to explain Paul's all-encompassing vision of oneness (John Chrysostom, *Homilies on Romans* 28). There may have been reasons somewhat closer to home driving Paul to conceive of united human family. In the letter to the Romans, Paul depicts another, retrograde kind of unity – a humanity united in its subservience to death because of Adam's rebellion (Rom. 5:12-21) and, therefore, unified in its estrangement from God (Rom. 3:9-18). Whether possessing the Law or not (Rom. 2:12), humankind exhibits all the social trademarks of dislocation from God (Rom. 1:18-32; 2:17-29). In this hostility towards God, all people shared a common platform – Jew and gentile alike were equally adrift (Rom. 3:23). The Apostle may well also have pondered the unity forged under Imperial rule in the so-called *Pax Romana*; in all his travels, he saw different nationalities under Rome's headship and the relative political stability that had existed throughout the Mediterranean since the time of Augustus. He certainly knew of Imperial propaganda of the Roman peace, despite the apparent contempt he had for its genuineness (1 Thess. 5:3). While we may but speculate about the precise origins of Paul's conviction (to which I will briefly return at the end), he saw authentic oneness existing only in relational *pistis* with the living Messiah. The many nations over whom Abraham would eschatologically preside (Gen. 17:5; 18:18) began with his trust in the divine promise of Isaac's life, even though it was physically unfeasible. God would accept all people into right, reconciled relationship with him, if they would trust in the same way; to do this was to trust in the resurrected Messiah. This story underpins Galatians such that a narrative of unity punctuates its pages, as W. S. Campbell intimates:

> Indeed, Galatians opens with allusions to the unity of the gospel itself (1:6-9) as well as the unity of the Gentile mission under Paul's apostleship (1:10-24) and the unity of the church leaders in accepting Paul's authority with respect to the Gentile mission (2:1-10). Those who would upset the oneness of the gospel, Paul's leadership in preaching it, or the gospel's implications for the unity of Christ-believers are to be cursed (1:7-9) and opposed (2:4-5). (2013: 229)

As has been expressed in the book, although the authors are not primarily concerned with narratology, the arguments presented here rely on a sensitivity to the 'backstory' which Paul's polemic assumes. At the epicentre of this back narrative is the risen Christ, alive and in relationship with the Galatian disciples.

The risen Christ relates to the Christ believers through *pistis* – a trust characterized by a lifestyle of loyalty. The ubiquitous Pauline designation of believers being 'in Christ' depicts their comprehensive relationship with the living Christ. A number of theorists have suggested what exactly Paul is attempting to summarize with the term; for Deissmann (1912), 'in Christ' language was a resonance of the Damascus Christophany and pointed initially to Paul's (and by extension all Christians') sense of mystical closeness to the risen Jesus. It was to be understood literally as a locative dative term (139–40). Schweitzer (1931) famously pressed the idea of mystical union further to suggest that being 'in Christ' referred to disciples continually experiencing the death and resurrection of Jesus – a suggestion finding potential support in 2 Cor. 4:10 (1931: 225; cf. Stewart 1935: 147). Hans Conzelmann utterly rejected the mystical reading of ἐν Χριστῷ, seeing rather a reference to the 'objective saving work' of Christ (1969: 209–10; Bultmann had earlier over-simplistically, albeit not wholly inaccurately, reduced the term to a metaphor for 'Christian'; 1951: 311). Many have opted for some manner of participatory formula; Sanders emphasizing that participation in Christ's suffering was central to being 'in Christ' (1977: 447, 505–6) and Gorman arguing persuasively that being in Christ is being caught up into his body and sharing in his narrative of death and covenant faithfulness to God (2019: 28). Oakes goes considerably beyond earlier and current scholarship demonstrating that this relational function of the risen Christ is the heartbeat of the Christology of Galatians.

Sophisticated forays into the use of *pistis* in ancient religious and secular literature have gone some way in establishing what Paul meant by it. Hay has shown how in Hellenized Jewish literature, *pistis* implies the 'objective basis for faith' and that Paul could have employed such a reading (1989: 461–76). Teresa Morgan's landmark study of *pistis* and *fides* treats Paul's usages of the former as an attempt at a three-way relational dynamic by which it is 'precisely the fact that Christ is both faithful to God and worthy of God's trust, trustworthy by human beings and trusted by them, that enables him to take those who *pisteuein* into righteousness' (2015: 274). N. Gupta acutely observes how

πίστις functions for Paul anthropologically, epistemologically, and socially as the way believers relate to God through the Christ-relation, which is necessarily thoughtful and participatory (socially, volitionally, existentially, etc.). (2019: 189)

Sierksma-Agteres reads Pauline *pistis* language against the backdrop of the ancient Mediterranean moral praxis of imitation, and particularly in the philosophical topos of assimilation to God. She argues that the chain of mimesis between philosophical masters and their succession of students is a model for understanding how *pistis* (and particularly *pistis Christou*) represents the imitation of Christ in order to become like God (Sierksma-Agteres 2016: 119–53).

M. Bates argues that the culmination of the gospel is the enthronement of Messiah and, as such, *pistis* ought to be understood as 'allegiance'. His reasoning lies in the Pauline emphasis on the gospel bringing about the practical obedience characteristic of allegiance to a king – what Bates refers to as 'enacted allegiance' (2017: 86). In Hagen-Pifer's exegetical synthesis of 'righteousness' and 'participation' in Pauline thought, she notes that faith is 'the means by which the Christ-event envelops believers as his life attaches to those who trust in him' (2019: 156).

Oakes demonstrates that the Christ of Galatians is not primarily presented in *pistis* relation to God, but to people. Oakes further demonstrates how this is also borne out in the references to *pistis Christou*. The current war of words over the term probably originates from the end of the nineteenth century and Johannes Haußleiter's declaration in support of the subjective genitive reading that

> Ich behaupte, die Empfänger und ersten Leser des Briefes konnten die Worte unmöglich in dem Sinne verstehen 'rechtfertigend den, der aus dem Glauben an Jesus ist. (1891: 109–45)

> [I maintain that the recipients and first readers of the letter could not possibly understand the words in the sense of 'justifying him whose faith is in Jesus.] (Boakye's translation)

Shortly after, Prescott Jernegan (1896) attempted a reading connecting human and divine agency. Human faith was a derivative of Christ's own faith, and, as such

> faith in Christ is, then, neither wholly ethical nor mystical. Evoked by authority, confirmed by reason, 'working by love', it becomes a life from God in which there are but two pulsations; the one Christ revealing himself, the other the believer, confessing Christ. (202)

Richard Hays most forcefully revived the debate and there has been considerable support for reading the term as a subjective genitive, but this underplays what is very apparent in the Christological statements in Galatians – Christ lives, loves and acts on behalf of people loyal to him and to whom he reciprocates that loyalty.

This living Christ is also the focal point of prophetic redemption eschatology. Embedded in the prophetic foretelling of deliverance from captivity, rescue from exile, revival from suppression or liberation from domination within Israel's turbulent political history, is a recurring narrative descriptor – the story of new life emerging from death. The metaphorical new life formulations in Israel's scriptures signified moments in her history where only direct divine intervention could reverse some sociopolitical disaster (as I have previously argued in Boakye 2017: 30). In light of the literal death-to-life event of Jesus's resurrection, these texts took on fresh significance for Paul and furnished his arguments with a unique impetus. Paul may well have had to counter the presupposed scriptural position of his adversaries who infiltrated Galatia (as many postulate; e.g., Stanley 2004: 120; Hietanen 2007: 102; Das 2016: 23–4) or had to use scripture in some way to issue a 'guilty verdict' on his opponents to justify marginalizing them (Martin 1995: 461), forcing Paul's hand into employing a scriptural rhetoric, but this cannot be the whole story. It partially explains which texts he appeals to, but not why he contextualizes them in the fashion he does. It is insufficient to suggest that he simply offered his own spin on the same texts his opponents employed (not least of all because he interprets some passages in a conventional manner, such as Lev. 19:18 in Gal. 5:14, and some intertexts, e.g. Deut. 21:23, do not appear to serve the objectives of either Paul or his interlocutors in any unambiguous way – something else must have driven Paul's intertextual methodologies). More thoroughgoing and persuasive schemes for explaining Pauline recourse to the Bible in Galatians are not uncommon (Bonneau 1997: 62–5; Garlington 1997: 86; Silva 2001: 253–5). The lack of any real mention of the resurrection of Jesus in Galatians, however, detracts from the significance of the living, risen Christ when scholars consider Paul's recourse to the Bible. Paul understood scripture through the lens of the risen Christ; he quoted it to demonstrate how the manifestations of new life in scripture prefigured the reanimating energy of the risen Christ. To this end, the narratives of Isaac's birth and the liberation of God's people from captivity to pagans prefigured the resurrection of Jesus. The resurrection, in turn, modelled the ontological dynamics of the justification of the faithful. These components are the interconnected elements of a biblical theology of new life.

It is not just Paul's appeal to Scripture which exhibits the centrality of new life emerging from death, that is, revivification, in Galatians. The notion is deeply embedded in the polemic of the letter itself. Paul described Jesus as

τοῦ δόντος ἑαυτὸν ὑπὲρ τῶν ἁμαρτιῶν ἡμῶν, ὅπως ἐξέληται ἡμᾶς ἐκ τοῦ αἰῶνος τοῦ ἐνεστῶτος πονηροῦ.

[*the one giving himself on behalf* of our sins, so as to rescue us from the age of the present evil.] (Gal. 1:4; Boakye's translation; emphasis added)

Later (in the context of his personal experience of the risen Jesus), he is described as τοῦ ἀγαπήσαντός με καὶ *παραδόντος ἑαυτὸν ὑπὲρ ἐμοῦ.*

[the one having loved me and *given himself over* on my *behalf.*] (Gal. 2:20c; Boakye's translation)

The italicized sections show Paul's thought process; Jesus had achieved in Paul specifically what he had come to do for the world at large. As such, the Apostle can write ζῶ δὲ οὐκέτι ἐγώ, ζῆ δὲ ἐν ἐμοὶ Χριστός· ὃ δὲ νῦν ζῶ ἐν σαρκί, ἐν πίστει ζῶ τῇ τοῦ υἱοῦ τοῦ θεοῦ. Paul was alive in an unprecedented way, alive because the risen Christ enlivened him – this was his rescue from the age of the present evil. If readers consider the very similar statement about believing gentiles – those having 'crucified' the 'flesh' because they are 'of Christ' and now 'alive' by virtue of the Spirit (Gal. 5:24-25) – the motif becomes even more explicit. It reaches full bloom in Gal. 6:14-15; through the cross of Christ, the cosmos itself had suffered crucifixion with respect to Paul, as he had indeed suffered crucifixion in relation to it (outlined earlier in the letter in 2:19). On this basis (γὰρ at the beginning of 6:15), Paul discounts the external markers of Jewish/non-Jewish identity, for the only significant entity is what has been 'newly created' (*kainē ktisis*). In other words, that which emerged from the crucified cosmos and in which such ethnic boundaries can no longer pose a threat to the oneness of God's family.

My co-author and I agree that one of Paul's key objectives in his appeal to the Galatians was to ratify authentic unity within socio-ethnic diversity in the community. Paul pursues this by directly addressing the intra-ecclesiological breakdown of communications instigated by the troublemakers. In Oakes's reading, Paul developed a counter-polemical strategy against his opponents' attempt to bully gentiles into being circumcised. In so doing, Paul transposed his argument into an appeal for unity. In the same move, he also challenged the pseudo-gospel of the agitators which posed a substantive threat to church unity; not only did gentiles need to resist circumcision, but believing Jews and gentiles needed to live in reciprocal *agape* without either party surrendering ground on the basis of ethnicity (Gal. 5:6; 6:15) or manufacturing an artificial unity based on the sort of assimilationist cultural blending Rome usually promoted (Leppä 2012: 69; Ehrensperger 2016: 197–201). As such, in the reading of Oakes, establishing this unity is Paul's most pressing concern. Oakes thus bookends the declaration of unity in Christ in Gal. 3:26-29 with the narrative of disunity relayed in Gal. 2:11-14, and so the central argument of the letter runs between these sections.

As per the conclusion of Gal. 3:28, Paul's desire for unity within diversity among the faithful extended beyond ethnic harmony. In reflecting on how the verse informs egalitarian male-female partnership in the community, Cooney states:

> When human differences are accepted and respected, then they will not be lived in unacceptable ways with which we are only too familiar. Rather, they will be embraced so that they are meant to be enriching in any local Christian community rather than a source of division. (2008: 102)

Similarly, Lo gives vent to how unity is both a matter of interpretation of Paul's theological outlook and a new social reality, noting that with Gal. 3:28

> Paul is not suggesting, [then], that there are no differences in social reality, but there should be a new kind of equality and unity that is lifted from social reality to a new level of relationship and values. In Christ there is a new reality. The social reality and theological interpretation are not demarcated, then, in Paul's mind. (2009: 193)

In my own reading, establishing this precious unity was a mammoth task for Paul; the socio-ethnic unity he sought for the Galatian Jesus assemblies was intended to be a microcosm of the same unity within the New Covenant people of God. As such, Paul had to outline a basis for a unity between believers as profound and compelling as the Torah was for the unity of Israel. Paul determined that the basis for true unity in diversity is the new life of the resurrected Christ, which is mediated by the Spirit. The Law, being powerless to generate and mediate this life (Gal. 3:21) and having been given to Israel and not to the nations (Gal. 3:19-20), could not be the index of a multi-ethnic unity. The Law rather pointed to this new life and to the trust (*pistis*) which would instigate it. Christian Jews and gentiles experienced 'death' by co-crucifixion with the Messiah as a precursor to rebirth (Gal. 2:19-20; 5:24-25). Death in Paul's arguments often referred to something other than the end of physical life – it was a conceptually loaded idea like the Stoics, who concluded that hedonists and those closed off to knowledge were 'dead' (Seneca, *Lucil.* 60.4; Epictetus, *Discourses* 1.13.5). In Galatians, when in reference to people other than Jesus (1:1; 2:21), death (particularly death by co-crucifixion, which links the death to the death of Jesus) is an eschatological terminus and the precursor for revivification and righteousness.

Disambiguating how Paul perceived the role of the Law relies on unravelling the clearest statement he makes regarding its restrictions – its inability to revivify related in Gal. 3:21. Two other associated quandaries are the meaning of Spirit in 3:14 and contextualization of restoration eschatology linked with the prophetic New Covenant texts. Objections to all three positions are predictable – some may challenge the hermeneutic weight being placed on Gal. 3:21; some may wish to limit the scope of Spirit in 3:14 to a motif signalling the new age (Isa. 44:3; Joel 2:28-32); the absence of explicit intertextual links with Jeremiah or Ezekiel in Galatians may also be cause for question. To the first objection, I reiterate both that nowhere is such a direct answer given as to Torah's limitations (not even in Romans 7, Paul's most sustained treatment of the place of Torah) and that the text is corroborated by Gal. 2:19-20 and 3:11-12. To the second, I would suggest that the presence of the Spirit as an eschatological signpost is attested in Gal. 3:3-5; the salient issue in Gal. 3:14 is how Paul attributes the designation 'Spirit' to the promise given to Abraham. To the final objection I would argue that (1) Paul is clearly versed in the contours of the New Covenant prophecies (1 Cor. 11:25; 2 Cor 3:6); (2) he is certainly cognizant of the salient texts (Jer. 31:1, 9; Ezek. 37:27, cited in 2 Cor. 6:17); and (3) Galatians has in its narrative foreground a story of new life emerging from deadness marking the definitive liberation from captivity, in a moment instigated by the Spirit, by which God's people would experience a revolutionary ability to engage with the divine will. Consequently, Paul's story of justification and Ezekiel's story of restoration have an almost irresistible shared theological-narrative core.

Of course, the thrust of Gal. 3:21 is that God never intended to give a written Law that could generate life, and so the Law was never intended to justify humanity. This leaves open the question of God's intention for giving the Law at all (Gal. 3:19a). It seems that in the Apostle Paul's theologizing, such a question could only be accurately addressed retroactively, in light of God's work in the Messiah. Ezekiel pre-empted the day when Yahweh would place his Spirit in his people (Ezek. 37:14; cf. 36:27), causing them to be uniquely responsive to his ordinances (Ezek. 37:24; cf. 36:27). There is general scholarly consensus that this moment of Spirit internalization in Ezekiel corresponds to the tenet of Jeremiah's New Covenant portrait (Jer. 31:33) which describes the inscription of the Law on the hearts of the people (Block 1989: 39; Woodhouse 1991: 17). Once again, looking through the retrospective lens of the Messiah's death and resurrection, and the Spirit activity amid the believing congregations in Galatia (Gal. 3:2-5), Paul could determine that the New Covenant blessings were being realized and the community's ethical praxis supervised by the Spirit.

At the beginning of these concluding thoughts, I proposed that Galatians goes some way towards allowing Paul to refract the intercommunity issues through the prism of his broader redemptive-historical vision, reshaped as this had been by the resurrection of Jesus. The issues in question involve a schism, or at least potential schism, along a particular fault line involving a party of gentiles persuaded by a rival doctrine. This doctrine had at its heart the question of whether non-Jewish people needed to embrace Jewish cultic practices in order to be inducted into the people of God. Paul's unambiguous response was that gentiles were in no way so obliged; however, in the melee, believers were ready to 'bite and devour' one another over their differences (Gal. 5:15), and Paul's epistle had to challenge the falsity of the competing claims, restore calm and explain why a social, non-hierarchical oneness in the community now was the only valid precursor for the eschatological salvation to come. The Law's purpose was not to bring humankind into right relation to God; the Law's objectives would be met when community *agape*, triggered by the Spirit (Gal. 5:14, 22), became the insignia of all believers, irrespective of their socio-ethnic categorization.

Paul's ambitious egalitarian vision, summed up in the so-called charter of unity in Gal. 3:28, was his rendition of the outworking of the promise to Abraham that all the nations would be blessed in him (Gen. 18:18). In some fashion, Christ-directed *pistis* was the bedrock of the entire enterprise. However, we can, of course, only speculate how indebted the Christology of Galatians is to the messianic beliefs Paul held before the Damascus Christophany and his association with the ancient Jesus movement. M. Hengel, R. Martin and others are likely correct to posit that knowing Paul's 'pre-Jesus movement' worldview is essential to understanding his later approach to life and mission. Consequently, interpreters are at something of a disadvantage trying to comprehend what led to this vision of oneness (Hengel 1991; Martin 1993: 5–102). There is some scant evidence that Paul may have exercised a circumcising mission to gentiles before he joined the Jesus movement, for example, Gal. 5:11 (D. Campbell 2011: 325–47; cf. Hardin 2013: 145–63). Paul may well have been a representative of the Jewish contingent who believed that gentiles could share in the blessings of salvation by joining Israel, and only altered the bounds of this conviction as a result of Damascus and accepting Jesus as Messiah (Donaldson 2006: 275–92). Perhaps, as Boyarin suggests, Paul's dream of a Platonic unity that transcended hierarchy and difference could be realized in Christ (1994: 7;

the all-embracing question of cosmic unity and how the many might originate from the one was a preoccupation of the so-called Pre-Socratic philosophers. From Thales who reckoned the great 'oneness' to be water, or Heraclitus who saw it as fire, to the extreme monism of Parmenides who considered multiplicity to be a sensory illusion, the unity of all things under one was a pressing ancient question). Paul may well have had an uneasy conscience about the seeming exclusion of gentiles and viewed the revelation of the risen Christ as the resolution (Davies 1948: 63). If Paul's 'zeal' for defending Torah (Gal. 1:13-14) truly echoed the tradition of Phinehas's zeal (Num. 25:7-11; Ps. 106:30-31; *Sir.* 45:23; *1 Macc.* 2:26, 54), then it is difficult to imagine that he had not been ruminating upon the position of gentiles in the divine economy long before his call to evangelize.

Further evidence, albeit both meagre and exegetically cumbersome, may exist in Gal. 3:19c-20 and receive support from Rom. 3:29-31. The Galatians text reads:

διαταγεὶς δι' ἀγγέλων ἐν χειρὶ μεσίτου. 20 ὁ δὲ μεσίτης ἑνὸς οὐκ ἔστιν, ὁ δὲ θεὸς εἷς ἐστιν.

[having been ratified through angels in the hand of a mediator. 20 And the mediator is not of one, but God is one.] (Boakye's translation)

The Law had been ratified through angels in the hand of a mediator – while there can be little doubt that Moses is in view here, it is the nature of the giving of Torah that is critical, and so Paul wisely does not name him. This is confirmed in v. 20 where the article defines him – he is the mediator. The mediator is not of one – but of one what? The key lies in the awkward clause in Gal. 3:16, and the lexical marker is ἑνός. There, the promises to Abraham were not spoken to him and to Israel (the many, represented by the ὡς ἐπὶ πολλῶν), but to Abraham and one (i.e. the one seed, represented by the ὡς ἐφ' ἑνός). In other words, it is in the 'one' that the promises would ultimately be fulfilled. The mediator is not of 'one multi-ethnic family'; he is only of the one ethnic family Israel. Hence, the next clause is critical – ὁ δὲ θεὸς εἷς ἐστιν (Gal. 3:20b) – echoing the very rallying cry of ethnic Israel: Ἄκουε, Ισραηλ, κύριος ὁ θεὸς ἡμῶν κύριος εἷς ἐστιν (Deut. 6:4). There is one God over all humanity, and not one deity for Jews and another for non-Jews, and so all must be brought together in the one. This 'bringing together' was prefigured in the moment of Abraham's *pistis* resulting in Isaac's life; it was fulfilled in the moment of people's *pistis* in relation to the risen Christ resulting in the new life. It is this scheme I suggest is corroborated in Rom. 3:29-31 (Rom. 3:30 contains the refrain εἷς ὁ θεὸς) and the picture filled out in Rom. 4:16-25.

Indeed, it is within this ideological matrix that Peter Oakes and I have moments of convergence and disagreement about Galatians and Paul's broader missiological enterprise. We cannot see into the Apostle's mind, but we can detect where he lays emphasis and paint a portrait of his objectives around it. In so doing, Oakes sees in Paul a Messianic believer committed to the divine ideal of the universal brotherhood and sisterhood of humankind in Christ, and one ready to go into religious combat to defend the ideal and protect it from corruption. I see in Paul a frustrated and zealous Yahwist whose world has been rocked by a present time resurrection – one that has caused him to rethink, reorder and reshape his social world, inherited tradition and God-given purpose around it. At key moments, what we both see in Paul and in Galatians coalesces. It is our shared hope that in this volume, readers can interpret these moments to illuminate their own understanding of Paul's vision.

REFERENCES

Abegg, Martin G. (1999). '4QMMT C 27, 31 and "Works Righteousness"'. *Dead Sea Discoveries* 6.2 (Studies in Qumran Law): 139–47.

Adeyemi, Femi (2006). 'The New Covenant Law and the Law of Christ'. *BibSac* 163: 438–52.

Alexander, T. Desmond (1997). 'Further Observations on the Term "Seed" in Genesis'. *Tyndale Bulletin* 48: 363–7.

Allen, Leslie C. (2008). *Jeremiah: A Commentary*. Louisville, KY: Westminster John Knox.

Allison Jr, Dale C. (2010). *Constructing Jesus: Memory, Imagination, and History*. Grand Rapids, MI: Baker Academic.

Aris, R. (1969). 'St. Paul's Use of the Old Testament in the Letter to the Galatians'. *Journal of the Christian Brethren Research Fellowship* 17: 9–13.

Badiou, Alain (2003). *Saint Paul: The Foundation of Universalism*. Translated by Ray Brassier. Stanford: Stanford University Press.

Barclay, John M. G. (1986). 'Paul and the Law: Observations on Some Recent Debates'. *Themelios* 12: 5–15.

Barclay, John M. G. (1988). *Obeying the Truth: A Study of Paul's Ethics in Galatians*. Studies in the New Testament and Its World. Edinburgh: T&T Clark.

Barclay, John M. G. (2014). 'Grace and the Countercultural Reckoning of Worth: Community Construction in Galatians 5–6'. In *Galatians and Christian Theology: Justification, the Gospel, and Ethics in Paul's Letter*, edited by Mark W. Elliott, Scott J. Hafemann, N. T. Wright and John Frederick, 306–17. Grand Rapids, MI: Baker Academic.

Barclay, John M. G. (2015). *Paul and the Gift*. Grand Rapids, MI: Eerdmans.

Barth, Karl (1968). *The Epistle to the Romans*. Oxford: Oxford University Press.

Bates, Matthew W. (2017). *Salvation by Allegiance Alone: Rethinking Faith, Works, and the Gospel of Jesus the King*. Grand Rapids, MI: Baker Academic.

Bates, Matthew W. (2019). *Gospel Allegiance: What Faith in Jesus Misses for Salvation in Christ*. Grand Rapids, MI: Brazos.

Baur, F. C. (1876). *Paul the Apostle of Jesus Christ: His Life and Work, his Epistles and his Doctrine*. Translated by E. Zeller, revised by A. Menzies. London: Williams & Norgate.

Bayes, Jonathan F. (2000). *The Weakness of the Law: God's Law and the Christian in New Testament Perspective*. Milton Keynes: Paternoster.

Beale, Gregory K. (2005). 'The Old Testament Background of Paul's Reference to "the Fruit of the Spirit" in Galatians 5:22'. *Bulletin for Biblical Research* 15: 1–38.

Beale, Gregory K. (2011). *A New Testament Biblical Theology: The Unfolding of the Old Testament in the New*. Grand Rapids, MI: Baker Academic.

References

Betz, Hans Dieter (1979). *Galatians: A Commentary on Paul's Letter to the Churches in Galatia*. Hermeneia. Philadelphia, PA: Fortress.

Bird, Michael F. (2003). '"Raised for Our Justification": A Fresh Look at Romans 4:25'. *Colloquium* 35: 31–46.

Bird, Michael F. (2007). *The Saving Righteousness of God: Studies on Paul, Justification and the New Perspective*. Eugene, OR: Wipf & Stock.

Bird, Michael F. (2016). *An Anomalous Jew: Paul among Jews, Greeks, and Romans*. Grand Rapids, MI: Eerdmans.

Bird, Michael F., and Preston M. Sprinkle, eds. (2009). *The Faith of Jesus Christ: Exegetical, Biblical, and Theological Studies*. Milton Keynes: Paternoster.

Black II, C. Clifton (1984). 'Pauline Perspectives on Death in Romans 5–8'. *Journal of Biblical Literature* 103: 413–33.

Bligh, J. (1969). *Galatians: A Discussion of St. Paul's Epistle*. London: St Paul.

Block, Daniel I. (1989). 'The Prophet of the Spirit: The Use of *RWḤ* in the Book of Ezekiel'. *Journal of the Evangelical Theological Society* 32: 27–49.

Block, Daniel I. (1992). 'Beyond the Grave: Ezekiel's Vision of Death and Afterlife'. *Bulletin for Biblical Research* 2: 113–41.

Boakye, Andrew K. (2017). *Death and Life: Resurrection, Restoration and Rectification in Paul's Letter to the Galatians*. Eugene, OR: Wipf & Stock.

Bock, Darrell (1987). *Proclamation from Prophecy and Pattern: Lucan Old Testament Christology*. Journal for the Study of the New Testament Supplement 12. Sheffield: JSOT.

Bonneau, Normand (1997). 'The Logic of Paul's Argument on the Curse of the Law in Galatians 3:10–14'. *Novum Testamentum* 39: 60–80.

Booker, Christopher (2004). *The Seven Basic Plots: Why We Tell Stories*. London: Continuum.

Bowker, John (1969). *The Targums and Rabbinic Literature: An Introduction to Jewish Interpretations of Scripture*. Cambridge: Cambridge University Press.

Boyarin, Daniel A. (1993). 'Was Paul an Anti-Semite? A Reading of Galatians 3–4'. *Union Seminary Quarterly Review* 47: 47–80.

Boyarin, Daniel A. (1994, 1997). *A Radical Jew: Paul and the Politics of Identity*. Berkeley: University of California Press.

Braswell, J. P. (1991). '"The Blessing of Abraham" versus "The Curse of the Law": Another Look at Gal. 3:10–13'. *Westminster Theological Journal* 53: 73–92.

Brondos, David A. (2001). 'The Cross and the Curse: Galatians 3:13 and Paul's Doctrine of Redemption'. *Journal for the Study of the New Testament* 81: 3–32.

Bruce, F. F. (1982). *The Epistle to the Galatians: A Commentary on the Greek Text*. New International Greek Testament Commentary. Grand Rapids, MI: Eerdmans.

Bryant, Robert A. (2001). *The Risen Crucified Christ in Galatians*. Atlanta, GA: Society of Biblical Literature.

Bultmann, Rudolf (1951). *Theology of the New Testament*. Translated by Kendrick Grobel. New York: Scribner's.

Bultmann, Rudolf (1964). 'ΔΙΚΑΙΟΣΥΝΗ ΘΕΟΥ'. *Journal of Biblical Literature* 83: 12–16.

Bultmann, Rudolf (1976). *The Second Letter to the Corinthians*. Translated by R. A. Harrisville. Minneapolis, MN: Augsburg.

Burton, Ernest De Witt (1920). *A Critical and Exegetical Commentary on the Epistle to the Galatians*. New York: Scribner's.

Byrne, Brendan (1996). *Romans*. Sacra Pagina. Collegeville: Liturgical Press.

Cain, Andrew (2010). *Jerome: Commentary on Galatians*. Washington, DC: Catholic University of America Press.

Callan, Terrance (2006). *Dying and Rising with Christ: The Theology of Paul the Apostle*. Mahwah, NJ: Paulist.

Calvert Koyzis, Nancy (2004). *Paul, Monotheism and the People of God: The Significance of Abraham Traditions for Early Judaism and Christianity*. London: T&T Clark.

Campbell, Douglas A. (2005). *The Quest for Paul's Gospel: A Suggested Strategy*. Edinburgh: T&T Clark.

Campbell, Douglas A. (2009). *The Deliverance of God: An Apocalyptic Rereading of Justification in Paul*. Grand Rapids, MI: Eerdmans.

Campbell, Douglas A. (2011). 'Galatians 5:11: Evidence of an Early Law-Observant Mission by Paul?' *New Testament Studies* 57: 325–47.

Campbell, Douglas A. (2013). *The Deliverance of God: An Apocalyptic Rereading of Justification in Paul*. Grand Rapids, MI: Eerdmans.

Campbell, William S. (2008). *Paul and the Creation of Christian Identity*. London: T&T Clark.

Campbell, William S. (2013). 'Unity in the Community: Rereading Galatians 2:15–21'. In *The Unrelenting God: God's Action in Scripture (Essays in Honour of Beverley Roberts Gaventa)*, edited by David J. Downs and Matthew L. Skinner, 226–41. Grand Rapids, MI: Eerdmans.

Caneday, Ardel (1989). 'Redeemed from the Curse of the Law: The Use of Deut. 21:22–23 in Gal. 3:13'. *Trinity Journal* 10: 185–209.

Carson, D. A., P. T. O'Brien and M. A. Seifrid (eds) (2001). *Justification and Variegated Nomism: The Complexities of Second Temple Judaism*, vol. I. Tübingen: Mohr Siebeck.

Castelli, Elizabeth A. (1991). *Imitating Paul: A Discourse of Power*. Louisville, KY: Westminster John Knox.

Chandler, Christopher N. (2013). '"Love Your Neighbour as Yourself": (Leviticus 19:18b) in Early Jewish-Christian Exegetical Practice and Missional Formulation'. In *What Does the Scripture Say? Studies in the Function of Scripture in Early Judaism and Christianity: The Synoptic Gospels*, edited by Craig A. Evans and H. Daniel Zacharias, 12–56. London: Bloomsbury.

Charry, Ellen T. (2003). 'The Grace of God and the Law of Christ'. *Interpretation* 57: 34–44.

Ciampa, Roy E. (1998). *The Presence and Function of Scripture in Galatians 1 and 2*. Tübingen: Mohr Siebeck.

Collins, C. John (2003). 'Galatians 3:16: What Kind of Exegete was Paul?' *Tyndale Bulletin* 54: 75–86.

Conzelmann, Hans (1969). *An Outline of the Theology of the New Testament*. Translated by John Bowden. New York: Harper & Row.

Cooney, Monica (2008). 'Men and Women as Equal Partners in Christian Community'. *Ecumenical Review* 60: 100–3.

Cosgrove, Charles H. (1987). 'Justification in Paul: A Linguistic and Theological Reflection'. *Journal of Biblical Literature* 106: 653–70.

Cosgrove, Charles H. (1988). *The Cross and the Spirit: A Study in the Argument and Theology of Galatians*. Macon, GA: Mercer University Press.

Cranford, Michael (1994). 'The Possibility of Perfect Obedience: Paul and an Implied Premise in Gal. 3:10 and 5:3'. *Novum Testamentum* 37: 242–58.

Crook, Zeba A. (2004). *Reconceptualising Conversion: Patronage, Loyalty, and Conversion in the Religions of the Ancient Mediterranean*. Beihefte zur Zeitschrift für die neutestamentliche Wissenschaft 130. Berlin: Walter de Gruyter.

Dahl, Nils A. (1977). *Studies in Paul: Theology for the Early Christian Mission*. Minneapolis, MN: Augsburg.

Das, A. Andrew (2014). *Galatians*. Concordia Commentary. St Louis, MO: Concordia.

Das, A. Andrew (2016). *Paul and the Stories of Israel: Grand Thematic Narratives in Galatians*. Minneapolis, MN: Fortress.

Davies, William D. (1948). *Paul and Rabbinic Judaism*. London: SPCK.

de Boer, Martinus (2011). *Galatians: A Commentary*. The New Testament Library. Louisville, KY: Westminster John Knox.

Deissmann, G. Adolf. (1972) [1912]. *Paul: A Study in Social and Religious History*. Translated by W. E. Wilson. Gloucester, MA: Peter Smith.

DeMaris, Richard E. (2008). *The New Testament in Its Ritual World*. London: Routledge.

Dimant, Devorah (2000). 'Resurrection, Restoration, and Time-Curtailing in Qumran, Early Judaism, and Christianity'. *Revue de Qumran* 19.4: 527–48.

Donaldson, Terence L. (2006). *Paul and the Gentiles: Remapping the Apostle's Convictional World*. Minneapolis, MN: Fortress.

Downs, David, and Benjamin Lappenga (2019). *The Faithfulness of the Risen Christ: Pistis and the Exalted Lord in the Pauline Letters*. Waco, TX: Baylor University Press.

Dunn, James D. G. (1983). 'The New Perspective on Paul'. *Bulletin of the John Ryland's Library* 65: 95–122.

Dunn, James D. G. (1988a). *Romans 1–8*. Word Biblical Commentary 38A. Dallas, TX: Word.

Dunn, James D. G. (1988b). *Romans 9–16*. Word Biblical Commentary 38B. Dallas, TX: Word.

Dunn, James D. G. (1992). 'Yet Once More – the Works of the Law: A Response'. *Journal for the Study of the New Testament* 46: 99–117.

Dunn, James D. G. (1993). *The Epistle to the Galatians*. London: A&C Black.

Dunn, James D. G. (1997). '4QMMT and Galatians 1'. *New Testament Studies* 43: 147–53.

Dunn, James D. G. (2008). 'ΕΚ ΠΙΣΤΕΩΣ: A Key to the Meaning of ΠΙΣΤΙΣ ΧΡΙΣΤΟΥ'. In *The Word Leaps the Gap: Essays on Scripture and Theology in Honor of Richard B. Hays*, edited by J. Ross Wagner, C. Kavin Rowe and A. Katherine Grieb, 351–66. Grand Rapids, MI: Eerdmans.

Eastman, Susan G. (2006). '"Cast Out the Slave Woman and Her Son": The Dynamics of Exclusion and Inclusion in Galatians 4.30'. *Journal for the Study of the New Testament* 28: 309–33.

Ehrensperger, K. (2016). 'The Pauline Ἐκκλησίαι and Images of Community in Enoch Traditions'. In *Paul the Jew: Rereading the Apostle as a Figure of Second Temple Judaism*, edited by Gabriele Boccaccini and Carlos Segovia, 183–216. Minneapolis, MN: Fortress.

Eisenbaum, Pamela (2000). 'Paul as the New Abraham'. In *Paul and Politics (Ekklesia, Israel, Imperium, Interpretation): Essays in Honour of Krister Stendahl*, edited by Richard A. Horsley, 130–45. Harrisburg, PA: Trinity Press International.

Eisenbaum, Pamela (2009). *Paul Was Not a Christian: The Original Message of a Misunderstood Apostle*. New York: Harper Collins.

Elliott, John H. (2011). 'Social-Scientific Criticism: Perspective, Process and Payoff: Evil Eye Accusation at Galatia as Illustration of the Method'. *HTS Theological Studies* 67, www.hts.org.za/index.php/HTS/article/view/858/1454.

Eschner, Christina (2019). *Essen im antiken Judentum und Urchristentum: Diskurse zur sozialen Bedeutung von Tischgemeinschaft, Speiseverboten und Reinheitsvorschriften*. Ancient Judaism and Early Christianity 108. Leiden: Brill.

Esler, Philip F. (2006). 'Paul's Contestation of Israel's Ethnic Memory of Abraham in Galatians 3'. *Biblical Theology Bulletin* 36: 23–34.

Fee, Gordon D. (1994). *God's Empowering Presence: The Holy Spirit in the Letters of Paul*. Peabody, MA: Hendrickson.

Fitzmyer, Joseph A. (1993). *Romans: A New Translation with Introduction and Commentary*. Anchor Yale Bible 33. New Haven, CT: Yale University Press.

Fowl, Stephen (1994). 'Who Can Read Abraham's Story? Allegory and Interpretive Power in Galatians'. *Journal for the Study of the New Testament* 55: 77–95.

Freud, Sigmund (1922). *Beyond the Pleasure Principle*, 2nd German edn. London: International Psychoanalytical Press.

Gager, John G. (2000). *Reinventing Paul*. Oxford: Oxford University Press.

Garlington, Don (1997). 'Role Reversal and Paul's Use of Scripture in Galatians 3.10–13'. *Journal for the Study of the New Testament* 65: 85–121.

Garroway, Joshua D. (2018). *The Beginning of the Gospel: Paul, Philippi, and the Origins of Christianity*. Cham: Palgrave Macmillan.

Gaston, Lloyd (1982). 'Angels and Gentiles in Early Judaism and in Paul (Gal 3:19)'. *Studies in Religion* 11: 65–75.

Gaston, Lloyd (1987). *Paul and the Torah*. Vancouver: University of British Columbia Press.

Gathercole, Simon J. (2004). 'Torah, Life and Salvation: Leviticus 18:5 in Early Judaism and the New Testament', In *From Prophecy to Testament: The Function of the Old Testament in the New*, edited by Craig A. Evans, 131–50. Peabody, MA: Hendrickson.

Gaventa, Beverley R. (1986). 'Galatians 1 and 2: Autobiography as Paradigm'. *Novum Testamentum* 28: 309–26.

George, Timothy (1994). *The New American Commentary: Galatians*. Nashville, TN: Broadman & Holman.

Gignilliat, Mark (2007). *Paul and Isaiah's Servants: Paul's Theological Reading of Isaiah 40–66 in 2 Corinthians 5:14–6:10*. New York: T&T Clark.

Gilthvedt, Gary E. (2016). *Dying and Deliverance: Searching Paul's Law-Gospel Tension*. Eugene, OR: Wipf & Stock.

Glatzer, Nahum N. (1961). *Franz Rosenzweig: His Life and Thought*. New York: Schocken.

Gorman, Michael J. (2009). *Inhabiting the Cruciform God: Kenosis, Justification, and Theosis in Paul's Narrative Soteriology*. Grand Rapids, MI: Eerdmans.

Gorman, Michael J. (2019). *Participating in Christ: Explorations in Paul's Theology and Spirituality*. Grand Rapids, MI: Baker Academic.

Grayston, Kenneth (1990). *Dying, We Live: A New Enquiry into the Death of Christ in the New Testament*. London: Darton, Longman & Todd.

Green, B. G. (2014). *Covenant and Commandment: Works, Obedience and Faithfulness in the Christian Life*. Downers Grove, IL: InterVarsity.

Greenberg, Moshe (1990). 'Three Conceptions of the Torah in Hebrew Scriptures'. In *Die Hebräische Bibel und ihre zweifache Nachgeschichte*, Festscrift for Rolf Rendtorff, edited by Erhard Blum, 365–78. Neukirchen-Vluyn: Neukirchener.

Gualtieri, Antonio R. (1982). 'The Resurrection of Jesus as Transformational Myth'. *Encounter* 43: 177–83.

Gupta, Nijay (2019). *Paul and the Language of Faith*. Grand Rapids, MI: Eerdmans.

Hafemann, Scott J. (1997). 'Paul and the Exile of Israel in Galatians 3–4'. In *Exile: Old Testament, Jewish and Christian Conceptions*, edited by James M. Scott, 329–71. Leiden: Brill.

Hafemann, Scott J. (2005). *Paul, Moses, and the History of Israel: The Letter/Spirit Contrast and the Argument from Scripture in 2 Corinthians 3*. Waynesboro, GA: Paternoster.

Hagen Pifer, Jeanette (2019). *Faith as Participation: An Exegetical Study of Some Key Pauline Texts*. Wissenschaftliche Untersuchungen zum Neuen Testament 2.486. Tübingen: Mohr Siebeck.

Hansen, Bruce (2010). 'All of You Are One': The Social Vision of Gal. 3.28, 1 Cor. 12.13 and Col. 3.11*. Library of New Testament Studies 409. London: T&T Clark.

Hansen, G. Walter (1989). *Abraham in Galatians: Epistolary and Rhetorical Contexts*. Journal for the Study of the New Testament Supplement. Sheffield: Continuum.

Hansen, G. Walter (1994). *Galatians*. IVP New Testament Commentary. Downers Grove, IL: InterVarsity.

Hardin, Justin K. (2013). 'If I Still Proclaim Circumcision (Galatians 5:11a): Paul, the Law, and Gentile Circumcision'. *Journal for the Study of Paul and His Letters* 3: 145–63.

Harink, Douglas (2013). *Paul among the Postliberals: Pauline Theology beyond Christendom and Modernity*. Eugene, OR: Wipf & Stock.

Harmon, Matthew S. (2010). *She Must and Shall Go Free: Paul's Isaianic Gospel in Galatians*. Beihefte zur Zeitschrift für die neutestamentliche Wissenschaft 168. Berlin: Walter de Gruyter.

Harvey, David S. (2012). ' "Upside-Down Honour" and the Spirit of the Faithful Son in Galatians'. *Journal of the European Pentecostal Theological Association* 32: 61–74.

Harvey, David S. (2018). 'Saving Face in Galatia: ΕΥΠΡΟΣΩΠΕΩ and Concern for Honour in the Argument of Paul's Letter'. In *Scripture as Social Discourse: Social-Scientific Perspectives on Early Jewish and Christian Writings*, edited by Jessica M. Keady, Todd E. Klutz and C. A. Strine, 183–95. London: Bloomsbury T&T Clark.

Haußleiter, Johannes (1891). *Der Glaube Jesu Christi und der Christliche Glaube: Ein Beitrag zur Erklaerung des Roemersbriefes*. Erlangen: Andreas Deichert.

Hay, David M. (1989). 'Pistis as Ground for Faith in Hellenized Judaism and Paul'. *Journal of Biblical Literature* 108: 461–76.

Hays, Richard B. (1987). 'Christology and Ethics in Galatians: The Law of Christ'. *Catholic Biblical Quarterly* 49: 268–90.

Hays, Richard B. (1989). *Echoes of Scripture in the Letters of Paul*. New Haven, CT: Yale University Press.

Hays, Richard B. (2000). 'The Letter to the Galatians: Introduction, Commentary, and Reflections'. In *The New Interpreter's Bible* 11, edited by Leander E. Keck, 181–348. Nashville, TN: Abingdon.

Hays, Richard B. (2002). *The Faith of Jesus Christ: The Narrative Substructure of Galatians 3:1–4:11*, 2nd edn. Grand Rapids, MI: Eerdmans.

Hengel, Martin (1991). *The Pre-Christian Paul*. Philadelphia, PA: Trinity Press International.

Hertz, J. H. (1950). *The Pentateuch and Haftorahs*. London: Soncino.

Hietanen, Mika (2007). *Paul's Argumentation in Galatians: A Pragma-Dialectical Analysis*. New York: T&T Clark.

Hong, In-Gyu (1993). *The Law in Galatians*. Journal for the Study of the New Testament Supplement Series 81. Sheffield: JSOT Press.

Hooker, Morna D. (1990). *From Adam to Christ*. Cambridge: Cambridge University Press.

Hooker, Morna D. (2008). 'On Becoming the Righteousness of God: Another Look at 2 Cor 5:21'. *Novum Testamentum* 50.4: 358–75.

Horrell, David G. (2017). 'Paul, Inclusion, and Whiteness: Particularising Interpretation'. *Journal for the Study of the New Testament* 40: 123–47.

Hubing, Jeff (2015). *Crucifixion and New Creation: The Strategic Purpose of Galatians 6:11–17*. Library of New Testament Studies 508. London: Bloomsbury T&T Clark.

Hübner, Hans (1984). *Law in Paul's Thought: A Contribution to the Development of Pauline Theology*. Translated by J. C. G. Greig. Studies in the New Testament and Its World. New York: T&T Clark.

Hunn, Debbie (2015). 'Galatians 3.10–12: Assumptions and Argumentation'. *Journal for the Study of the New Testament* 37: 253–66.

Irons, Charles Lee (2015). *The Righteousness of God: A Lexical Examination of the Covenant-Faithfulness Interpretation*. Tübingen: Mohr Siebeck.

Jernegan, Prescott F. (1896). 'The Faith of Jesus Christ'. *Biblical World* 8: 198–202.

References

Jewett, Robert (2007). *Romans: A Commentary*. Hermeneia. Minneapolis, MN: Fortress.

Jobes, Karen H. (1993). 'Jerusalem, Our Mother: Metalepsis and Intertextuality in Galatians 4:21–31'. *Westminster Theological Journal* 55: 299–320.

Johnson Hodge, Caroline (2007). *If Sons, then Heirs: A Study of Kinship and Ethnicity in the Letters of Paul*. Oxford: Oxford University Press.

Jolivet, Ira (2009). 'Christ the TELOS in Romans 10:4 as Both Fulfillment and Termination of the Law'. *Restoration Quarterly* 51: 13–30.

Juncker, Günther H. (2007). 'Children of Promise: Spiritual Paternity and Patriarch Typology in Galatians and Romans'. *Bulletin for Biblical Research* 17: 131–60.

Kahl, Brigitte (2010). *Galatians Re-imagined: Reading with the Eyes of the Vanquished*. Minneapolis, MN: Fortress.

Kahl, Brigitte (2014). 'Galatians'. In *Fortress Commentary on the Bible: The New Testament*, edited by Margaret Aymer, Cynthia Briggs Kittredge and David A. Sánchez, 503–25. Minneapolis, MN: Fortress.

Käsemann, Ernst (1969). ' "The Righteousness of God" in Paul'. In *New Testament Questions of Today*, translated by W. J. Montague, 168–82. Philadelphia, PA: Fortress.

Käsemann, Ernst (1980). *Commentary on Romans*. Grand Rapids, MI: Eerdmans.

Keesmaat, Sylvia C. (2004). 'The Psalms in Romans and Galatians'. In *The Psalms in the New Testament*, edited by Steve Moyise and Maarten J. J. Menken, 139–61. New York: T&T Clark.

Kim, Jung Hoon (2004). *The Significance of Clothing Imagery in the Pauline Corpus*. London: T&T Clark.

Kim, Seyoon (2012). 'Paul as an Eschatological Herald'. In *Paul as Missionary: Identity, Activity, Theology, and Practice*, edited by Trevor J. Burke and Brian S. Rosner, 9–24. Library of New Testament Studies 420. London: Bloomsbury.

Kimber Buell, Denise, and Caroline Johnson Hodge (2004). 'The Politics of Interpretation: The Rhetoric of Race and Ethnicity in Paul'. *Journal of Biblical Literature* 123: 235–51.

Kreitzer, L. J. (1993). 'Resurrection'. In *Dictionary of Paul and His Letters*, edited by Gerald F. Hawthorne, Ralph P. Martin and Daniel G. Reid, 805–12. Downers Grove, IL: InterVarsity.

Kruse, Colin (2014). 'Paul the Law and the Spirit'. *Paradosis* 1: 1–48.

Laney, J. Carl (1990). 'The Prophets and Social Concern', *Bibliotheca Sacra* 147: 32–43.

Leale, Thomas H. (1892). *The Preacher's Complete Homiletic Commentary on the First Book of Moses Called Genesis*. New York: Funk & Wagnalls.

Lee, Chee-Chiew (2013). *The Blessing of Abraham, the Spirit, and Justification in Galatians: Their Relationship and Significance for Understanding Paul's Theology*. Eugene, OR: Wipf & Stock.

Leppä, Heikki (2012). 'The Torah in Galatians'. In *The Torah in the Ethics of Paul*, edited by Martin Meiser, 59–69. New York: T&T Clark.

Levenson, Jon D. (1993). *The Death and Resurrection of the Beloved Son: The Transformation of Child Sacrifice in Judaism and Christianity*. New Haven, CT: Yale University Press.

Levison, John R. (1993). 'Creation and New Creation'. In *Dictionary of Paul and His Letters*, edited by Gerald F. Hawthorne, Ralph P. Martin and Daniel G. Reid, 189–90. Leicester: InterVarsity.

Lewis, John G. (2005). *Looking for Life: The Role of 'Theo-Ethical Reasoning' in Paul's Religion*. London: T&T Clark.

Litwak, Kenneth D. (2005). *Echoes of Scripture in Luke-Acts: Telling the History of God's People Intertextually*. New York: T&T Clark.

Lo, Lung-Kwong (2009). 'Paul and Ethnicity: The Paradigm of Glocalization'. In *Jesus and Paul: Global Perspectives in Honor of James D.G. Dunn for His 70th Birthday*, edited by B. J. Oropeza, C. K. Robertson and Douglas C. Mohrmann, 184–98. New York: T&T Clark.

Longenecker, Richard N. (1990). *Galatians*. Word Biblical Commentary 41. Dallas, TX: Word.

Lührmann, Dieter (1992). *Galatians: A Continental Commentary*. Translated by O. C. Dean Jr. Minneapolis, MN: Fortress.

Lull, David J. (1986). ' "The Law Was Our Pedagogue": A Study in Galatians 3:19–25'. *Journal of Biblical Literature* 105: 481–98.

Luther, Martin (2007) [1520]. *Concerning Christian Liberty: With, Letter of Martin Luther to Pope Leo X*. Fort Worth: RDMC.

Macaskill, Grant (2013). *Union with Christ in the New Testament*. Oxford: Oxford University Press.

Macaskill, Grant (2019). *Living in Union with Christ: Paul's Gospel and Christian Moral Identity*. Grand Rapids, MI: Baker Academic.

Macchia, Frank D. (2001). 'Justification through New Creation: The Holy Spirit and the Doctrine by Which the Church Stands or Falls'. *Theology Today* 58: 202–17.

Macchia, Frank D. (2017). 'The Spirit and God's Return to Indwell a People: A Systematic Theologian's Response to N.T. Wright's Reading of Paul's Pneumatology'. In *God and the Faithfulness of Paul: A Critical Examination of the Pauline Theology of N.T. Wright*, edited by Christoph Heilig, J. Thomas Hewitt and Michael F. Bird, 623–44. Minneapolis, MN: Fortress.

Manning, Gary T. (2004). *Echoes of a Prophet: The Use of Ezekiel in the Gospel of John and in Literature of the Second Temple*. New York: T&T Clark.

Marchal, Joseph A. (2006). *Hierarchy, Unity, and Imitation: A Feminist Rhetorical Analysis of Power Dynamics in Paul's Letter to the Philippians*. Academia Biblica 24. Atlanta, GA: Society of Biblical Literature.

Marchal, Joseph A. (2012). 'Queer Approaches: Improper Relations with Pauline Letters', In *Studying Paul's Letters: Contemporary Perspectives and Methods*, edited by Joseph A. Marchal, 209–27. Minneapolis, MN: Fortress.

Martin, Raymond A. (1993). *Studies in the Life and Ministry of Paul and Related Issues*. Lewiston, NY: Edwin Mellen.

Martin, T. (1995). 'Apostasy to Paganism: The Rhetorical Stasis of the Galatian Controversy'. *Journal of Biblical Literature* 114: 437–61.

Martyn, J. Louis (1985). 'Apocalyptic Antinomies in Paul's Letter to the Galatians'. *New Testament Studies* 31: 410–24.

Martyn, J. Louis (1995). 'Christ, the Elements of the Cosmos, and the Law in Galatians'. In *The Social World of the First Christians: Essays in Honour of*

Wayne A. Meeks, edited by L. Michael White and O. Larry Yarbrough, 16–39. Minneapolis, MN: Fortress.

Martyn, J. Louis (1997). *Galatians: A New Translation with Introduction and Commentary*. The Anchor Bible 33A. New York: Doubleday.

Martyn, J. Louis (2000). 'The Apocalyptic Gospel in Galatians'. *Interpretation* 54: 246–66.

Matera, Frank (2010). *Romans*. Grand Rapids, MI: Baker Academic.

Matlock, R. Barry (2009). 'Saving Faith: The Rhetoric and Semantics of πίστις in Paul'. In *The Faith of Jesus Christ: Exegetical, Biblical, and Theological Studies*, edited by Michael F. Bird and Preston M. Sprinkle, 73–89. Milton Keynes: Paternoster.

McKnight, Scot (2000). 'The Ego and "I": Galatians 2:19 in New Perspective'. *Word & World* 20: 272–80.

Medina, Richard W. (2010). 'Life and Death Viewed as Physical and Lived Spaces: Some Preliminary Thoughts from Proverbs'. *Zeitschrift fur die Alttestamentliche Wissenschaft* 122: 199–211.

Mohrmann, Douglas C. (2009). 'Of "Doing" and "Living": The Intertextual Semantics of Leviticus 18:5 in Galatians and Romans'. In *Jesus and Paul: Global Perspectives in Honour of James D.G. Dunn for His 70th Birthday*, edited by B. J. Oropeza, C. K. Robertson and Douglas C. Mohrmann, 164–6. London: T&T Clark.

Moo, Douglas J. (2010). 'Creation and New Creation'. *Bulletin of Biblical Research* 20: 39–60.

Moo, Douglas J. (2013). *Galatians*. Baker Exegetical Commentary on the New Testament. Grand Rapids, MI: Baker Academic.

Morales, Rodrigo (2010). *The Spirit and the Restoration of Israel: New Exodus and New Creation Motifs in Galatians*. Tübingen: Mohr Siebeck.

Morgan, Robert (1997). *Romans*. Sheffield: Sheffield Academic.

Morgan, Teresa (2015). *Roman Faith and Christian Faith*: Pistis and Fides *in the Early Roman Empire and Early Churches*. Oxford: Oxford University Press.

Mounce, Robert H. (1995). *Romans*. Nashville, TN: Broadman & Holman.

Moyise, Steve (2001). *Paul and Scripture*. London: SPCK.

Munck, Johannes (1959). *Paul and the Salvation of Mankind*. Richmond, VA: John Knox.

Nanos, Mark D. (1996). *The Mystery of Romans: The Jewish Context of Paul's Letter*. Minneapolis, MN: Fortress.

Nanos, Mark D. (2002). *The Irony of Galatians: Paul's Letter in First-Century Context*. Minneapolis, MN: Fortress.

Neutel, Karin B. (2015). *A Cosmopolitan Ideal: Paul's Declaration' Neither Jew Nor Greek, Neither Slave Nor Free Nor Male and Female' in the Context of First-Century Thought*. Library of New Testament Studies 513. London: Bloomsbury.

Noegel, Scott B. (2003). 'Abraham's Ten Trials and a Biblical Numerical Convention'. *Jewish Bible Quarterly* 31: 73–83.

Noth, Martin (1981) *The Deuteronomistic History*. Journal for the Study of the New Testament Supplement Series 15. Sheffield: JSOT (German original; Halle: Niemeyer, 1943).

Oakes, Peter (2015). *Galatians*. Paideia Commentaries on the New Testament. Grand Rapids, MI: Baker Academic.

Oakes, Peter (2018). '*Pistis* as Relational Way of Life in Galatians'. *Journal for the Study of the New Testament* 40: 255–75.

O'Brien, Peter T. (2004). 'Was Paul Converted?' In *Justification and Variegated Nomism* II: *The Paradoxes of Paul*, edited by D. A. Carson, Peter T. O'Brien and Mark A. Seifrid, 361–92. Wissenschaftliche Untersuchungen Zum Neuen Testament 2.181. Tübingen: Mohr Siebeck.

Ota, Shuji (2016). 'The Holistic Pistis and Abraham's Faith (Galatians 3)'. *Hitotsubashi Journal of Arts and Sciences* 57: 1–12.

Peterson, Norman (1985). *Rediscovering Paul: Philemon and the Sociology of Paul's Narrative World*. Philadelphia, PA: Fortress.

Popkes, Wilard (2005). 'Two Interpretations of "Justification" in the New Testament: Reflections on Galatians 2:15–21 and James 2:21–25'. *Studia Theologica* 59: 129–46.

Portefaix, Lilian (1988). *Sisters Rejoice: Paul's Letter to the Philippians and Luke-Acts as Received by First-Century Philippian Women*. Coniectanea Biblica NT 20. Uppsala/Stockholm: Almqvist & Wiksell.

Porter, Stanley, and Andrew Pitts (2009). 'Πίστις with a Preposition and Genitive Modifier: Lexical, Semantic, and Syntactic Considerations in the πίστις Χριστοῦ Discussion'. In *The Faith of Jesus Christ: Exegetical, Biblical, and Theological Studies*, edited by Michael F. Bird and Preston M. Sprinkle, 33–53. Milton Keynes: Paternoster.

Pyne, Robert A. (1995). 'The Seed, the Spirit and the Blessing of Abraham'. *Biblotheca Sacra* 152: 211–22.

Rad, Gerhard von. (1977). *Biblical Interpretations in Preaching*. Translated by John E. Steely. Nashville, TN: Abingdon.

Räisänen, Heikki (1985). 'Galatians 2.16 and Paul's Break with Judaism'. *New Testament Studies* 31: 543–53.

Räisänen, Heikki (1987). *Paul and the Law*. Tübingen: Mohr Siebeck.

Rand, Thomas A. (1995). 'A Call to KOINONIA: A Rhetorical Analysis of Galatians 5:25–6:10'. *Proceedings (Eastern Great Lakes Biblical Society)* 15: 79–92.

Richardson, Peter (1973). 'Spirit and Letter: A Foundation for Hermeneutics'. *Evangelical Quarterly* 45: 208–18.

Rosner, Brian (2013). *Paul and the Law: Keeping the Commandments of God*. Downers Grove, IL: InterVarsity.

Sanders, E. P. (1977). *Paul and Palestinian Judaism: A Comparison of Patterns of Religion*. London: SCM.

Sanders, E. P. (1983). *Paul, the Law, and the Jewish People*. London: SCM.

Schliesser, Benjamin (2016). '"Christ-Faith" as an Eschatological Event (Galatians 3.23–26): A "Third View" on Πίστις Χριστοῦ'. *Journal for the Study of the New Testament* 38: 277–300.

Schreiner, Thomas R. (1984). 'Is Perfect Obedience to the Law Possible? A Re-examination of Galatians 3:10'. *Journal of the Evangelical Theological Society* 27: 151–60.

Schreiner, Thomas R. (1991). ' "Works of Law" in Paul'. *Novum Testamentum* 33: 217–44.

Schreiner, Thomas R. (1993). 'Works of the Law'. *Dictionary of Paul and His Letters*, edited by Gerald F. Hawthorne, Ralph P. Martin and Daniel G. Reid, 975–7. Downers Grove, IL: InterVarsity.

Schreiner, Thomas R. (2010). *Galatians: An Exegetical Commentary on the New Testament*. Grand Rapids, MI: Zondervan.

Schwartz, Daniel R. (1983). 'Two Pauline Allusions to the Redemptive Mechanism of the Crucifixion'. *Journal of Biblical Literature* 102: 259–68.

Schweitzer, Albert (1931). *The Mysticism of Paul the Apostle*. Translated by C. T. Campion. London: A&C Black.

Scott, James M. (1992). *Adoption as Sons of God: An Exegetical Investigation into the Background of ΥΙΟΘΕΣΙΑ in the Pauline Corpus*. Tübingen: Mohr Siebeck.

Scott, James M. (1993a). 'For as Many as Are of the Works of the Law are under a Curse (Galatians 3:10)'. In *Paul and the Scriptures of Israel*, edited by Craig A. Evans and James A. Sanders, 187–221. Journal for the Study of the New Testament Supplement 83. Sheffield: Sheffield Academic.

Scott, James M. (1993b). 'Paul's Use of Deuteronomic Tradition'. *Journal of Biblical Literature* 112: 645–65.

Scott, James M., ed. (2017). *Exile: A Conversation with N.T. Wright*. Downers Grove, IL: InterVarsity.

Sierksma-Agteres, Suzan J. M. (2016). 'Imitation in Faith: Enacting Paul's Ambiguous *Pistis Christou* Formulations on a Greco-Roman Stage'. *International Journal of Philosophy and Theology* 77.3: 119–53.

Silva, Moisés (2001). 'Abraham, Faith, and Works: Paul's Use of Scripture in Galatians 3:6–14'. *Westminster Theological Journal* 63: 251–67.

Silva, Moisés (2004). 'Faith versus Works of Law in Galatians'. In *Justification and Variegated Nomism* II: *The Paradoxes of Paul*, edited by D. A. Carson, Peter T. O'Brien and Mark A. Seifrid, 217–48. Wissenschaftliche Untersuchungen Zum Neuen Testament 2.181. Tübingen: Mohr Siebeck.

Sim, David C. (2006). 'The Appearances of the Risen Christ to Paul: Identifying Their Implications and Complications'. *Australian Biblical Review* 54: 1–12.

Smith, Dennis E., and Hal Taussig, eds. (2012). *Meals in the Early Christian World: Social Formation, Experimentation, and Conflict at the Table*. New York: Palgrave Macmillan.

Sprinkle, Preston M. (2008). *Law and Life: The Interpretation of Leviticus 18:5 in Early Judaism and in Paul*. Tübingen: Mohr Siebeck.

Sprinkle, Preston M. (2009). 'Πίστις Χριστοῦ as an Eschatological Event'. In *The Faith of Jesus Christ: Exegetical, Biblical, and Theological Studies*, edited by Michael F. Bird and Preston M. Sprinkle, 165–84. Milton Keynes: Paternoster.

Stanley, Christopher D. (2004). *Arguing with Scripture: The Rhetoric of Quotations in the Letters of Paul*. New York: T&T Clark.

Stewart, J. S. (1935). *A Man in Christ*. London: Hodder & Stoughton.

Strelan, John G. (1975). 'Burden-Bearing and the Law of Christ: A Re-examination of Galatians 6:2'. *Journal of Biblical Literature* 94.2: 266–76.

Taubes, Jacob (2004). *The Political Theology of Paul.* Translated by D. Hollander. Stanford: Stanford University Press.

Taylor, John W. (2004). 'From Faith to Faith: Romans 1:17 in the Light of Greek Idiom'. *New Testament Studies* 50: 337–48.

Thate, Michael J., Kevin J. Vanhoozer and Constantine R. Campbell, eds. (2014). *'In Christ' in Paul: Explorations in Paul's Theology of Union and Participation.* Wissenschaftliche Untersuchungen zum Neuen Testament 2.384. Tübingen: Mohr Siebeck.

Thielman, Frank (1994). *Paul and the Law: A Contextual Approach.* Downers Grove, IL: InterVarsity.

Thomas, Robert L. (2005). 'Hermeneutics of the New Perspective on Paul'. *Master's Seminary Journal* 16: 293–316.

Thompson, James W. (2011). *Moral Formation according to Paul: The Context and Coherence of Pauline Ethics.* Grand Rapids, MI: Baker Academic.

Trick, Bradley R. (2016). *Abrahamic Descent, Testamentary Adoption, and the Law in Galatians: Differentiating Abraham's Sons, Seed, and Children of Promise.* Boston: Brill.

Tromp, Johannes (2007). ' "Can these Bones Live?" Ezekiel 37:1–14 and Eschatological Resurrection'. In *The Book of Ezekiel and Its Influence,* edited by Henk Jan de Jonge and Johannes Tromp, 61–78. Hampshire: Ashgate.

Turley, Stephen Richard (2015). *The Ritualized Revelation of the Messianic Age: Washings and Meals in Galatians and 1 Corinthians.* London: Bloomsbury T&T Clark.

Ulrichs, Karl Friedrich (2007). *Christusglaube: Studien zum Syntagma* pistis Christou *und zum paulinischen Verständnis von Glaube und Rechtfertigung.* Wissenschaftliche Untersuchungen zum Neuen Testament 2.227. Tübingen: Mohr Siebeck.

Uro, Risto (2016). *Ritual and Christian Beginnings: A Socio-cognitive Analysis.* Oxford: Oxford University Press.

Uzukwu, Gesila Nneka (2015). *The Unity of Male and Female in Jesus Christ: An Exegetical Study of Galatians 3.28c in Light of Paul's Theology of Promise.* London: Bloomsbury T&T Clark.

van der Horst, P. W. (1978). *The Sentences of Pseudo-Phocylides.* Studia in Veteris Testamenti Pseudepigrapha 4. Leiden: Brill.

von Rad, Gerhard (1977) [1959]. *Biblical Interpretations in Preaching.* Translated by John E. Steely. Nashville, TN: Abingdon.

Wakefield, Andrew H. (2003). *Where to Live: The Hermeneutical Significance of Paul's Citations from Scripture in Galatians 3:1–14.* Academia Biblica. Leiden: Brill.

Wallis, Wilber B. (1969). 'Irony in Jeremiah's Prophecy of a New Covenant'. *JETS* 12.2: 107–10.

Watson, Francis (2004). *Paul and the Hermeneutics of Faith.* New York: T&T Clark.

Watson, Francis (2009). 'By Faith (of Christ): An Exegetical Dilemma and its Scriptural Solution'. In *The Faith of Jesus Christ: Exegetical, Biblical, and Theological Studies,* edited by Michael F. Bird and Preston M. Sprinkle, 147–63. Milton Keynes: Paternoster.

References

Weima, Jeffrey A. D. (1995). 'The Pauline Letter Closings: Analysis and Hermeneutical Significance'. *Bulletin for Biblical Research* 5: 177–98.

Westerholm, Stephen (1984). 'Letter and Spirit: The Foundation of Pauline Ethics'. *New Testament Studies* 30: 229–48.

Westerholm, Stephen (1988). *Israel's Law and the Church's Faith: Paul and His Recent Interpreters*. Grand Rapids, MI: Eerdmans.

Westerholm, Stephen (2008). 'Finnish Contributions to the Debate on Paul and the Law'. In *The Nordic Paul: Finnish Approaches to Pauline Theology*, edited by Lars Aejmelaeus and Antii Mustakallio, 3–16. Library of New Testament Studies 374. New York: T&T Clark.

Williams, Sam K. (1987). 'Justification and the Spirit in Galatians'. *Journal for the Study of the New Testament* 29: 91–100.

Williams, Sam K. (1988). 'Promise in Galatians: A Reading of Paul's Reading of Scripture'. *Journal of Biblical Literature* 107: 709–20.

Williams, Sam K. (1997). *Galatians*. Abingdon New Testament Commentaries. Nashville, TN: Abingdon.

Willits, Joel (2005). 'Isa. 54:1 in Gal. 4:24b-27: Reading Genesis in Light of Isaiah'. *Zeitschrift für die Neutestamentliche Wissenschaft und die Kunde der Älteren Kirche* 96: 188–210.

Wilson, Todd A. (2005). 'Under Law in Galatians: A Pauline Theological Abbreviation'. *Journal of Theologial Studies* 56: 362–92.

Wilson, Todd A. (2006). 'The Law of Christ and the Law of Moses: Reflections on a Recent Trend in Interpretation'. *Currents in Biblical Research* 5: 123–44.

Winger, Michael (2000). 'The Law of Christ'. *New Testament Studies* 46: 537–46.

Winter, Bruce W. (1994). *Seek the Welfare of the City: Christians as Benefactors and Citizens*. First-Century Christians in the Graeco-Roman World. Carlisle: Paternoster.

Witherington III, Ben (1998). *Grace in Galatia: A Commentary on St. Paul's Letter to the Galatians*. Edinburgh: T&T Clark.

Woodhouse, John (1991). 'The Spirit in the Book of Ezekiel'. In *Spirit of the Living God*, edited by B. G. Webb, 1–22. Explorations 5. Sydney: Lancer.

Wright, N. T. (1991). *The Climax of the Covenant: Christ and the Law in Pauline Theology*. Edinburgh: T&T Clark.

Wright, N. T. (1992). *The New Testament and the People of God*. London: SPCK.

Wright, N. T. (1994). 'Gospel and Theology in Galatians'. In *Gospel in Paul: Studies on Corinthians, Galatians and Romans for Richard N. Longenecker*, edited by L. Ann Jervis and Peter Richardson, 222–39. Sheffield: Sheffield Academic.

Wright, N. T. (1995). 'Romans and the Theology of Paul'. In *Pauline Theology 3: Romans*, edited by David M. Hay and E. Elizabeth Johnson, 30–67. Minneapolis, MN: Fortress.

Wright, N. T. (1996). *Jesus and the Victory of God*. London: SPCK.

Wright, N. T. (1997). *What Saint Paul Really Said*. Grand Rapids, MI: Eerdmans.

Wright, N. T. (2003). *The Resurrection of the Son of God*. London: SPCK.

Wright, N. T. (2005). *Paul: In Fresh Perspective*. London: SPCK.

Wright, N. T. (2013). *Paul and the Faithfulness of God*. London: SPCK.

Wright, Tom (2002). *Paul for Everyone: Galatians and Thessalonians*. London: SPCK.

Yates, John W. (2008). *The Spirit and Creation in Paul*. Tübingen: Mohr Siebeck.

Zetterholm, Magnus (2009). *Approaches to Paul: A Student's Guide to Recent Scholarship*. Minneapolis, MN: Fortress.

ANCIENT SOURCES INDEX

Ancient Sources Index

MODERN AUTHORS INDEX

Modern Authors Index

Mounce, Robert H. 93
Moyise, Steve 39–40
Munck, Johannes 161

Nanos, Mark D. 110
Neutel, Karin B. 7
Noth, Martin 50

Oakes, Peter 3, 5–7, 18–20, 26, 29, 36,
	52, 70, 140, 145, 150, 152, 154, 163,
	164, 166, 171
O'Brien, Peter T. 43
Ota, Shuji 36

Peterson, Norman 23
Pitts, Andrew 15, 16
Popkes, Wilard 99
Portefaix, Lilian 135
Porter, Stanley E. 15, 16
Pyne, Robert A. 58

Räisänen, Heikki 71, 109, 126
Rand, Thomas A. 70
Richardson, Peter 126
Rosner, Brian 54
Rosenzweig, Franz 110

Sanders, E. P. 46, 49, 52, 71, 109, 110,
	111, 150, 163
Schliesser, Benjamin 6, 17–18, 30
Schreiner, Thomas R. 45, 48, 56, 111
Schwartz, Daniel R. 56–7
Schweitzer, Albert 162
Scott, James M. 49–50, 89, 104, 118
Segal, Alan 104
Sierksma–Agteres, Susan J. M. 163
Silva, Moisés 41, 50, 57, 165
Sim, David C. 72
Smith, Dennis E. 149
Sprinkle, Preston M. 17, 53

Stanley, Christopher D. 40–1, 46, 165
Stendahl, Krister 48, 110
Stowers, Stanley 48
Strelan, John G. 69

Taubes, Jacob 71
Taussig, Hal 149
Taylor, John W. 94
Thate, Michael J. 1
Thielman, Frank 51
Thomas, Robert L. 110
Thompson, James W. 68
Tolkien, J. R. R. 75
Trick, Bradley R. 46, 65
Turley, Stephen Richard 92

Ulrichs, Karl Friedrich 18
Uro, Risto 148

van der Horst, Pieter W. 66–7
von Rad, Gerhard 82

Wakefield, Andrew H. 20
Wallis, Wilber B. 125
Watson, Francis 17, 20, 50, 66
Weima, Jeffrey A. D. 96
Westerholm, Stephen 112, 126
Wilder, William N. 104
Williams, Sam K. 17, 18, 44, 57, 73, 108
Willits, Joel 62
Wilson, Todd A. 47, 69
Winger, Michael 69
Winter, Bruce W. 104, 146
Witherington III, Ben 79
Woodhouse, John 168
Wright, N. T. 16, 17, 23, 29, 46, 50,
	59, 79, 88, 90, 102, 104, 109,
	120, 136–9

Yates, John W. 123

SUBJECT INDEX